| | |
|---|---|
| First Published in April 2003 | 1,000 copies |
| Second Edition - February 2010 | 4,000 copies |
| Third Edition - May 2012 to December 2023 | 42,000 copies |
| Reprint - August 2025 | 7,000 copies |

Published by:
**Chinmaya Prakashan**
The Publications Division of
**Central Chinmaya Mission Trust**
Sandeepany Sadhanalaya
Saki Vihar Road, Powai, Mumbai - 400 072. India.
Tel.: +91-22-2803 4900
E-mail: ccmtpublications@chinmayamission.com
Website: www.chinmayamission.com

Distribution Centre in the USA:
**Chinmaya Publications West**
560 Bridgetown Pike
Feasterville, PA 19053-7240, USA
Tel.: (215) 396-0390, Fax: (215) 396-9710
E-mail: publications@chinmayamission.org
Website: www.chinmayapublications.com

Printed by: SAP Print Solutions Pvt. Ltd., Mumbai

ISBN: 978-81-7597-471-5

# SHRIMAD BHAGAVAD-GITA

CENTRAL CHINMAYA MISSION TRUST

# Transliteration and Pronunciation Guide

In this book, Devanagari characters are transliterated according to the scheme adopted by the International Congress of Orientalists at Athens in 1912. In it one fixed pronunciation value is given to each letter; f, q, w, x and z are not called to use.

| Devanagari | Transliteration | Sounds Like |
|---|---|---|
| अ | a | son |
| आ | ā | father |
| इ | i | different |
| ई | ī | feel |
| उ | u | full |
| ऊ | ū | boot |
| ऋ | ṛ | rhythm* |
| ॠ | ṝ | ** |
| ऌ | ḷ | ** |
| ए | e | evade |
| ऐ | ai | delight |
| ओ | o | core |
| औ | au | now |
| क् | k | calm |
| ख् | kh | khan |
| ग् | g | gate |
| घ् | gh | ghost |
| ङ् | ṅ | ankle* |
| च् | c | chuckle |
| छ् | ch | witch* |
| ज् | j | justice |
| झ् | jh | Jhansi |
| ञ् | ñ | banyan |
| ट् | ṭ | tank |
| ठ् | ṭh | ** |
| ड् | ḍ | dog |
| ढ् | ḍh | adhesive* |
| ण् | ṇ | under* |
| त् | t | tabla |
| थ् | th | thumb |
| द् | d | this |
| ध् | dh | Gandhi |
| न् | n | nose |
| प् | p | pen |
| फ् | ph | phantom* |
| ब् | b | boil |
| भ् | bh | abhor |
| म् | m | mind |
| य् | y | yes |
| र् | r | right |
| ल् | l | love |
| व् | v | very |
| श् | ś | shut |
| ष | ṣ | sugar |
| स् | s | simple |
| ह् | h | happy |
| ं | ṁ | improvise |
| ः | ḥ | ** |
| क्ष् | kṣ | action |
| त्र् | tr | three* |
| ज्ञ् | jñ | gnosis |
| ऽ | ' | a silent 'a' |

* These letters don't have an exact English equivalent. An approximation is given here.
** These sounds cannot be approximated in English words.

# CONTENTS

***

# PREFACE

*Śrīmad Bhagavad-gītā,* is unique among the body of scriptural literature for the simple, practical and relevant style with which it presents the essence of the Hindu way of life.

Sage Vyāsa, through the mouth of Lord Kṛṣṇa, masterfully brings the teachings of the Upaniṣads from secluded forests and tranquil mountains to our familiar world of agitations, chaos and whirlwind activity. The *Gītā's* teachings can be practised in the midst of even the most harrowing of situations – a fratricidal war. Śrī Kṛṣṇa's teaching is not confined to the rare few, who are pure and devout seekers of Truth. It addresses all of us, complete with our confusions, delusions and fear. The *Gītā* can guide us from our current pitiable condition to the most exalted state of supreme beatitude, and therein lies her glory.

This book is dedicated to Swami Chinmayananda, who, through his Gītā Jñāna Yajñas revived this most remarkable scripture and spread its message around the world.

We are deeply grateful to Shri Kaushik Rindani and Shri Pradeep Kharwal, who have poured immense efforts into bringing this book out.

Date : **Central Chinmaya Mission Trust**

21/02/2010 Mumbai - 400 072.

***

*Read.*
*Reflect.*
*Digest.*
*Discover the*
*Courage to*
*live the Geeta*
*Way - of - life.*
*The Joy*
*arising*
*in your*
*bosom is the*
*SWAROOPA*
*of the Flute*
*bearer of*
*Brindavan.*

Arjuna's Grief

# Chapter 1

## *Yoga of Arjuna's Grief*

धृतराष्ट्र उवाच
धर्मक्षेत्रे कुरुक्षेत्रे समवेता युयुत्सवः ।
मामकाः पाण्डवाश्चैव किमकुर्वत सञ्जय ।।१।।

*dhṛtarāṣṭra uvāca*

*dharmakṣetre kurukṣetre samavetā yuyutsavaḥ,*
*māmakāḥ pāṇḍavāścaiva kimakurvata sañjaya. (1)*

Dhṛtarāṣṭra said :

O Sañjaya! What did my people & Pāṇḍavas do after having assembled in the holy land of Kurukṣetra, eager to fight the battle?

सञ्जय उवाच
दृष्ट्वा तु पाण्डवानीकं व्यूढं दुर्योधनस्तदा ।
आचार्यमुपसङ्गम्य राजा वचनमब्रवीत् ।। २ ।।

*sañjaya uvāca*

*dṛṣṭvā tu pāṇḍavānīkaṁ vyūḍhaṁ duryodhanastadā,*
*ācāryamupasaṅgamya rājā vacanamabravīt. (2)*

Sañjaya said :

Having seen the army of the Pāṇḍavas drawn up in battle array, King Duryodhana then approached his teacher (Droṇa) and spoke these words.

पश्यैतां पाण्डुपुत्राणामाचार्य महतीं चमूम् ।
व्यूढां द्रुपदपुत्रेण तव शिष्येण धीमता ।। ३ ।।

*paśyaitāṁ pāṇḍuputrāṇāmācārya mahatīṁ camūm,*
*vyūḍhāṁ drupadaputreṇa tava śiṣyeṇa dhīmatā. (3)*

Behold, O Teacher! This mighty army of the sons of Pāṇḍu arrayed by the son of Drupada, thy wise disciple.

अत्र शूरा महेष्वासा भीमार्जुनसमा युधि ।
युयुधानो विराटश्च द्रुपदश्च महारथः ।। ४ ।।

*atra śūrā maheṣvāsā bhīmārjunasamā yudhi,*
*yuyudhāno virāṭaśca drupadaśca mahārathaḥ.* (4)

Here are heroes, mighty archers like Yuyudhāna, Virāṭa and Drupada, who are equal in battle to Bhīma and Arjuna, each commanding eleven thousand archers.

धृष्टकेतुश्चेकितानः काशिराजश्च वीर्यवान् ।
पुरुजित्कुन्तिभोजश्च शैब्यश्च नरपुङ्गवः ।। ५ ।।

*dhṛṣṭaketuścekitānaḥ kāśirājaśca vīryavān,*
*purujitkuntibhojaśca śaibyaśca narapuṅgavaḥ.* (5)

Dhṛṣṭaketu, Cekitāna, and the valiant king of Kāśī, Purujit and Kuntibhoja and Śaibya, the best of men.

युधामन्युश्च विक्रान्त उत्तमौजाश्च वीर्यवान् ।
सौभद्रो द्रौपदेयाश्च सर्व एव महारथाः ।।६ ।।

*yudhāmanyuśca vikrānta uttamaujāśca vīryavān,*
*saubhadro draupadeyāśca sarva eva mahārathāḥ.* (6)

The strong Yudhāmanyu and the brave Uttamaujā, the son of Subhadrā and the sons of Draupadi, all of them, divisional commanders.

अस्माकं तु विशिष्टा ये तान्निबोध द्विजोत्तम ।
नायका मम सैन्यस्य सञ्ज्ञार्थं तान्ब्रवीमि ते ।। ७।।

*asmākaṁ tu viśiṣṭā ye tānnibodha dvijottama,*
*nāyakā mama sainyasya sañjñārthaṁ tānbravīmi te. (7)*

Know also, O best among the twice-born, the names of those who are the most distinguished amongst ourselves, the leaders of my army; these I name to thee for thy information.

भवान्भीष्मश्च कर्णश्च कृपश्च समितिञ्जयः ।
अश्वत्थामा विकर्णश्च सौमदत्तिस्तथैव च ।। ८।।

*bhavānbhīṣmaśca karṇaśca kṛpaśca samitiñjayaḥ,*
*aśvatthāmā vikarṇaśca saumadattistathaiva ca. (8)*

Yourself and Bhīṣma, and Karṇa and also Kṛpa, the victorious in war; Aśvatthāmā, Vikarṇa and so also Bhūriśravā, the son of Somadatta.

अन्ये च बहवः शूरा मदर्थे त्यक्तजीविताः ।
नानाशस्त्रप्रहरणाः सर्वे युद्धविशारदाः ।। ९ ।।

*anye ca bahavaḥ śūrā madarthe tyaktajīvitāḥ,*
*nānāśastrapraharaṇāḥ sarve yuddhaviśāradāḥ. (9)*

And many other heroes, who are determined to give up their lives for my sake, armed with various weapons and missiles, all well-skilled in battle.

अपर्याप्तं तदस्माकं बलं भीष्माभिरक्षितम् ।
पर्याप्तं त्विदमेतेषां बलं भीमाभिरक्षितम् ।। १० ।।

*aparyāptaṁ tadasmākaṁ balaṁ bhīṣmābhirakṣitam,*
*paryāptaṁ tvidameteṣāṁ balaṁ bhīmābhirakṣitam. (10)*

This army of ours, defended by Bhīṣma is insufficient, whereas, that army of theirs defended by Bhīma is sufficient.

OR

This army of ours protected by Bhīṣma is unlimited, whereas, that army of theirs protected by Bhīma is limited.

अयनेषु च सर्वेषु यथाभागमवस्थिताः ।
भीष्ममेवाभिरक्षन्तु भवन्तः सर्व एव हि ।। ११ ।।

*ayaneṣu ca sarveṣu yathābhāgamavasthitāḥ,*
*bhīṣmamevābhirakṣantu bhavantaḥ sarva eva hi. (11)*

Therefore, do you all, stationed in your respective positions in the several divisions of the army, protect Bhīṣma alone.

तस्य सञ्जनयन्हर्षं कुरुवृद्धः पितामहः ।
सिंहनादं विनद्योच्चैः शङ्खं दध्मौ प्रतापवान् ।।१२।।

*tasya sañjanayanharṣaṁ kuruvṛddhaḥ pitāmahaḥ,*
*siṁhanādaṁ vinadyoccaiḥ śaṅkhaṁ dadhmau pratāpavān. (12)*

His glorious grandsire (Bhīṣma), the oldest of the Kauravas, in order to cheer Duryodhana, now sounded aloud a lion's roar and blew his conch.

ततः शङ्खाश्च भेर्यश्च पणवानकगोमुखाः ।
सहसैवाभ्यहन्यन्त स शब्दस्तुमुलोऽभवत् ।। १३ ।।

*tataḥ śaṅkhāśca bheryaśca paṇavānakagomukhāḥ,*
*sahasaivābhyahanyanta sa śabdastumulo'bhavat.* (13)

Then (following Bhīṣma), conches and kettle-drums, tabors, drums and cow-horns blared forth quite suddenly and the sound was tremendous.

ततः श्वेतैर्हयैर्युक्ते महति स्यन्दने स्थितौ ।
माधवः पाण्डवश्चैव दिव्यौ शङ्खौ प्रदध्मतुः ।।१४।।

*tataḥ śvetairhayairyukte mahati syandane sthithau,*
*mādhavaḥ pāṇḍavaścaiva divyau śaṅkhau pradadhmatuḥ.* (14)

Then, also Mādhava and the son of Pāṇḍu, seated in their magnificent chariot yoked with white horses, blew their divine conches.

पाञ्चजन्यं हृषीकेशो देवदत्तं धनञ्जयः ।
पौण्ड्रं दध्मौ महाशङ्खं भीमकर्मा वृकोदरः ।।१५।।

*pāñcajanyaṁ hṛṣīkeśo devadattaṁ dhanañjayaḥ,*
*pauṇḍraṁ dadhmau mahāśaṅkhaṁ bhīmakarmā vṛkodaraḥ.* (15)

Hṛṣīkeśa blew the Pāñchajanya and Dhanañjaya (Arjuna) blew the Devadatta and Vṛkodara (Bhīma), the doer of terrible deeds, blew the great conch, named Pauṇḍra.

अनन्तविजयं राजा कुन्तीपुत्रो युधिष्ठिरः ।
नकुलः सहदेवश्च सुघोषमणिपुष्पकौ ।।१६।।

*anantavijayaṁ rājā kuntīputro yudhiṣṭhiraḥ,*
*nakulaḥ sahadevaśca sughoṣamaṇipuṣpakau. (16)*

King Yudhiṣṭhira, the son of Kuntī, blew the Anantavijaya; Nakula and Sahadeva blew the Sughoṣa and the Maṇipuṣpaka.

काश्यश्च परमेष्वासः शिखण्डी च महारथः ।
धृष्टद्युम्नो विराटश्च सात्यकिश्चापराजितः ।।१७।।

*kāśyaśca parameṣvāsaḥ śikhaṇḍī ca mahārathaḥ,*
*dhṛṣṭadyumno virāṭaśca sātyakiścāparājitaḥ. (17)*

The king of Kāśī, an excellent archer, Śikhaṇḍī, the mighty commander of eleven thousand archers, Dhṛṣṭadyumna and Virāṭa and Sātyaki, the unconquered;

द्रुपदो द्रौपदेयाश्च सर्वशः पृथिवीपते ।
सौभद्रश्च महाबाहुः शङ्खान्दध्मुः पृथक् पृथक् ।।१८।।

*drupado draupadeyāśca sarvaśaḥ pṛthivīpate,*
*saubhadraśca mahābāhuḥ śaṅkhāndadhmuḥ pṛthak pṛthak. (18)*

Drupada and the sons of Draupadi, O Lord of the earth, and the son of Subhadrā the mighty armed, blew their respective conches.

स घोषो धार्तराष्ट्राणां हृदयानि व्यदारयत् ।
नभश्च पृथिवीं चैव तुमुलो व्यनुनादयन् ।।१९।।

*sa ghoṣo dhārtarāṣṭrāṇāṁ hṛdayāni vyadārayat,*
*nabhaśca pṛthivīṁ caiva tumulo vyanunādayan. (19)*

That tumultuous sound rent the hearts of (the people of) Dhṛtarāṣṭra's party and made both heaven and earth reverberate.

अथ व्यवस्थितान्दृष्ट्वा धार्तराष्ट्रान् कपिध्वजः ।
प्रवृत्ते शस्त्रसम्पाते धनुरुद्यम्य पाण्डवः ।।२०।।
हृषीकेशं तदा वाक्यमिदमाह महीपते ।

*atha vyavasthitāndṛṣṭvā dhārtarāṣṭrān kapidhvajaḥ,*
*pravṛtte śastrasampāte dhanurudyamya pāṇḍvaḥ. (20)*
*hṛṣīkeṣaṁ tadā vākyamidamāha mahīpate*

Then, seeing the people of Dhṛtarāṣṭra's party standing arrayed and the discharge of weapons about to begin, Arjuna, the son of Pāṇḍu, whose ensign was a monkey, took up his bow and said these words to Kṛṣṇa (Hṛṣīkeśa), O Lord of the earth!

अर्जुन उवाच
सेनयोरुभयोर्मध्ये रथं स्थापय मेऽच्युत ।।२१।।
यावदेतान्निरीक्षेऽहं योद्धुकामानवस्थितान् ।
कैर्मया सह योद्धव्यमस्मिन्रणसमुद्यमे ।।२२।।

*arjuna uvāca*
*senyorubhayormadhye rathaṁ sthāpaya me'cyuta. (21)*
*yāvadetānnirīkṣe'haṁ yoddhukāmānavasthitān,*
*kairmayā saha yoddhavyamasminraṇasamudyame. (22)*

Arjuna said:

In the midst of the two armies, place my chariot, O Achyuta, that I may behold those who stand here desirous of fighting and, on the eve of this battle, let me know with whom I must fight.

योत्स्यमानानवेक्षेऽहं य एतेऽत्र समागताः ।
धार्तराष्ट्रस्य दुर्बुद्धेर्युद्धे प्रियचिकीर्षवः ।।२३।।

*yotsyamānānavekṣe'haṁ ya ete'tra samāgatāḥ*
*dhārtarāṣṭrasya durbuddheryuddhe priyacikīrṣavaḥ. (23)*

For, I desire to observe those who are assembled here for the fight, wishing to please, in battle, the evil-minded sons of Dhṛtarāṣṭra.

सञ्जय उवाच
एवमुक्तो हृषीकेशो गुडाकेशेन भारत ।
सेनयोरुभयोर्मध्ये स्थापयित्वा रथोत्तमम् ।।२४।।

*sañjaya uvāca*
*evamukto hṛṣīkeśo guḍākeśena bhārata,*
*senayorubhayormadhye sthāpayitvā rathottamam. (24)*

Sañjaya said :
Thus, addressed by Guḍākeśa, O Bhārata (here meaning

Dhṛtarāṣṭra), Hṛṣīkeśa, having stationed the best of chariots between the two armies....

भीष्मद्रोणप्रमुखतः सर्वेषां च महीक्षिताम् ।
उवाच पार्थ पश्यैतान् समवेतान्कुरूनिति ।।२५।।

*bhīṣmadroṇapramukhataḥ sarveṣāṁ ca mahīkṣitām,*
*uvāca pārtha paśyaitān samavetānkurūniti. (25)*

In front of Bhīṣma and Droṇa, and all the rulers of the earth, the Lord said, "O Pārtha, behold these Kurus gathered together".

तत्रापश्यत्स्थितान् पार्थः पितॄनथ पितामहान् ।
आचार्यान्मातुलान्भ्रातॄन्पुत्रान्पौत्रान्सखींस्तथा ।।२६।।

*tatrāpaśyatsthitānpārthaḥ pitṝnatha pitāmahān,*
*ācāryānmātulānbhrātṝnputrānpautrānsakhīṁstathā. (26)*

Then, Pārtha saw stationed there in both the armies, fathers, grandfathers, teachers, maternal uncles, brothers, sons, grandsons and friends too.

**श्वशुरान् सुहृदश्चैव सेनयोरुभयोरपि ।**
**तान्समीक्ष्य स कौन्तेयः सर्वान्बन्धूनवस्थितान् ।।२७।।**

*śvaśurān suhṛdaścaiva senayorubhayorapi,*
*tānsamīkṣya sa kaunteyaḥ sarvānbandhūnavasthitān.* (27)

(He saw) Fathers-in-law and friends also in both the armies. Then the son of Kuntī, seeing all these kinsmen thus standing arrayed, spoke thus sorrowfully, filled with deep pity.

**कृपया परयाविष्टो विषीदन्निदमब्रवीत् ।**

**अर्जुन उवाच**

**दृष्ट्वेमं स्वजनं कृष्ण युयुत्सुं समुपस्थितम् ।।२८।।**

*kṛpayā parayāviṣṭo viṣīdannidamabravīt*

*arjuna uvāca*

*dṛṣṭvemaṁ svajanaṁ kṛṣṇa yuyutsuṁ samupasthitam.* (28)

Arjuna said:

Seeing these my kinsmen, O Kṛṣṇa, arrayed, eager to fight.....

सीदन्ति मम गात्राणि मुखं च परिशुष्यति ।
वेपथुश्च शरीरे मे रोमहर्षश्च जायते ।।२९।।

*sīdanti mama gātrāṇi mukhaṁ ca pariśuṣyati,*
*vepathuśca śarīre me romaharṣaśca jāyate. (29)*

My limbs fail and my mouth is parched, my body quivers and my hair stands on end.....

गाण्डीवं स्रंसते हस्तात्त्वक्चैव परिदह्यते ।
न च शक्नोम्यवस्थातुं भ्रमतीव च मे मनः ।।३०।।

*gāṇḍīvaṁ sraṁsate hastāttvakcaiva paridahyate,*
*na ca śaknomyavasthātuṁ bhramatīva ca me manaḥ. (30)*

The Gāṇḍīva-bow slips from my hand and my skin burns all over; I am also unable to stand and my mind is whirling round, as it were....

निमित्तानि च पश्यामि विपरीतानि केशव ।
न च श्रेयोऽनुपश्यामि हत्वा स्वजनमाहवे ।।३१।।

*nimittāni ca paśyāmi viparītāni keśava,*
*na ca śreyo'nupaśyāmi hatvā svajanamāhave. (31)*

And I see adverse omens, O Keśava. Nor do I see any good, in killing my kinsmen in battle....

न काङ्क्षे विजयं कृष्ण न च राज्यं सुखानि च ।
किं नो राज्येन गोविन्द किं भोगैर्जीवितेन वा ।।३२।।

*na kāṅkṣe vijayaṁ kṛṣṇa na ca rājyaṁ sukhāni ca,*
*kiṁ no rājyena govinda kiṁ bhogairjīvitena vā. (32)*

For, I desire not victory, O Kṛṣṇa, nor kingdom, nor pleasures. Of what avail is dominion to us, O Govinda? Of what avail are pleasures or even life itself ?....

येषामर्थे काङ्क्षितं नो राज्यं भोगाः सुखानि च ।
त इमेऽवस्थिता युद्धे प्राणांस्त्यक्त्वा धनानि च ।।३३।।

*yeṣāmarthe kāṅkṣitaṁ no rājyaṁ bhogāḥ sukhāni ca,*
*ta ime'vasthitā yuddhe prāṇāṁstyaktvā dhanāni ca. (33)*

They, for whose sake we desire kingdom, enjoyment and pleasures, stand here in battle, having renounced life and wealth....

आचार्याः पितरः पुत्रास्तथैव च पितामहाः ।
मातुलाः श्वशुराः पौत्राः श्यालाः सम्बन्धिनस्तथा ।।३४।।

*ācāryāḥ pitaraḥ putrāstathaiva ca pitāmahāḥ,*
*mātulāḥ śvaśurāḥ pautrāḥ śyālāḥ sambandhinastathā.* (34)

Teachers, fathers, sons and also grandfathers, maternal uncles, fathers-in-law, grandsons, brothers-in-law and other relatives....

एतान्न हन्तुमिच्छामि घ्नतोऽपि मधुसूदन ।
अपि त्रैलोक्यराज्यस्य हेतोः किं नु महीकृते ।।३५।।

*etānna hantumicchāmi ghnato'pi madhusūdana,*
*api trailokyarājyasya hetoḥ kiṁ nu mahīkṛte.* (35)

These, I do not wish to kill, though they may kill me, O Madhusūdana, even for the sake of dominion over the three worlds; how much less for the sake of the earth.

निहत्य धार्तराष्ट्रान्नः का प्रीतिः स्याज्जनार्दन ।
पापमेवाश्रयेदस्मान्हत्वैतानाततायिनः ।।३६।।

*nihatya dhārtarāṣṭrānnaḥ kā prītiḥ syājjanārdana,*
*pāpamevāśrayedasmānhatvaitānātatāyinaḥ. (36)*

Killing these sons of Dhṛtarāṣṭra, what pleasure can be ours, O Janārdana ? Sin alone will be our gain by killing these felons.

तस्मान्नार्हा वयं हन्तुं धार्तराष्ट्रान् स्वबान्धवान् ।
स्वजनं हि कथं हत्वा सुखिनः स्याम माधव ।।३७।।

*tasmānnārhā vayaṁ hantuṁ dhārtarāṣṭrān svabāndhavān,*
*svajanaṁ hi kathaṁ hatvā sukhinaḥ syāma mādhava. (37)*

Therefore, we shall not kill sons of Dhṛtarāṣṭra, our relatives; for how can we be happy by killing our own people, O Mādhava?

यद्यप्येते न पश्यन्ति लोभोपहतचेतसः ।
कुलक्षयकृतं दोषं मित्रद्रोहे च पातकम् ।।३८।।

*yadyapyete na paśyanti lobhopahatacetasaḥ,*
*kulakṣayakṛtaṁ dośaṁ mitradrohe ca pātakam. (38)*

Though these, with their intelligence clouded by greed, see no evil in the destruction of the families in the society and no sin in their cruelty to friends...

कथं न ज्ञेयमस्माभिः पापादस्मान्निवर्तितुम् ।
कुलक्षयकृतं दोषं प्रपश्यद्भिर्जनार्दन ।।३९।।

*katham na jñeyamasmābhiḥ pāpādasmānnivartitum,*
*kulakṣayakṛtam doṣam prapaśyadbhirjanārdana. (39)*

Why should not we, who clearly see evil in the destruction of the family units, learn to turn away from this sin, O Janārdana?

कुलक्षये प्रणश्यन्ति कुलधर्माः सनातनाः ।
धर्मे नष्टे कुलं कृत्स्नमधर्मोऽभिभवत्युत ।।४०।।

*kulakṣaye praṇaśyanti kuladharmāḥ sanātanāḥ,*
*dharme naṣṭe kulam kṛtsnamadharmo'bhibhavatyuta. (40)*

In the destruction of a family, the immemorial religious rites of that family perish; on the destruction of spirituality, impiety indeed overcomes the whole family.

अधर्माभिभवात्कृष्ण प्रदुष्यन्ति कुलस्त्रियः ।
स्त्रीषु दुष्टासु वार्ष्णेय जायते वर्णसङ्करः ।।४१।।

*adharmābhibhavātkṛṣṇa praduṣyanti kulastriyaḥ,*
*strīṣu duṣṭāsu vārṣṇeya jāyate varṇasaṅkaraḥ. (41)*

By the prevalence of impiety, O Kṛṣṇa, the women of the family become corrupt; and women being corrupted, O descendent of the Vṛṣṇi clan, there arises 'intermingling of castes' (varṇasaṅkara).

सङ्करो नरकायैव कुलघ्नानां कुलस्य च ।
पतन्ति पितरो ह्येषां लुप्तपिण्डोदकक्रियाः ।।४२।।

*saṅkaro narakāyaiva kulaghnānāṁ kulasya ca,*
*patanti pitaro hyeṣāṁ luptapiṇḍodakakriyāḥ. (42)*

'Confusion of caste' leads the slayer of the family to hell; for their forefathers fall, deprived of the offerings of piṇḍa (rice ball) and water (libations).

दोषैरेतैः कुलघ्नानां वर्णसङ्करकारकैः ।
उत्साद्यन्ते जातिधर्माः कुलधर्माश्च शाश्वताः ।।४३।।

*doṣairetaiḥ kulaghnānāṁ varṇasaṅkarakārakaiḥ,*
*utsādyante jātidharmāḥ kuladharmāśca śāśvatāḥ. (43)*

By these evil deeds of the 'destroyers of the family', which cause confusion of castes, the eternal religious rites of the caste and the family are destroyed.

उत्सन्नकुलधर्माणां मनुष्याणां जनार्दन ।
नरकेऽनियतं वासो भवतीत्यनुशुश्रुम ।।४४।।

*utsannakuladharmāṇāṁ manuṣyāṇāṁ janārdana,*
*narake'niyataṁ vāso bhavatītyanuśuśruma. (44)*

We have heard, O Janārdana, that it is inevitable for those men, in whose families the religious practices have been destroyed, to dwell in hell for an unknown period of time.

अहो बत महत्पापं कर्तुं व्यवसिता वयम् ।
यद्राज्यसुखलोभेन हन्तुं स्वजनमुद्यताः ।।४५।।

*aho bata mahatpāpaṁ kartuṁ vyavasitā vayam,*
*yadrājyasukhalobhena hantuṁ svajanamudyatāḥ. (45)*

Alas! We are involved in a great sin, in that we are prepared to kill our kinsmen, from greed for the pleasures of the kingdom.

यदि मामप्रतीकारमशस्त्रं शस्त्रपाणयः ।
धार्तराष्ट्रा रणे हन्युस्तन्मे क्षेमतरं भवेत् ।।४६।।

*yadi māmapratīkāramaśastraṁ śastrapāṇayaḥ,*
*dhārtarāṣṭrā raṇe hanyustanme kṣemataraṁ bhavet. (46)*

If the sons of Dhṛtarāṣṭra, 'weapons in hand', slay me in battle, unresisting and unarmed, that would be better for me.

सञ्जय उवाच
एवमुक्त्वार्जुनः सङ्ख्ये रथोपस्थ उपाविशत् ।
विसृज्य सशरं चापं शोकसंविग्नमानसः ।।४७।।

*sañjaya uvāca*

*evamuktvārjunaḥ saṅkhye rathopastha upāviśat,*
*visṛjya saśaraṁ cāpaṁ śokasaṁvignamānasaḥ. (47)*

Sañjaya said :

Having thus spoken in the midst of the battlefield, Arjuna sat down on the seat of the chariot, casting away his bow and arrow, with a mind distressed with sorrow.

ॐ तत्सदिति श्रीमद्भगवद्गीतासूपनिषत्सु
ब्रह्मविद्यायां योगशास्त्रे
श्रीकृष्णार्जुनसंवादेऽर्जुनविषादयोगो
नाम प्रथमोऽध्यायः

*om tatsaditi śrimadbhagavadgītāsūpaniṣatsu*
*brahmavidyāyāṁ yogaśāstre*
*śrīkṛṣṇārjunasaṁvāde'rjunaviṣādayogo*
*nāma prathamo'dhyāyaḥ*

Thus, in the Upaniṣads of the glorious Bhagavad-gītā, in the science of the eternal, in the scripture of yoga, in the dialogue betwen Śrī Kṛṣṇa and Arjuna, the first discourse ends entitled:

THE YOGA OF ARJUNA - GRIEF

* * *

Yoga of Knowledge

# Chapter 2

## *Yoga of Knowledge (Sāṅkhya)*

सञ्जय उवाच
तं तथा कृपयाविष्टमश्रुपूर्णाकुलेक्षणम् ।
विषीदन्तमिदं वाक्यमुवाच मधुसूदनः ।।१।।

*sañjaya uvāca*
*taṁ tathā kṛpayāviṣṭamaśrupūrṇākulekṣaṇam,*
*viṣīdantamidaṁ vākyamuvāca madhusūdanaḥ. (1)*

Sañjaya said :
To him, who was thus overcome with pity and despondency, with eyes full of tears, and agitated, Madhusūdana (the destroyer of Madhu, the demon) spoke these words.

श्रीभगवानुवाच

कुतस्त्वा कश्मलमिदं विषमे समुपस्थितम् ।
अनार्यजुष्टमस्वर्ग्यमकीर्तिकरमर्जुन ।।२।।

*śrībhagavānuvāca*

*kutastvā kaśmalamidaṁ viṣame samupasthitam,*
*anāryajuṣṭamasvargyamakīrtikaramarjuna. (2)*

The Blessed Lord said :

Whence is this perilous condition come upon thee, this dejection, unlike of Āryan, heaven-excluding, disgraceful, O Arjuna?

क्लैब्यं मा स्म गमः पार्थ नैतत्त्वय्युपपद्यते ।
क्षुद्रं हृदयदौर्बल्यं त्यक्त्वोत्तिष्ठ परंतप ।।३।।

*klaibyaṁ mā sma gamaḥ pārtha naitattvayyupapadyate,*
*kṣudraṁ hṛdayadaurbalyaṁ tyaktvottiṣṭha parantapa. (3)*

Yield not to impotence, O Pārtha! It does not befit thee. Cast off this mean weakness of heart! Stand up, O Parantapa (scorcher of foes) !

अर्जुन उवाच
कथं भीष्ममहं सङ्ख्ये द्रोणं च मधुसूदन ।
इषुभिः प्रतियोत्स्यामि पूजार्हावरिसूदन ।।४।।

*arjuna uvāca*

*kathaṁ bhīṣmamahaṁ saṅkhye droṇaṁ ca madhusūdana,*
*iṣubhiḥ pratiyotsyāmi pūjārhāvarisūdana. (4)*

Arjuna said :

How, O Madhusūdana, shall I, in battle, fight with arrows against Bhīṣma and Droṇa, who are fit to be worshipped, O destroyer of enemies!

गुरूनहत्वा हि महानुभावान्
श्रेयो भोक्तुं भैक्ष्यमपीह लोके ।
हत्वार्थकामांस्तु गुरूनिहैव
भुञ्जीय भोगान् रुधिरप्रदिग्धान् ।।५।।

*gurūnahatvā hi mahānubhāvān*
*śreyo bhoktuṁ bhaikṣyamapīha loke,*
*hatvārthakāmāṁstu gurūnihaiva*
*bhuñjīya bhogān rudhirapradigdhān. (5)*

Better indeed in this world, is to eat even the bread of beggary than to slay the most noble of teachers. But, if I kill them, all my enjoyments of wealth and desires, even in this world, will be stained with blood.

न चैतद्विद्मः कतरन्नो गरीयो-
यद्वा जयेम यदि वा नो जयेयुः ।
यानेव हत्वा न जिजीविषाम-
स्तेऽवस्थिताः प्रमुखे धार्तराष्ट्राः ।।६ ।।

*na caitadvidmaḥ kataranno garīyo-*
*yadvā jayema yadi vā no jayeyuḥ,*
*yāneva hatvā na jijīviṣāma-*
*ste'vasthitāḥ pramukhe dhārtarāṣṭrāḥ. (6)*

I can scarcely say which will be better; that we should conquer them or that they should conquer us. Even the sons of Dhṛtarāṣṭra, after slaying whom, we do not wish to live, stand facing us.

कार्पण्यदोषोपहतस्वभावः
पृच्छामि त्वां धर्मसम्मूढचेताः ।

यच्छ्रेयः स्यान्निश्चितं ब्रूहि तन्मे
शिष्यस्तेऽहं शाधि मां त्वां प्रपन्नम् ।। ७।।

*kārpaṇyadoṣopahatasvabhāvaḥ*
*pṛcchāmi tvāṁ dharmasammuḍhacetāḥ,*
*yacchreyaḥ syānniścitaṁ brūhi tanme*
*śiṣyaste'haṁ śādhi māṁ tvāṁ prapannam. (7)*

My heart is overpowered by the taint of pity; my mind is confused as to duty. I ask Thee. Tell me decisively what is good for me. I am Thy disciple. Instruct me, I have taken refuge in Thee.

न हि प्रपश्यामि ममापनुद्याद्
यच्छोकमुच्छोषणमिन्द्रियाणाम् ।
अवाप्य भूमावसपत्नमृद्धं-
राज्यं सुराणामपि चाधिपत्यम् ।।८।।

*na hi prapaśyāmi mamāpanudyād*
*yacchokamucchoṣaṇamindriyāṇām,*
*avāpya bhūmāvasapatnamṛddhaṁ-*
*rājyaṁ surāṇāmapi cādhipatyam. (8)*

I do not see that it would remove this sorrow that burns up my senses, even if I should attain prosperous and unrivalled dominion on earth, or even lordship over the gods.

सञ्जय उवाच
एवमुक्त्वा हृषीकेशं गुडाकेशः परन्तप ।
न योत्स्य इति गोविन्दमुक्त्वा तूष्णीं बभूव ह ॥९॥

*sañjaya uvāca*
*evamuktvā hṛṣīkeśaṁ guḍākeśaḥ parantapa,*
*na yotsya iti govindamuktvā tūṣṇīṁ babhūva ha. (9)*

Sañjaya said :
Having spoken thus to Hṛṣīkeśa, Guḍākeśa, the destroyer of foes, said to Govinda: "I will not fight" and became silent.

तमुवाच हृषीकेशः प्रहसन्निव भारत ।
सेनयोरुभयोर्मध्ये विषीदन्तमिदं वचः ॥१०॥

*tamuvāca hṛṣīkeśaḥ prahasanniva bhārata,*
*senayorubhayormadhye viṣīdantamidaṁ vacaḥ. (10)*

To him, who was despondent in the midst of the two armies, Hṛṣīkeśa as if smiling, 'O Bhārata', spoke these words.

श्रीभगवानुवाच
अशोच्यानन्वशोचस्त्वं प्रज्ञावादांश्च भाषसे ।
गतासूनगतासूंश्च नानुशोचन्ति पण्डिताः ।।११।।

*śrībhagavānuvāca*
*aśocyānanvaśocastvaṁ prajñāvādāṁśca bhāṣase,*
*gatāsūnagatāsūṁśca nānuśocanti paṇḍitāḥ. (11)*

The Blessed Lord said:
You have grieved for those that should not be grieved for; yet, you speak words of wisdom. The wise grieve neither for the living nor for the dead.

न त्वेवाहं जातु नासं न त्वं नेमे जनाधिपाः ।
न चैव न भविष्यामः सर्वे वयमतः परम् ।।१२।।

*na tvevāhaṁ jātu nāsaṁ na tvaṁ neme janādhipāḥ,*
*na caiva na bhaviṣyāmaḥ sarve vayamataḥ param. (12)*

It is not that at any time (in the past), indeed was I not, nor were you, nor these rulers of men. Nor verily, shall we ever cease to be hereafter.

देहिनोऽस्मिन्यथा देहे कौमारं यौवनं जरा ।
तथा देहान्तरप्राप्तिर्धीरस्तत्र न मुह्यति ।।१३।।

*dehino'sminyathā dehe kaumāraṁ yauvanaṁ jarā,*
*tathā dehāntaraprāptirdhīrastatra na muhyati. (13)*

Just as in this body the embodied (soul) passes into childhood, youth and old age, so also does he pass into another body; the firm man does not grieve at it.

मात्रास्पर्शास्तु कौन्तेय शीतोष्णसुखदुःखदाः ।
आगमापायिनोऽनित्यास्तांस्तितिक्षस्व भारत ।।१४।।

*mātrāsparśāstu kaunteya śītoṣṇasukhaduḥkhadāḥ,*
*āgamāpāyino'nityāstāṁstitikṣasva bhārata. (14)*

The contacts of senses with objects, O son of Kuntī, which cause heat and cold, pleasure and pain, have a beginning and an end; they are impermanent. Endure them bravely, O descendant of Bharata.

यं हि न व्यथयन्त्येते पुरुषं पुरुषर्षभ ।
समदुःखसुखं धीरं सोऽमृतत्वाय कल्पते ।।१५।।

*yaṁ hi na vyathayantyete puruṣaṁ puruṣarṣabha,*
*samaduḥkhasukhaṁ dhīraṁ so'mṛtatvāya kalpate. (15)*

That firm man whom surely these afflict not, O chief among men, to whom pleasure and pain are the same, is fit for realising the immortality of the Self.

नासतो विद्यते भावो नाभावो विद्यते सतः ।
उभयोरपि दृष्टोऽन्तस्त्वनयोस्तत्त्वदर्शिभिः ।।१६।।

*nāsato vidyate bhāvo nābhāvo vidyate sataḥ,*
*ubhayorapi dṛṣṭo'ntastvanayostattvadarśibhiḥ. (16)*

The unreal has no existence; there is no non-existence of the Real; the truth about both these has been seen by the knowers of the Truth (or the seers of the Essence).

अविनाशि तु तद्विद्धि येन सर्वमिदं ततम् ।
विनाशमव्ययस्यास्य न कश्चित्कर्तुमर्हति ।।१७।।

*avināśi tu tadviddhi yena sarvamidaṁ tatam,*
*vināśamavyayasyāsya na kaścitkartumarhati. (17)*

Know That to be indestructible by which all this is pervaded. None can cause the destruction of That – the Imperishable.

अन्तवन्त इमे देहा नित्यस्योक्ताः शरीरिणः ।
अनाशिनोऽप्रमेयस्य तस्माद्युध्यस्व भारत ।।१८।।

*antavanta ime dehā nityasyoktāḥ śarīriṇaḥ,*
*anāśino'prameyasya tasmādyudhyasva bhārata. (18)*

It is said that these bodies of the embodied Self have an end. The Self is eternal, indestructible, incomprehensible. Therefore, fight, O Bhārata.

य एनं वेत्ति हन्तारं यश्चैनं मन्यते हतम् ।
उभौ तौ न विजानीतो नायं हन्ति न हन्यते ।।१९।।

*ya enaṁ vetti hantāraṁ yaścainaṁ manyate hatam,*
*ubhau tau na vijānīto nāyaṁ hanti na hanyate. (19)*

He, who takes the self to be the slayer and he, who thinks he is slain; neither of them knows. He slays not, nor is he slain.

न जायते म्रियते वा कदाचि-
न्नायं भूत्वा भविता वा न भूयः।
अजो नित्यः शाश्वतोऽयं पुराणो-
न हन्यते हन्यमाने शरीरे ॥२०॥

*na jāyate mriyate vā kadāci-*
*nnāyaṁ bhūtvā bhavitā vā na bhūyaḥ,*
*ajo nityaḥ śāśvato'yaṁ purāṇo-*
*na hanyate hanyamāne śarīre. (20)*

He is not born, nor does He ever die; after having been, He again ceases not to be; unborn, eternal, changeless and ancient, He is not killed when the body is killed.

वेदाविनाशिनं नित्यं य एनमजमव्ययम् ।
कथं स पुरुषः पार्थ कं घातयति हन्ति कम् ॥२१॥

*vedāvināśinaṁ nityaṁ ya enamajamavyayam,*
*kathaṁ sa puruṣaḥ pārtha kaṁ ghātayati hanti kam.* (21)

Whosoever knows Him to be indestructible, eternal, unborn and inexhaustible, how can that man slay O Pārtha, or cause others to be slain?

वासांसि जीर्णानि यथा विहाय
नवानि गृह्णाति नरोऽपराणि ।
तथा शरीराणि विहाय जीर्णा-
न्यन्यानि संयाति नवानि देही ।।२२।।

*vāsāṁsi jīrṇāni yathā vihāya*
*navāni gṛhṇāti naro'parāṇi,*
*tathā śarīrāṇi vihāya jīrṇā-*
*nyanyāni saṁyāti navāni dehī.* (22)

Just as a man casts off his worn out clothes and puts on new ones, so also the embodied Self casts off its worn out bodies and enters new ones.

नैनं छिन्दन्ति शस्त्राणि नैनं दहति पावकः ।
न चैनं क्लेदयन्त्यापो न शोषयति मारुतः ।।२३।।

*nainaṁ chindanti śastrāṇi nainaṁ dahati pāvakaḥ,*
*na cainaṁ kledayantyāpo na śoṣayati mārutaḥ.* (23)

Weapons cleave It not, fire burns It not, water moistens It not, wind dries It not.

अच्छेद्योऽयमदाह्योऽयमक्लेद्योऽशोष्य एव च ।
नित्यः सर्वगतः स्थाणुरचलोऽयं सनातनः ।।२४।।

*acchedyo'yamadāhyo'yamakledyo'śoṣya eva ca,*
*nityaḥ sarvagataḥ sthāṇuracalo'yaṁ sanātanaḥ.* (24)

This Self cannot be cut, nor burnt, nor moistened, nor dried up. It is eternal, all-pervading, stable, immovable and ancient.

अव्यक्तोऽयमचिन्त्योऽयमविकार्योऽयमुच्यते ।
तस्मादेवं विदित्वैनं नानुशोचितुमर्हसि ।।२५।।

*avyakto'yamacintyo'yamavikāryo'yamucyate,*
*tasmādevaṁ viditvainaṁ nānuśocitumarhasi.* (25)

This (Self) is said to be unmanifest, unthinkable and unchangeble. Therefore, knowing This to be such, you should not grieve.

अथ चैनं नित्यजातं नित्यं वा मन्यसे मृतम् ।
तथापि त्वं महाबाहो नैवं शोचितुमर्हसि ।।२६।।

*atha cainaṁ nityajātaṁ nityaṁ vā manyase mṛtam,*
*tathāpi tvaṁ mahābāho naivaṁ śocitumarhasi. (26)*

But, even if you think of him as being constantly born and constantly dying, even then, O mighty-armed, you should not grieve.

जातस्य हि ध्रुवो मृत्युर्ध्रुवं जन्म मृतस्य च ।
तस्मादपरिहार्येऽर्थे न त्वं शोचितुमर्हसि ।।२७।।

*jātasya hi dhruvo mṛtyurdhruvaṁ janma mṛtasya ca,*
*tasmādaparihārye'rthe na tvaṁ śocitumarhasi. (27)*

Indeed, certain is death for the born, and certain is birth for the dead; therefore, over the inevitable, you should not grieve.

अव्यक्तादीनि भूतानि व्यक्तमध्यानि भारत ।
अव्यक्तनिधनान्येव तत्र का परिदेवना ।।२८।।

*avyaktādīni bhūtāni vyaktamadhyāni bhārata,*
*avyaktanidhanānyeva tatra kā paridevanā. (28)*

Beings were unmanifest in the beginning, and unmanifest again in their end, seem to be manifest in the middle, O Bhārata. What then, is there to grieve about?

आश्चर्यवत्पश्यति कश्चिदेन-
माश्चर्यवद्वदति तथैव चान्यः ।
आश्चर्यवच्चैनमन्यः शृणोति
श्रुत्वाप्येनं वेद न चैव कश्चित् ।।२९।।

*āscaryavatpaśyati kaścidena-*
*māścaryavadvadati tathaiva cānyaḥ,*
*āścaryavaccainamanyaḥ śṛṇoti*
*śrutvāpyenaṁ veda na caiva kaścit. (29)*

One sees This as a wonder; another speaks of This as a wonder; another hears of This as a wonder; yet, having heard, none understands This at all!

देही नित्यमवध्योऽयं देहे सर्वस्य भारत ।
तस्मात्सर्वाणि भूतानि न त्वं शोचितुमर्हसि ।।३०।।

*dehī nityamavadhyo'yaṁ dehe sarvasya bhārata,*
*tasmātsarvāṇi bhūtāni na tvaṁ śocitumarhasi. (30)*

This – the Indweller in the body of everyone is ever indestructible, O Bhārata; and, therefore, you should not grieve for any creature.

स्वधर्ममपि चावेक्ष्य न विकम्पितुमर्हसि ।
धर्म्याद्धि युद्धाच्छ्रेयोऽन्यत्क्षत्रियस्य न विद्यते ।।३१।।

*svadharmamapi cāvekṣya na vikampitumarhasi,*
*dharmyāddhi yuddhācchreyo'nyatkṣatriyasya na vidyate. (31)*

Further, looking at thy own duty, thou ought not to waver, for there is nothing higher for a kṣatriya than a righteous war.

यदृच्छया चोपपन्नं स्वर्गद्वारमपावृतम् ।
सुखिनः क्षत्रियाः पार्थ लभन्ते युद्धमीदृशम् ।।३२।।

*yadṛcchayā copapannaṁ svargadvāramapāvṛtam,*
*sukhinaḥ kṣatriyāḥ pārtha labhante yuddhamīdṛśam. (32)*

Happy indeed are the kṣatriyas, O Pārtha, who are called to fight in such a battle that comes of itself as an open door to heaven.

अथ चेत्त्वमिमं धर्म्यं सङ्ग्रामं न करिष्यसि ।
ततः स्वधर्मं कीर्तिं च हित्वा पापमवाप्स्यसि ।।३३।।

*atha cettvamimaṁ dharmyaṁ saṁgrāmaṁ na kariṣyasi,*
*tataḥ svadharmaṁ kīrtiṁ ca hitvā pāpamavāpṣyasi.* (33)

But, if you will not fight this righteous war, then having abandoned your own duty and fame, you shall incur sin.

अकीर्तिं चापि भूतानि कथयिष्यन्ति तेऽव्ययाम् ।
सम्भावितस्य चाकीर्तिर्मरणादतिरिच्यते ।।३४।।

*akīrtiṁ cāpi bhūtāni kathayiṣyanti te'vyayām,*
*sambhāvitasya cākīrtirmaraṇādatiricyate.* (34)

People too will recount your everlasting dishonour; and to one who has been honoured, dishonour is more than death.

भयाद्रणादुपरतं मंस्यन्ते त्वां महारथाः ।
येषां च त्वं बहुमतो भूत्वा यास्यसि लाघवम् ।।३५।।

*bhayādraṇāduparataṁ maṁsyante tvāṁ mahārathāḥ,*
*yeṣāṁ ca tvaṁ bahumato bhūtvā yāsyasi lāghavam. (35)*

The great battalion commanders will think that you have withdrawn from the battle through fear; and you will be looked down upon by those who had thought much of you and your heroism in the past.

अवाच्यवादांश्च बहून्वदिष्यन्ति तवाहिताः ।
निन्दन्तस्तव सामर्थ्यं ततो दुःखतरं नु किम् ।।३६।।

*avācyavādāṁśca bahūnvadiṣyanti tavāhitāḥ,*
*nindantastava sāmarthyaṁ tato duḥkhataraṁ nu kim. (36)*

And many unspeakable words will your enemies speak cavilling about your powers. What can be more painful than this?

हतो वा प्राप्स्यसि स्वर्गं जित्वा वा भोक्ष्यसे महीम् ।
तस्मादुत्तिष्ठ कौन्तेय युद्धाय कृतनिश्चयः ।।३७।।

*hato vā prāpsyasi svargaṁ jitvā vā bhokṣyase mahīm,*
*tasmāduttiṣṭha kaunteya yuddhāya kṛtaniścayaḥ. (37)*

Slain, you will obtain heaven; victorious, you will enjoy the earth; therefore, stand up, O son of Kuntī, resolved to fight.

सुखदुःखे समे कृत्वा लाभालाभौ जयाजयौ ।
ततो युद्धाय युज्यस्व नैवं पापमवाप्स्यसि ।।३८।।

*sukhaduḥkhe same kṛtvā lābhālābhau jayājayau,*
*tato yuddhāya yujyasva naivaṁ pāpamavāpsyasi. (38)*

Having made pleasure and pain, gain and loss, victory and defeat the same, engage in battle for the sake of battle; thus, you shall not incur sin.

एषा तेऽभिहिता साङ्ख्ये बुद्धिर्योगे त्विमां शृणु ।
बुद्ध्या युक्तो यया पार्थ कर्मबन्धं प्रहास्यसि ।।३९।।

*eṣā te'bhihitā sāṅkhye buddhiryoge tvimāṁ śṛṇu,*
*buddhyā yukto yayā pārtha karmabandhaṁ prahāsyasi. (39)*

This, which has been taught to thee, is wisdom concerning sāṅkhya. Now listen to the wisdom concerning yoga, having known which, O Pārtha, you shall cast off the 'bonds of action'.

नेहाभिक्रमनाशोऽस्ति प्रत्यवायो न विद्यते ।
स्वल्पमप्यस्य धर्मस्य त्रायते महतो भयात् ॥४०॥

*nehābhikramanāśo'sti pratyavāyo na vidyate,*
*svalpamapyasya dharmasya trāyate mahato bhayāt.* (40)

In this, there is no loss of effort, nor is there any harm (production of contrary results). Even a little of this knowledge, even a little practice of this yoga, protects one from the great fear.

व्यवसायात्मिका बुद्धिरेकेह कुरुनन्दन ।
बहुशाखा ह्यनन्ताश्च बुद्धयोऽव्यवसायिनाम् ॥४१॥

*vyavasāyātmikā buddhirekeha kurunandana,*
*bahuśākha hyanantāśca buddhayo'vyavasāyinām.* (41)

Here, O Joy of the Kurus (Kurunandana) there is but a single pointed determination; many-branched and endless are the thoughts of the irresolute.

यामिमां पुष्पितां वाचं प्रवदन्त्यविपश्चितः ।
वेदवादरताः पार्थ नान्यदस्तीति वादिनः ।।४२।।

*yāmimaṁ puṣpitāṁ vācaṁ pravadantyavipaścitaḥ,*
*vedavādaratāḥ pārtha nānyadastīti vādinaḥ. (42)*

Flowery speech is uttered by the unwise, taking pleasure in the eulogising words of Vedas, O Pārtha, saying, 'there is nothing else'.

कामात्मानः स्वर्गपरा जन्मकर्मफलप्रदाम् ।
क्रियाविशेषबहुलां भोगैश्वर्यगतिं प्रति ।।४३।।

*kāmātmānaḥ svargaparā janmakarmaphalapradām,*
*kriyāviśeṣabahulāṁ bhogaiśvaryagatiṁ prati. (43)*

Full of desires, having heaven as their goal, they utter flowery words, which promise new birth as the reward of their actions, and prescribe various specific actions for the attainment of pleasure and lordship.

भोगैश्वर्यप्रसक्तानां तयापहृतचेतसाम् ।
व्यवसायात्मिका बुद्धिः समाधौ न विधीयते ।।४४।।

*bhogaiśvaryaprasaktānāṁ tayāpahṛtacetasām,*
*vyavasāyātmikā buddhiḥ samādhau na vidhīyate.* (44)

For, those who cling to joy and lordship, whose minds are drawn away by such teaching, are neither determinate and resolute nor are they fit for steady meditation and samādhi.

त्रैगुण्यविषया वेदा निस्त्रैगुण्यो भवार्जुन ।
निर्द्वन्द्वो नित्यसत्त्वस्थो निर्योगक्षेम आत्मवान् ।।४५।।

*traiguṇyaviṣayā vedā nistraiguṇyo bhavārjuna,*
*nirdvandvo nityasattvastho niryogakṣema ātmavān.* (45)

The Vedas deal with the three attributes; be you above these three attributes (guṇas), O Arjuna, free yourself from the pairs of opposites, and ever remain in the sattva (goodness), freed from all thoughts of acquisition and preservation, and be established in the Self.

यावानर्थ उदपाने सर्वतः सम्प्लुतोदके ।
तावान्सर्वेषु वेदेषु ब्राह्मणस्य विजानतः ।।४६।।

*yāvānartha udapāne sarvataḥ samplutodake,*
*tāvānsarveṣu vedeṣu brāhmaṇasya vijānataḥ. (46)*

To the brāhmaṇa who has known the Self, all the Vedas are of as much use as is a reservoir of water in a place where there is flood everywhere.

कर्मण्येवाधिकारस्ते मा फलेषु कदाचन ।
मा कर्मफलहेतुर्भूर्मा ते सङ्गोऽस्त्वकर्मणि ।।४७।।

*karmaṇyevādhikāraste mā phaleṣu kadācana,*
*mā karmaphalaheturbhūrmā te saṅgo'stvakarmaṇi. (47)*

Thy right is to work only, but never to its fruits; let not the fruit of action be thy motive, nor let thy attachment be to inaction.

योगस्थः कुरु कर्माणि सङ्गं त्यक्त्वा धनञ्जय ।
सिद्ध्यसिद्ध्योः समो भूत्वा समत्वं योग उच्यते ।।४८।।

*yogasthaḥ kuru karmāṇi saṅgaṁ tyaktvā dhanañjaya,*
*siddhyasiddhyoḥ samo bhūtvā samatvaṁ yoga ucyate. (48)*

Perform action O Dhanañjaya, abandoning attachment, being steadfast in yoga, and balanced in success and failure. "Evenness of mind is called yoga."

दूरेण ह्यवरं कर्म बुद्धियोगाद्धनञ्जय ।
बुद्धौ शरणमन्विच्छ कृपणाः फलहेतवः ।।४९।।

*dūreṇa hyavaraṁ karma buddhiyogāddhanañjaya,*
*buddhau śaraṇamanviccha kṛpaṇāḥ phalahetavaḥ. (49)*

Far lower than the yoga of wisdom is action, O Dhanañjaya. Seek thou refuge in wisdom; wretched are they whose motive is the fruit.

बुद्धियुक्तो जहातीह उभे सुकृतदुष्कृते ।
तस्माद्योगाय युज्यस्व योगः कर्मसु कौशलम् ।।५०।।

*buddhiyukto jahātīha ubhe suktṛtaduṣkṛte,*
*tasmādyogāya yujyasva yogaḥ karmasu kauśalam. (50)*

Endowed with the wisdom of 'evenness of mind', one casts off in this life both good deeds and evil deeds; therefore, devote yourself to yoga. 'Skill in action is yoga.'

कर्मजं बुद्धियुक्ता हि फलं त्यक्त्वा मनीषिणः ।
जन्मबन्धविनिर्मुक्ताः पदं गच्छन्त्यनामयम् ।।५१।।

*karmajaṁ buddhiyuktā hi phalaṁ tyaktvā manīṣiṇaḥ,*
*janmabandhavinirmuktāḥ padaṁ gacchantyanāmayam. (51)*

The wise, possessed of knowledge, having abandoned the fruits of their actions and freed from the fetters of birth, go to the state which is beyond all evil.

यदा ते मोहकलिलं बुद्धिर्व्यतितरिष्यति ।
तदा गन्तासि निर्वेदं श्रोतव्यस्य श्रुतस्य च ।। ५२।।

*yadā te mohakalilaṁ buddhirvyatitariṣyati,*
*tadā gantāsi nirvedaṁ śrotavyasya śrutasya ca. (52)*

When your intellect crosses the mire of delusion, you shall attain to indifference as to what has been heard and what is yet to be heard.

श्रुतिविप्रतिपन्ना ते यदा स्थास्यति निश्चला ।
समाधावचला बुद्धिस्तदा योगमवाप्स्यसि ।। ५३।।

*śrutivipratipannā te yadā sthāsyati niścalā,*
*samādhāvacalā buddhistadā yogamavāpsyasi.* (53)

When your intellect, though perplexed by what you have heard, shall stand immovable and steady in the Self, then you shall attain Self-Realisation.

अर्जुन उवाच
स्थितप्रज्ञस्य का भाषा समाधिस्थस्य केशव ।
स्थितधीः किं प्रभाषेत किमासीत व्रजेत किम् ।।५४।।

*arjuna uvāca*
*sthitaprajñasya kā bhāṣā samādhisthasya keśava,*
*sthitadhīḥ kiṁ prabhāṣeta kimāsīta vrajeta kim.* (54)

Arjuna said :

What, O Keśava, is the description of him who has steady wisdom and who is merged in the superconscious state? How does one of steady wisdom speak, how does he sit, how does he walk?

श्रीभगवानुवाच
प्रजहाति यदा कामान्सर्वान्पार्थ मनोगतान् ।
आत्मन्येवात्मना तुष्टः स्थितप्रज्ञस्तदोच्यते ।।५५।।

*śrībhagavānuvāca*
*prajahāti yadā kāmānsarvānpārtha manogatān,*
*ātmanyevātmanā tuṣṭaḥ sthitaprajñastadocyate. (55)*

The Blessed Lord said :
When a man completely casts off, O Pārtha, all the desires of the mind and is satisfied in the Self by the Self, then is he said to be one of steady wisdom.

दुःखेष्वनुद्विग्नमनाः सुखेषु विगतस्पृहः ।
वीतरागभयक्रोधः स्थितधीर्मुनिरुच्यते ।।५६।।

*duḥkheṣvanudvignamanāḥ sukheṣu vigataspṛhaḥ,*
*vītarāgabhayakrodhaḥ sthitadhīrmunirucyate. (56)*

He, whose mind is not shaken up by adversity, and who, in prosperity does not hanker after pleasures, who is free from attachment, fear and anger is called a Sage of steady Wisdom.

यः सर्वत्रानभिस्नेहस्तत्तत्प्राप्य शुभाशुभम् ।
नाभिनन्दति न द्वेष्टि तस्य प्रज्ञा प्रतिष्ठिता ।।५७।।

*yaḥ sarvatrānabhisnehastattatprāpya śubhāśubham,*
*nābhinandati na dveṣṭi tasya prajñā pratiṣṭhitā. (57)*

He, who is everywhere without attachment, on meeting with anything good or bad, who neither rejoices nor hates, his wisdom is fixed.

यदा संहरते चायं कूर्मोऽङ्गानीव सर्वशः ।
इन्द्रियाणीन्द्रियार्थेभ्यस्तस्य प्रज्ञा प्रतिष्ठिता ।।५८।।

*yadā saṁharate cāyaṁ kūrmo'ṅgānīva sarvaśaḥ,*
*indriyāṇīndriyārthebhyastasya prajñā pratiṣṭhitā. (58)*

When like the tortoise, which withdraws its limbs from all sides, he withdraws his senses from the sense objects, then his wisdom becomes steady.

विषया विनिवर्तन्ते निराहारस्य देहिनः ।
रसवर्जं रसोऽप्यस्य परं दृष्ट्वा निवर्तते ।।५९।।

*viṣayā vinivartante nirāhārasya dehinaḥ,*
*rasavarjaṁ raso'pyasya paraṁ dṛṣṭvā nivartate. (59)*

The objects of the senses turn away from the abstinent man leaving the longing (behind); but his longing also leaves him upon seeing the Supreme.

यततो ह्यपि कौन्तेय पुरुषस्य विपश्चितः ।
इन्द्रियाणि प्रमाथीनि हरन्ति प्रसभं मनः ।।६०।।

*yatato hyapi kaunteya puruṣasya vipaścitaḥ,*
*indriyāṇi pramāthīni haranti prasabhaṁ manaḥ. (60)*

The turbulent senses, O son of Kuntī, do violently carry away the mind of a wise man, though he (may) be striving to control them.

तानि सर्वाणि संयम्य युक्त आसीत मत्परः ।
वशे हि यस्येन्द्रियाणि तस्य प्रज्ञा प्रतिष्ठिता ।।६१।।

*tāni sarvāṇi saṁyamya yukta āsīta matparaḥ,*
*vaśe hi yasyendriyāṇi tasya prajñā pratiṣṭhitā. (61)*

Having restrained them all, He should sit steadfast, intent on Me; his wisdom is steady whose senses are under control.

ध्यायतो विषयान्पुंसः सङ्गस्तेषूपजायते ।
सङ्गात्सञ्जायते कामः कामात्क्रोधोऽभिजायते ।।६२।।

*dhyāyato viṣayānpuṁsaḥ saṅgasteṣūpajāyate,*
*saṅgātsañjāyate kāmaḥ kāmātkrodho'bhijāyate. (62)*

When a man thinks of objects, attachment for them arises; from attachment desire is born; from desire arises anger....

क्रोधाद्भवति सम्मोहः सम्मोहात्स्मृतिविभ्रमः ।
स्मृतिभ्रंशाद् बुद्धिनाशो बुद्धिनाशात्प्रणश्यति ।।६३।।

*krodhādbhavati sammohaḥ sammohātsmṛtivibhramaḥ,*
*smṛtibhraṁśād buddhināśo buddhināśātpraṇaśyati. (63)*

From anger comes delusion; from delusion, loss of memory; from loss of memory, the destruction of discrimination; from destruction of discrimination, he perishes.

रागद्वेषवियुक्तैस्तु विषयानिन्द्रियैश्चरन् ।
आत्मवश्यैर्विधेयात्मा प्रसादमधिगच्छति ।।६४।।

*rāgadveṣaviyuktaistu viṣayānindriyaiścaran,*
*ātmavaśyairvidheyātmā prasādamadhigacchati.* (64)

But the self-controlled man moving among objects with his senses under restraint and free from both attraction and repulsion, attains peace.

प्रसादे सर्वदुःखानां हानिरस्योपजायते ।
प्रसन्नचेतसो ह्याशु बुद्धिः पर्यवतिष्ठते ।।६५।।

*prasāde sarvaduḥkhānāṁ hānirasyopajāyate,*
*prasannacetaso hyāśu buddhiḥ paryavatiṣṭhate.* (65)

In that peace all pains are destroyed; for, the intellect of the tranquil minded soon becomes steady.

नास्ति बुद्धिरयुक्तस्य न चायुक्तस्य भावना ।
न चाभावयतः शान्तिरशान्तस्य कुतः सुखम् ।।६६।।

*nāsti buddhirayuktasya na cāyuktasya bhāvanā,*
*na cābhāvayataḥ śantiraśāntasya kutaḥ sukham. (66)*

There is no knowledge (of the Self) to the unsteady; and to the unsteady no meditation; and to the unmeditative no peace; to the peaceless, how can there be happiness?

इन्द्रियाणां हि चरतां यन्मनोऽनुविधीयते ।
तदस्य हरति प्रज्ञां वायुर्नावमिवाम्भसि ।।६७।।

*indriyāṇāṁ hi caratāṁ yanmano'nuvidhīyate,*
*tadasya harati prajñāṁ vāyurnāvamivāmbhasi. (67)*

For, the mind which follows in the wake of the wandering senses, carries away his discrimination, as the wind carries away a boat on the waters.

तस्माद्यस्य महाबाहो निगृहीतानि सर्वशः ।
इन्द्रियाणीन्द्रियार्थेभ्यस्तस्य प्रज्ञा प्रतिष्ठिता ।।६८।।

*tasmādyasya mahābāho nigṛhītāni sarvaśaḥ,*
*indriyāṇīndriyārthebhyastasya prajñā pratiṣṭhitā. (68)*

Therefore, O mighty-armed, his knowledge is steady whose senses are completely restrained from sense objects.

या निशा सर्वभूतानां तस्यां जागर्ति संयमी ।
यस्यां जाग्रति भूतानि सा निशा पश्यतो मुनेः ।।६९।।

*yā niśā sarvabhūtānāṁ tasyāṁ jāgarti saṁyamī,*
*yasyāṁ jāgrati bhūtāni sā niśā paśyato muneḥ. (69)*

That, which is night to all beings, in that the self-controlled man keeps awake; where all beings are awake, that is the night for the Sage (Muni) who sees.

आपूर्यमाणमचलप्रतिष्ठं-
समुद्रमापः प्रविशन्ति यद्वत् ।
तद्वत्कामा यं प्रविशन्ति सर्वे
स शान्तिमाप्नोति न कामकामी ।। ७० ।।

*āpūryamāṇamacalapratiṣṭhaṁ-*
*samudramapaḥ praviśanti yadvat,*
*tadvatkāmā yaṁ praviśānti sarve*
*sa śāntimāpnoti na kāmakāmī. (70)*

He (Man of Perfection) attains peace into whom all desires enter as waters enter the ocean, which filled from all sides, remains unmoved, but not the 'desirer of desires'.

विहाय कामान्यः सर्वान्पुमांश्चरति निःस्पृहः ।
निर्ममो निरहङ्कारः स शान्तिमधिगच्छति ।।७१।।

*vihāya kāmānyaḥ sarvānpumāṁścarati niḥspṛhaḥ,*
*nirmamo nirahaṅkāraḥ sa śāntimadhigacchati. (71)*

That man attains peace who, abandoning all desires, moves about without longing, without the sense of 'I-ness' and 'my-ness'.

एषा ब्राह्मी स्थितिः पार्थ नैनां प्राप्य विमुह्यति ।
स्थित्वास्यामन्तकालेऽपि ब्रह्मनिर्वाणमृच्छति ।।७२।।

*eṣā brāhmī sthitiḥ pārtha naināṁ prāpya vimuhyati,*
*sthitvāsyāmantakāle'pi brahmanirvāṇamṛcchati. (72)*

This is the Brāhmika state, O son of Pṛthā. Attaining this, none is deluded. Being established therein, even at the end of life, one attains to oneness with Brahman.

ॐ तत्सदिति श्रीमद्भगवद्गीतासूपनिषत्सु
ब्रह्मविद्यायां योगशास्त्रे श्रीकृष्णार्जुनसंवादे
साङ्ख्ययोगो नाम द्वितीयोऽध्यायः

*om tatsaditi śrimadbhagavadgītāsūpaniṣatsu*
*brahmavidyāyāṁ yogaśāstre śrīkṛṣṇārjunasaṁvāde*
*sāṅkhyayogo nāma dvitīyo'dhyāyaḥ.*

Thus, in the Upaniṣads of the glorious Bhagavad-gītā, in the science of the eternal, in scripture of yoga, in the dialogue between Śrī Kṛṣṇa and Arjuna, the second discourse ends entitled:

THE YOGA OF KNOWLEDGE (SĀṄKHYA)

***

Yoga of Action

# Chapter 3

## *Yoga of Action (Karma-yoga)*

अर्जुन उवाच

ज्यायसी चेत्कर्मणस्ते मता बुद्धिर्जनार्दन ।
तत्किं कर्मणि घोरे मां नियोजयसि केशव ।।१।।

*arjuna uvāca*

*jyāyasī cetkarmaṇaste matā buddhirjanārdana,*
*tatkiṁ karmaṇi ghore māṁ niyojayasi keśava. (1)*

Arjuna said :

If it be thought by you that 'knowledge' is superior to 'action,' O Janārdana, why then, do you, O Keśava, engage me in this terrible action?

व्यामिश्रेणेव वाक्येन बुद्धिं मोहयसीव मे ।
तदेकं वद निश्चित्य येन श्रेयोऽहमाप्नुयाम् ।।२।।

*vyāmiśreṇeva vākyena buddhiṁ mohayasīva me,*
*tadekaṁ vada niścitya yena śreyo'hamāpnuyām.* (2)

With this apparently perplexing speech you confuse, as it were, my understanding; therefore, tell me that 'one' way by which, I, for certain, may attain the Highest.

श्रीभगवानुवाच
लोकेऽस्मिन्द्विविधा निष्ठा पुरा प्रोक्ता मयानघ ।
ज्ञानयोगेन साङ्ख्यानां कर्मयोगेन योगिनाम् ।।३।।

*śrībhagavānuvāca*

*loke'smindvividhā niṣṭhā purā proktā mayānagha,*
*jñānayogena sāṅkhyānāṁ karmayogena yoginām.* (3)

The Blessed Lord said :

In this world there is a twofold path, as said before, O sinless one; the 'path of knowledge' of the sāṅkhyans and the 'path of action' of the yogins.

न कर्मणामनारम्भान्नैष्कर्म्यं पुरुषोऽश्नुते ।
न च सन्न्यसनादेव सिद्धिं समधिगच्छति ।।४।।

*na karmaṇāmanārambhānnaiṣkarmyaṁ puruṣo'śnute,*
*na ca sannyasanādeva siddhiṁ samadhigacchati.* (4)

Not by non-performance of action does man reach 'actionlessness'; nor by mere renunciation does he attain perfection.

न हि कश्चित्क्षणमपि जातु तिष्ठत्यकर्मकृत् ।
कार्यते ह्यवशः कर्म सर्वः प्रकृतिजैर्गुणैः ।।५।।

*na hi kaścitkṣaṇamapi jātu tiṣṭhatyakarmakṛt,*
*kāryate hyavaśaḥ karma sarvaḥ prakṛtijairguṇaiḥ.* (5)

Verily, none can ever remain, even for a moment, without performing action; for, everyone is made to act helplessly, indeed, by the qualities born of prakṛti (nature).

कर्मेन्द्रियाणि संयम्य य आस्ते मनसा स्मरन् ।
इन्द्रियार्थान्विमूढात्मा मिथ्याचारः स उच्यते ।।६।।

*karmendriyāṇi saṁyamya ya āste manasā smaran,*
*indriyārthānvimūḍhātmā mithyācāraḥ sa ucyate. (6)*

He who, restraining the organs of action, sits thinking in his mind of the sense objects, he, of deluded understanding, is called a hypocrite.

यस्त्विन्द्रियाणि मनसा नियम्यारभतेऽर्जुन ।
कर्मेन्द्रियैः कर्मयोगमसक्तः स विशिष्यते ।।७।।

*yastvindriyāṇi manasā niyamyārabhate'rjuna,*
*karmendriyaiḥ karmayogamasaktaḥ sa viśiṣyate. (7)*

But, whosoever, controlling the senses by the mind, O Arjuna, engages his organs of action in Karma-yoga, without attachment, he excels.

नियतं कुरु कर्म त्वं कर्म ज्यायो ह्यकर्मणः ।
शरीरयात्रापि च ते न प्रसिद्ध्येदकर्मणः ।।८।।

*niyataṁ kuru karma tvaṁ karma jyāyo hyakarmaṇaḥ,*
*śarīrayātrāpi ca te na prasiddhyedakarmaṇaḥ. (8)*

You perform (your) bounden duty; for, action is superior to inaction. Even the maintenance of the body would not be possible for you by inaction.

यज्ञार्थात्कर्मणोऽन्यत्र लोकोऽयं कर्मबन्धनः ।
तदर्थं कर्म कौन्तेय मुक्तसङ्गः समाचर ।।९।।

*yajñārthātkarmaṇo'nyatra loko'yaṁ karmabandhanaḥ,*
*tadarthaṁ karma kaunteya muktasaṅgaḥ samācara. (9)*

The world is bound by actions other than those performed for the sake of sacrifice; do thou, therefore, O son of Kuntī, perform action for that sake (for yajña) alone, free from all attachments.

सहयज्ञाः प्रजाः सृष्ट्वा पुरोवाच प्रजापतिः ।
अनेन प्रसविष्यध्वमेष वोऽस्त्विष्टकामधुक् ।।१०।।

*sahayajñāḥ prajāḥ sṛṣṭvā purovāca prajāpatiḥ,*
*anena prasaviṣyadhvameṣa vo'stviṣṭakāmadhuk. (10)*

The Prajāpati (the Creator), having in the beginning (of creation) created mankind together with sacrifices, said, "By this shall you prosper; let this be the milch cow of your desires – kāmadhuk" (the mythological cow which yields all desired objects).

देवान्भावयतानेन ते देवा भावयन्तु वः ।
परस्परं भावयन्तः श्रेयः परमवाप्स्यथ ।।११।।

*devānbhāvayatānena te devā bhāvayantu vaḥ,*
*parasparaṁ bhāvayantaḥ śreyaḥ paramavāpsyatha. (11)*

With this, you do nourish the gods and may those devas nourish you; thus nourishing one another, you shall, attain the highest good.

इष्टान्भोगान्हि वो देवा दास्यन्ते यज्ञभाविताः।
तैर्दत्तानप्रदायैभ्यो यो भुङ्क्ते स्तेन एव सः ।।१२।।

*iṣṭānbhogānhi vo devā dāsyante yajñabhāvitāḥ,*
*tairdattānapradāyaibhyo yo bhuṅkte stena eva saḥ. (12)*

The devas, nourished by the sacrifice, will give you the desired objects. Indeed, he who enjoys objects given by the devas, without offering (in return) to them, is verily a thief.

**यज्ञशिष्टाशिनः सन्तो मुच्यन्ते सर्वकिल्बिषैः ।**
**भुञ्जते ते त्वघं पापा ये पचन्त्यात्मकारणात् ।।१३।।**

*yajñaśiṣṭāśinaḥ santo mucyante sarvakilbiṣaiḥ,*
*bhuñjate te tvaghaṁ pāpā ye pacantyātmakāraṇāt. (13)*

The righteous, who eat the remnants of the sacrifices are freed from all sins; but those sinful ones, who cook food (only) for their own sake, verily eat but sin.

**अन्नाद्भवन्ति भूतानि पर्जन्यादन्नसम्भवः ।**
**यज्ञाद्भवति पर्जन्यो यज्ञः कर्मसमुद्भवः ।।१४।।**

*annādbhavanti bhūtāni parjanyādannasambhavaḥ,*
*yajñādbhavati parjanyo yajñaḥ karmasamudbhavaḥ. (14)*

From food, come forth beings; from rain, food is produced; from sacrifice, arises rain and sacrifice is born of action.

**कर्म ब्रह्मोद्भवं विद्धि ब्रह्माक्षरसमुद्भवम् ।**
**तस्मात्सर्वगतं ब्रह्म नित्यं यज्ञे प्रतिष्ठितम् ।।१५।।**

*karma brahmodbhavaṁ viddhi brahmākṣarasamudbhavam,*
*tasmātsarvagataṁ brahma nityaṁ yajñe pratiṣṭhitam. (15)*

Know you that action comes from Brahmājī (the Creator) and Brahmājī comes from the Imperishable. Therefore, the all-pervading Brahman (God Principle) ever rests in sacrifice.

एवं प्रवर्तितं चक्रं नानुवर्तयतीह यः ।
अघायुरिन्द्रियारामो मोघं पार्थ स जीवति ।।१६।।

*evaṁ pravartitaṁ cakraṁ nānuvartayatīha yaḥ,*
*aghāyurindriyārāmo moghaṁ pārtha sa jīvati. (16)*

He, who does not follow here the wheel thus set revolving, is of a sinful life, rejoicing in the senses. He lives in vain, O son of Pṛthā.

यस्त्वात्मरतिरेव स्यादात्मतृप्तश्च मानवः ।
आत्मन्येव च सन्तुष्टस्तस्य कार्यं न विद्यते ।।१७।।

*yastvātmaratireva syādātmatṛptaśca mānavaḥ,*
*ātmanyeva ca santuṣṭastasya kāryaṁ na vidyate. (17)*

But, the man who rejoices only in the Self, who is satisfied with the Self, who is content in the Self alone, for him verily there is nothing (more) to be done.

नैव तस्य कृतेनार्थो नाकृतेनेह कश्चन ।
न चास्य सर्वभूतेषु कश्चिदर्थव्यपाश्रयः ॥१८॥

*naiva tasya kṛtenārtho nākṛteneha kaścana,*
*na cāsya sarvabhūteṣu kaścidarthavyapāśrayaḥ. (18)*

For him there is no interest whatever in what is done, or what is not done; nor does he depend upon any being for any object.

तस्मादसक्तः सततं कार्यं कर्म समाचर ।
असक्तो ह्याचरन्कर्म परमाप्नोति पूरुषः ॥१९॥

*tasmādasaktaḥ satataṁ kāryaṁ karma samācara,*
*asakto hyācarankarma paramāpnoti pūruṣaḥ. (19)*

Therefore, always perform action which should be done without attachment; for, by performing action without attachment man attains the Supreme.

कर्मणैव हि संसिद्धिमास्थिता जनकादयः ।
लोकसङ्ग्रहमेवापि सम्पश्यन्कर्तुमर्हसि ॥२०॥

*karmaṇaiva hi saṁsiddhimāsthitā janakādayaḥ,*
*lokasaṅgrahamevāpi sampaśyankartumarhasi. (20)*

Janaka and others attained Perfection verily through action only; even with a view to protecting the masses you should perform action.

यद्यदाचरति श्रेष्ठस्तत्तदेवेतरो जनः ।
स यत्प्रमाणं कुरुते लोकस्तदनुवर्तते ।।२१।।

*yadyadācarati śreṣṭhastattadevetaro janaḥ,*
*sa yatpramāṇaṁ kurute lokastadanuvartate. (21)*

Whatever a great man does, that other men also do (imitate); whatever he sets up as the standard, that the world (people) follows.

न मे पार्थास्ति कर्तव्यं त्रिषु लोकेषु किञ्चन ।
नानवाप्तमवाप्तव्यं वर्त एव च कर्मणि ।।२२।।

*na me pārthāsti kartavyaṁ triṣu lokeṣu kiñcana,*
*nānavāptamavāptavyaṁ varta eva ca karmaṇi. (22)*

There is nothing in the three worlds, O Pārtha, that has to be done by Me, nor is there anything unattained that should be attained by Me; yet, I engage myself in action.

यदि ह्यहं न वर्तेयं जातु कर्मण्यतन्द्रितः ।
मम वर्त्मानुवर्तन्ते मनुष्याः पार्थ सर्वशः ॥२३॥

*yadi hyahaṁ na varteyaṁ jātu karmaṇyatandritaḥ,*
*mama vartmānuvartante manuṣyāḥ pārtha sarvaśaḥ. (23)*

For, should I not ever engage myself in action without relaxation, men would in every way follow My path, O son of Pṛthā.

उत्सीदेयुरिमे लोका न कुर्यां कर्म चेदहम् ।
सङ्करस्य च कर्ता स्यामुपहन्यामिमाः प्रजाः ॥ २४॥

*utsīdeyurime lokā na kuryāṁ karma cedaham,*
*saṅkarasya ca kartā syāmupahanyāmimāḥ prajāḥ. (24)*

These worlds would perish, if I did not perform action; I would be the author of confusion of castes and would destroy these beings.

सक्ताः कर्मण्यविद्वांसो यथा कुर्वन्ति भारत ।
कुर्याद्विद्वांस्तथासक्तश्चिकीर्षुर्लोकसङ्ग्रहम् ।।२५।।

*saktāḥ karmaṇyavidvāṁso yathā kurvanti bhārata,*
*kuryādvidvāṁstathāsaktaścikīrṣurlokasaṅgraham. (25)*

As the ignorant men act from attachment to action, O Bhārata, so should the wise men act without attachment, wishing the welfare of the world.

न बुद्धिभेदं जनयेदज्ञानां कर्मसङ्गिनाम् ।
जोषयेत्सर्वकर्माणि विद्वान्युक्तः समाचरन् ।।२६।।

*na buddhibhedaṁ janayedajñānāṁ karmasaṅginām,*
*joṣayetsarvakarmāṇi vidvānyuktaḥ samācaran. (26)*

Let no wise man unsettle the minds of ignorant people, who are attached to action; he should engage them all in actions, himself fulfilling them with devotion.

प्रकृतेः क्रियमाणानि गुणैः कर्माणि सर्वशः।
अहङ्कारविमूढात्मा कर्ताहमिति मन्यते ।।२७।।

*prakṛteḥ kriyamāṇāni guṇaiḥ karmāṇi sarvaśaḥ,*
*ahaṅkāravimūḍhātmā kartāhamiti manyate. (27)*

All actions are performed, in all cases, merely by the qualities in nature (guṇas). He, whose mind is deluded by egoism, thinks 'I am the doer'.

तत्त्ववित्तु महाबाहो गुणकर्मविभागयोः ।
गुणा गुणेषु वर्तन्त इति मत्वा न सज्जते ।।२८।।

*tattvavittu mahābāho guṇakarmavibhāgayoḥ,*
*guṇā guṇeṣu vartanta iti matvā na sajjate. (28)*

But he, who knows the Truth, O mighty-armed, about the divisions of the qualities and (their) functions, and he, who knows that 'guṇas as senses' move amidst 'guṇas as objects', is not attached.

प्रकृतेर्गुणसम्मूढाः सज्जन्ते गुणकर्मसु ।
तानकृत्स्नविदो मन्दान्कृत्स्नविन्न विचालयेत् ।।२९।।

*prakṛterguṇasammūḍhāḥ sajjante guṇakarmasu,*
*tānakṛtsnavido mandānkṛtsnavinna vicālayet. (29)*

Those deluded by the qualities of nature (guṇas) are attached to the functions of the qualities. The Man of perfect Knowledge should not unsettle the foolish, who are of imperfect knowledge.

मयि सर्वाणि कर्माणि सन्न्यस्याध्यात्मचेतसा ।
निराशीर्निर्ममो भूत्वा युध्यस्व विगतज्वरः ।।३०।।

*mayi sarvāṇi karmāṇi sannyasyādhyātmacetasā,*
*nirāśirnirmamo bhūtvā yudhyasva vigatajvaraḥ. (30)*

Renouncing all actions in Me, with the mind centered on the Self, free from hope and egoism (ownership), free from (mental) fever, (you) do fight!

ये मे मतमिदं नित्यमनुतिष्ठन्ति मानवाः ।
श्रद्धावन्तोऽनसूयन्तो मुच्यन्ते तेऽपि कर्मभिः ।।३१।।

*ye me matamidaṁ nityamanutiṣṭhanti mānavāḥ,*
*śraddhāvanto'nasūyanto mucyante te'pi karmabhiḥ. (31)*

Those men, who constantly practise this teaching of Mine, full of faith and without cavilling, they too, are freed from actions.

ये त्वेतदभ्यसूयन्तो नानुतिष्ठन्ति मे मतम् ।
सर्वज्ञानविमूढांस्तान्विद्धि नष्टानचेतसः ।।३२।।

*ye tvetadabhyasūyanto nānutiṣṭhanti me matam,*
*sarvajñānavimūḍhāṁstānviddhi naṣṭānacetasaḥ.* (32)

But, those who carp at My teaching and do not practise it, deluded in all knowledge, and devoid of discrimination, know them to be doomed to destruction.

सदृशं चेष्टते स्वस्याः प्रकृतेर्ज्ञानवानपि ।
प्रकृतिं यान्ति भूतानि निग्रहः किं करिष्यति ।।३३।।

*sadṛśaṁ ceṣṭate svasyāḥ prakṛterjñānavānapi,*
*prakṛtiṁ yānti bhūtāni nigrahaḥ kiṁ kariṣyati.* (33)

Even a wise man acts in accordance with his own nature; beings will follow their own nature; what can restraint do?

इन्द्रियस्येन्द्रियस्यार्थे रागद्वेषौ व्यवस्थितौ ।
तयोर्न वशमागच्छेत्तौ ह्यस्य परिपन्थिनौ ।।३४।।

*indriyasyendriyasyārthe rāgadveṣau vyavasthitau,*
*tayorna vaśamāgacchettau hyasya paripanthinau.* (34)

Attachment and aversion for the objects of the senses abide in the senses; let none come under their sway; for, they are his foes.

श्रेयान्स्वधर्मो विगुणः परधर्मात्स्वनुष्ठितात् ।
स्वधर्मे निधनं श्रेयः परधर्मो भयावहः ।।३५।।

*śreyānsvadharmo viguṇaḥ paradharmātsvanuṣṭhitāt,*
*svadharme nidhanaṁ śreyaḥ paradharmo bhayāvahaḥ. (35)*

Better is one's own duty, though devoid of merit, than the duty of another well discharged. Better is death in one's own duty; the duty of another is fraught with fear (is productive of positive danger).

अर्जुन उवाच
अथ केन प्रयुक्तोऽयं पापं चरति पूरुषः ।
अनिच्छन्नपि वार्ष्णेय बलादिव नियोजितः ।।३६।।

*arjuna uvāca*

*atha kena prayukto'yaṁ pāpaṁ carati pūruṣaḥ,*
*anicchannapi vārṣṇeya balādiva niyojitaḥ. (36)*

Arjuna said:

But, impelled by what does man commit sin, though against his wishes, O Vārṣṇeya, constrained, as it were, by force?

श्रीभगवानुवाच

काम एष क्रोध एष रजोगुणसमुद्भवः ।
महाशनो महापाप्मा विद्ध्येनमिह वैरिणम् ।।३७।।

*śrībhagavānuvāca*

*kāma eṣa krodha eṣa rajoguṇasamudbhavaḥ,*
*mahāśano mahāpāpmā viddhyenamiha vairiṇam.* (37)

The Blessed Lord said:

It is desire, it is anger born of the 'active', all-devouring, all-sinful; know this as the foe here (in this world).

धूमेनाव्रियते वह्निर्यथादर्शो मलेन च ।
यथोल्बेनावृतो गर्भस्तथा तेनेदमावृतम् ।।३८।।

*dhūmenāvriyate vahniryathādarśo malena ca,*
*yatholbenāvṛto garbhastathā tenedamāvṛtam.* (38)

As fire is enveloped by smoke, as a mirror by dust, as an embryo by the womb, so this (wisdom) is enveloped by that (desire or anger).

आवृतं ज्ञानमेतेन ज्ञानिनो नित्यवैरिणा ।
कामरूपेण कौन्तेय दुष्पूरेणानलेन च ।।३९।।

*āvṛtaṁ jñānametena jñānino nityavairiṇā,*
*kāmarūpeṇa kaunteya duṣpūreṇānalena ca. (39)*

Enveloped, O son of Kuntī, is 'wisdom' by this constant enemy of the wise in the form of 'desire', which is difficult to appease, like fire.

इन्द्रियाणि मनो बुद्धिरस्याधिष्ठानमुच्यते ।
एतैर्विमोहयत्येष ज्ञानमावृत्य देहिनम् ।।४०।।

*indriyāṇi mano buddhirasyādhiṣṭhānamucyate,*
*etairvimohayatyeṣa jñānamāvṛtya dehinam. (40)*

The senses, the mind and the intellect are said to be its seat; through these, it deludes the embodied, by veiling his wisdom.

तस्मात्त्वमिन्द्रियाण्यादौ नियम्य भरतर्षभ ।
पाप्मानं प्रजहि ह्येनं ज्ञानविज्ञाननाशनम् ।।४१।।

*tasmāttvamindriyāṇyādau niyamya bharatarṣabha,*
*pāpmānaṁ prajahi hyenaṁ jñānavijñānanāśanam. (41)*

Therefore, O best of the Bhāratas, controlling first the senses, kill this sinful thing, the destroyer of knowledge and wisdom.

इन्द्रियाणि पराण्याहुरिन्द्रियेभ्यः परं मनः ।
मनसस्तु परा बुद्धिर्यो बुद्धेः परतस्तु सः ।।४२।।

*indriyāṇi parāṇyāhurindriyebhyaḥ paraṁ manaḥ,*
*manasastu parā buddhiryo buddheḥ paratastu saḥ. (42)*

They say that the senses are superior (to the body); superior to the senses is the mind; superior to the mind is the intellect; one who is even superior to the intellect is He, (the Ātman).

एवं बुद्धेः परं बुद्ध्वा संस्तभ्यात्मानमात्मना ।
जहि शत्रुं महाबाहो कामरूपं दुरासदम् ।।४३।।

*evaṁ buddheḥ paraṁ buddhvā saṁstabhyātmānamātmanā,*
*jahi śatruṁ mahābāho kāmarūpaṁ durāsadam. (43)*

Thus knowing Him, who is superior to intellect, and restraining the self by the Self, slay you, O mighty-armed, the enemy in the form of desire, no doubt, hard indeed to conquer.

ॐ तत्सदिति श्रीमद्भगवद्गीतासूपनिषत्सु
ब्रह्मविद्यायां योगशास्त्रे श्रीकृष्णार्जुनसंवादे
कर्मयोगो नाम तृतीयोऽध्यायः

*om tatsaditi śrīmadbhagavadgītāsūpaniṣatsu*
*brahmavidyāyāṁ yogaśāstre śrīkṛṣṇārjunasaṁvāde*
*karmayogo nāma tṛtīyo'dhyāyaḥ.*

Thus, in the Upaniṣads of the glorious Bhagavad-gītā, in the science of the eternal, in the scripture of yoga, in the dialouge between Śrī Kṛṣṇa and Arjuna, the third discourse ends entitled:

THE KARMA YOGA

***

Renunciation of Action in Knowledge

# Chapter 4

## *Yoga of Renunciation of Action in Knowledge*

श्रीभगवानुवाच

इमं विवस्वते योगं प्रोक्तवानहमव्ययम् ।
विवस्वान्मनवे प्राह मनुरिक्ष्वाकवेऽब्रवीत् ।।१।।

*śrībhagavānuvāca*

*imaṁ vivasvate yogaṁ proktavānahamavyayam,*
*vivasvānmanave prāha manurikṣvākave'bravīt. (1)*

The Blessed Lord said :

I taught this imperishable yoga to Vivasvān; Vivasvān taught to Manu; Manu taught it to Ikṣvāku.

एवं परम्पराप्राप्तमिमं राजर्षयो विदुः ।
स कालेनेह महता योगो नष्टः परन्तप ।।२।।

*evaṁ paramparāprāptamimaṁ rājarṣayo viduḥ,*
*sa kāleneha mahatā yogo naṣṭaḥ parantapa. (2)*

This knowledge, handed down thus, in regular succession, the royal sages knew. This yoga, by long lapse of time, has been lost here, O Parantapa (burner of the foes).

स एवायं मया तेऽद्य योगः प्रोक्तः पुरातनः ।
भक्तोऽसि मे सखा चेति रहस्यं ह्येतदुत्तमम् ।।३।।

*sa evāyaṁ mayā te'dya yogaḥ proktaḥ purātanaḥ,*
*bhakto'si me sakhā ceti rahasyaṁ hyetaduttamam. (3)*

That same ancient yoga has been today taught to you by Me, for you are My devotee and my friend. This is a supreme secret.

अर्जुन उवाच
अपरं भवतो जन्म परं जन्म विवस्वतः ।
कथमेतद्विजानीयां त्वमादौ प्रोक्तवानिति ।। ४।।

*arjuna uvāca*

*aparaṁ bhavato janma paraṁ janma vivasvataḥ,*
*kathametadvijānīyāṁ tvamādau proktavāniti. (4)*

Arjuna said :

Later was your birth, and prior was the birth of Vivasvān (Sun); - how am I to understand that you taught this yoga in the beginning?

श्रीभगवानुवाच

बहूनि मे व्यतीतानि जन्मानि तव चार्जुन ।
तान्यहं वेद सर्वाणि न त्वं वेत्थ परन्तप ।।५।।

*śrībhagavānuvāca*

*bahūni me vyatītāni janmāni tava cārjuna,*
*tānyahaṁ veda sarvāṇi na tvaṁ vettha parantapa.(5)*

The Blessed Lord said :

Many births of Mine have passed as well as yours, O Arjuna; I know them all but you know them not, O Parantapa (scorcher of foes).

अजोऽपि सन्नव्ययात्मा भूतानामीश्वरोऽपि सन् ।
प्रकृतिं स्वामधिष्ठाय सम्भवाम्यात्ममायया ।।६।।

*ajo'pi sannavyayātmā bhūtānāmīśvaro'pi san,*
*prakṛtiṁ svāmadhiṣṭhāya sambhavāmyātmamāyayā. (6)*

Though I am unborn and am of imperishable nature, and though I am the Lord of all beings, yet, ruling over My own nature, I take birth by My own māyā.

यदा यदा हि धर्मस्य ग्लानिर्भवति भारत ।
अभ्युत्थानमधर्मस्य तदात्मानं सृजाम्यहम् ।।७।।

*yadā yadā hi dharmasya glānirbhavati bhārata,*
*abhyutthānamadharmasya tadātmānaṁ sṛjāmyaham. (7)*

Whenever there is decay of righteousness, O Bhārata, and a rise of unrighteousness, then I manifest Myself.

परित्राणाय साधूनां विनाशाय च दुष्कृताम् ।
धर्मसंस्थापनार्थाय सम्भवामि युगे युगे ।।८।।

*paritrāṇāya sādhūnāṁ vināśāya ca duṣkṛtām,*
*dharmasaṁsthāpanārthāya sambhavāmi yuge yuge. (8)*

For the protection of the good, for the destruction of the wicked and for the establishment of righteousness, I am born in every age.

जन्म कर्म च मे दिव्यमेवं यो वेत्ति तत्त्वतः ।
त्यक्त्वा देहं पुनर्जन्म नैति मामेति सोऽर्जुन ।।९।।

*janma karma ca me divyamevaṁ yo vetti tattvataḥ,*
*tyaktvā dehaṁ punarjanma naiti māmeti so'rjuna.* (9)

He who thus knows, in true light, My divine birth and action; having abandoned the body, he is not born again; he comes to Me, O Arjuna.

वीतरागभयक्रोधा मन्मया मामुपाश्रिताः ।
बहवो ज्ञानतपसा पूता मद्भावमागताः ।।१०।।

*vītarāgabhayakrodhā manmayā māmupāśritāḥ,*
*bahavo jñānatapasā pūtā madbhāvamāgatāḥ.* (10)

Freed from attachment, fear and anger, absorbed in Me, taking refuge in Me, purified by the 'fire of knowledge', many have attained My Being.

ये यथा मां प्रपद्यन्ते तांस्तथैव भजाम्यहम् ।
मम वर्त्मानुवर्तन्ते मनुष्याः पार्थ सर्वशः ।।११।।

*ye yathā māṁ prapadyante tāṁstathaiva bhajāmyaham,*
*mama vartmānuvartante manuṣyāḥ pārtha sarvaśaḥ.(11)*

In whatever way men approach Me, even so do I reward them; My path do men tread in all ways, O son of Pṛthā.

काङ्क्षन्तः कर्मणां सिद्धिं यजन्त इह देवताः ।
क्षिप्रं हि मानुषे लोके सिद्धिर्भवति कर्मजा ।।१२।।

*kāṅkṣantaḥ karmaṇāṁ siddhiṁ yajanta iha devatāḥ,*
*kṣipraṁ hi mānuṣe loke siddhirbhavati karmajā. (12)*

They, who long for satisfaction from actions in this world, make sacrifices to the gods, because satisfaction is quickly obtained from actions in the world of objects.

चातुर्वर्ण्यं मया सृष्टं गुणकर्मविभागशः ।
तस्य कर्तारमपि मां विद्ध्यकर्तारमव्ययम् ।।१३।।

*cāturvarṇyaṁ mayā sṛṣṭaṁ guṇakarmavibhāgaśaḥ,*
*tasya kartāramapi māṁ viddhyakartāramavyayam. (13)*

The fourfold caste, has been created by Me, according to the differentiation of guṇa and karma; though I am the author thereof, know Me as non-doer and immutable.

न मां कर्माणि लिम्पन्ति न मे कर्मफले स्पृहा ।
इति मां योऽभिजानाति कर्मभिर्न स बध्यते ।।१४।

*na māṁ karmāṇi limpanti na me karmaphale spṛhā,*
*iti māṁ yo'bhijānāti karmabhirna sa badhyate. (14)*

Actions do not taint Me, nor have I any desire for the fruits of actions. He who knows Me thus, is not bound by his actions.

एवं ज्ञात्वा कृतं कर्म पूर्वैरपि मुमुक्षुभिः ।
कुरु कर्मैव तस्मात्त्वं पूर्वैः पूर्वतरं कृतम् ।।१५।।

*evaṁ jñātvā kṛtaṁ karma pūrvairapi mumukṣubhiḥ,*
*kuru karmaiva tasmāttvaṁ pūrvaiḥ pūrvataraṁ kṛtam. (15)*

Having known this, the ancient seekers after freedom, also performed action; therefore, you too, perform action, as did the ancients in the olden times.

किं कर्म किमकर्मेति कवयोऽप्यत्र मोहिताः ।
तत्ते कर्म प्रवक्ष्यामि यज्ज्ञात्वा मोक्ष्यसेऽशुभात् ।।१६।।

*kiṁ karma kimakarmeti kavayo'pyatra mohitāḥ,*
*tatte karma pravakṣyāmi yajjñātva mokṣyase'śubhāt.(16)*

What is action? What is inaction? As to this, even the wise are deluded. Therefore, I shall teach you 'action' (the nature of action and inaction), knowing which, you shall be liberated from the evil (of saṁsāra - the wheel of birth and death).

कर्मणो ह्यपि बोद्धव्यं बोद्धव्यं च विकर्मणः ।
अकर्मणश्च बोद्धव्यं गहना कर्मणो गतिः ।।१७।।

*karmaṇo hyapi boddhavyaṁ boddhavyaṁ ca vikarmaṇaḥ,*
*akarmaṇaśca boddhavyaṁ gahanā karmaṇo gatiḥ. (17)*

For, verily (the true nature) of right action should be known; also (that) of forbidden (or unlawful) action and of inaction; imponderable is the nature (path) of action.

कर्मण्यकर्म यः पश्येदकर्मणि च कर्म यः ।
स बुद्धिमान्मनुष्येषु स युक्तः कृत्स्नकर्मकृत् ।।१८।।

*karmaṇyakarma yaḥ paśyedakarmaṇi ca karma yaḥ,*
*sa buddhimānmanuṣyeṣu sa yuktaḥ kṛtsnakarmakṛt.* (18)

He, who recognises 'inaction in action' and 'action in inaction' is wise among men; he is a yogī and a true performer of all actions.

यस्य सर्वे समारम्भाः कामसङ्कल्पवर्जिताः ।
ज्ञानाग्निदग्धकर्माणं तमाहुः पण्डितं बुधाः ।।१९।।

*yasya sarve samārambhāḥ kāmasaṅkalpavarjitāḥ,*
*jñānāgnidagdhakarmāṇaṁ tamāhuḥ paṇḍitaṁ budhāḥ.* (19)

Whose undertakings are all devoid of desires and purposes, and whose actions have been burnt by the 'fire of knowledge', him the wise call a Sage.

त्यक्त्वा कर्मफलासङ्गं नित्यतृप्तो निराश्रयः ।
कर्मण्यभिप्रवृत्तोऽपि नैव किञ्चित्करोति सः ।।२०।।

*tyaktvā karmaphalāsaṅgaṁ nityatṛpto nirāśrayaḥ,*
*karmaṇyabhipravṛtto'pi naiva kiñcitkaroti saḥ. (20)*

Having abandoned attachment to the fruits of action, ever content, depending on nothing, he does not do anything, though engaged in actions.

निराशीर्यतचित्तात्मा त्यक्तसर्वपरिग्रहः ।
शारीरं केवलं कर्म कुर्वन्नाप्नोति किल्बिषम् ।।२१।।

*nirāśīryatacittātmā tyaktasarvaparigrahaḥ,*
*śārīraṁ kevalaṁ karma kurvannāpnoti kilbiṣam. (21)*

Without hope (desire), with the mind self controlled, having abandoned all sense of possessions, doing mere bodily action, he incurs no sin.

यदृच्छालाभसन्तुष्टो द्वन्द्वातीतो विमत्सरः ।
समः सिद्धावसिद्धौ च कृत्वापि न निबध्यते ।।२२।।

*yadṛcchālābhasantuṣṭo dvandvātīto vimatsaraḥ,*
*samaḥ siddhāvasiddhau ca kṛtvāpi na nibadhyate. (22)*

Content with what comes to him without effort, free from the pairs of opposites and envy, even-minded in success and failure, though acting he is not bound.

गतसङ्गस्य मुक्तस्य ज्ञानावस्थितचेतसः ।
यज्ञायाचरतः कर्म समग्रं प्रविलीयते ।।२३।।

*gatasaṅgasya muktasya jñānāvasthitacetasaḥ,*
*yajñāyācarataḥ karma samagraṁ pravilīyate.* (23)

Of one who is devoid of attachment, who is liberated, whose mind is established in knowledge, who acts for the sake of sacrifice, all his actions are dissolved.

ब्रह्मार्पणं ब्रह्म हविर्ब्रह्माग्नौ ब्रह्मणा हुतम् ।
ब्रह्मैव तेन गन्तव्यं ब्रह्मकर्मसमाधिना ।।२४।।

*brahmārpaṇaṁ brahma havirbrahmāgnau brahmaṇā hutam,*
*brahmaiva tena gantavyaṁ brahmakarmasamādhinā.* (24)

Brahman is the oblation; Brahman is the clarified butter, and so on, constituting the offerings; by Brahman is the oblation poured into the fire of Brahman; Brahman verily, shall be reached by him who always sees Brahman in all actions.

दैवमेवापरे यज्ञं योगिनः पर्युपासते ।
ब्रह्माग्नावपरे यज्ञं यज्ञेनैवोपजुह्वति ।।२५।।

*daivamevāpare yajñaṁ yoginaḥ paryupāsate,*
*brahmāgnāvapare yajñaṁ yajñenaivopajuhvati. (25)*

Some yogīs perform sacrifice to devas alone (deva-yajña); while others offer sacrifice of the Self (i.e. Ātman itself) as 'sacrifice (oblation) by the Self', in the 'fire of Brahman' (Brahma-yajña).

श्रोत्रादीनीन्द्रियाण्यन्ये संयमाग्निषु जुह्वति ।
शब्दादीन्विषयानन्य इन्द्रियाग्निषु जुह्वति ।।२६।।

*śrotrādīnīndriyāṇyanye saṁyamāgniṣu juhvati,*
*śabdādīnviṣayānanya indriyāgniṣu juhvati. (26)*

Some again offer hearing and other senses as sacrifice in the fire of restraint; others offer sound and other objects of senses as sacrifice in the fires of the senses.

सर्वाणीन्द्रियकर्माणि प्राणकर्माणि चापरे ।
आत्मसंयमयोगाग्नौ जुह्वति ज्ञानदीपिते ।।२७।।

*sarvāṇīndriyakarmāṇi prāṇakarmāṇi cāpare,*
*ātmasaṁyamayogāgnau juhvati jñānadīpite.* (27)

Others again sacrifice all the functions of the senses and the functions of the breath (vital energy) in the fire of the yoga of self-restraint, kindled by knowledge.

द्रव्ययज्ञास्तपोयज्ञा योगयज्ञास्तथापरे ।
स्वाध्यायज्ञानयज्ञाश्च यतयः संशितव्रताः ।।२८।।

*dravyayajñāstapoyajñā yogayajñāstathāpare,*
*svādhyāyajñānayajñāśca yatayaḥ saṁśitavratāḥ.* (28)

Others again offer wealth, austerity and yoga as sacrifice, while the ascetics of self-restraint and rigid vows offer study of scriptures and knowledge as sacrifice.

अपाने जुह्वति प्राणं प्राणेऽपानं तथापरे ।
प्राणापानगती रुद्ध्वा प्राणायामपरायणाः ।।२९।।

*apāne juhvati prāṇaṁ prāṇe'pānaṁ tathāpare,*
*prāṇāpānagatī ruddhvā prāṇāyāmaparāyaṇāḥ.* (29)

Others offer as sacrifice the outgoing breath in the incoming, and the incoming in the outgoing, restraining the courses of the outgoing and incoming breaths, solely absorbed in the restraint of breath.

अपरे नियताहाराः प्राणान्प्राणेषु जुह्वति ।
सर्वेऽप्येते यज्ञविदो यज्ञक्षपितकल्मषाः ।।३०।।

*apare niyatāhārāḥ prāṇānprāṇeṣu juhvati,*
*sarve'pyete yajñavido yajñakṣapitakalmaṣāḥ.* (30)

Others, with well-regulated diet, offer vital-airs in the Vital-Air. All these are knowers of sacrifice (yajña), whose sins are destroyed by sacrifice (yajña).

यज्ञशिष्टामृतभुजो यान्ति ब्रह्म सनातनम् ।
नायं लोकोऽस्त्ययज्ञस्य कुतोऽन्यः कुरुसत्तम ।।३१।।

*yajñaśiṣṭāmṛtabhujo yānti brahma sanātanam,*
*nāyaṁ loko'styayajñasya kuto'nyaḥ kurusattama.* (31)

The eaters of the nectar - remnant of the sacrifice (yajña) - go to the eternal Brahman. Even this world is not for the non-performer of sacrifice; how then the other (world), O best of the Kurus?

एवं बहुविधा यज्ञा वितता ब्रह्मणो मुखे ।
कर्मजान्विद्धि तान्सर्वानेवं ज्ञात्वा विमोक्ष्यसे ।।३२।।

*evaṁ bahuvidhā yajñā vitatā brahmaṇo mukhe,*
*karmajānviddhi tānsarvānevaṁ jñātvā vimokṣyase. (32)*

Thus innumerable sacrifices lie spread out before Brahman (literally at the mouth or face of Brahman), Know them all as born of action, and thus knowing, you shall be liberated.

श्रेयान्द्रव्यमयाद्यज्ञाज्ज्ञानयज्ञः परन्तप ।
सर्वं कर्माखिलं पार्थ ज्ञाने परिसमाप्यते ।।३३।।

*śreyāndravyamayādyajñājjñānayajñaḥ parantapa,*
*sarvaṁ karmākhilaṁ pārtha jñāne parisamāpyate. (33)*

Superior is knowledge-sacrifice to sacrifice with objects, O Parantapa. All actions in their entirety, O Pārtha, culminate in Knowledge.

तद्विद्धि प्रणिपातेन परिप्रश्नेन सेवया ।
उपदेक्ष्यन्ति ते ज्ञानं ज्ञानिनस्तत्त्वदर्शिनः ।।३४।।

*tadviddhi praṇipātena paripraśnena sevayā,*
*upadekṣyanti te jñānaṁ jñāninastattvadarśinaḥ.* (34)

Know that by long prostration, by question, and service; the wise who have realised the Truth will instruct you in (that) Knowledge.

यज्ज्ञात्वा न पुनर्मोहमेवं यास्यसि पाण्डव ।
येन भूतान्यशेषेण द्रक्ष्यस्यात्मन्यथो मयि ।।३५।।

*yajjñātvā na punarmohamevaṁ yāsyasi pāṇḍava,*
*yena bhūtānyaśeṣeṇa drakṣyasyātmanyatho mayi.* (35)

Knowing that, you shall not, O Pāṇḍava, again get deluded like this; and by that, you shall see all beings in your Self, and also in Me.

अपि चेदसि पापेभ्यः सर्वेभ्यः पापकृत्तमः ।
सर्वं ज्ञानप्लवेनैव वृजिनं सन्तरिष्यसि ।।३६।।

*api cedasi pāpebhyaḥ sarvebhyaḥ pāpakṛttamaḥ,*
*sarvaṁ jñānaplavenaiva vṛjinaṁ santariṣyasi. (36)*

Even if you are the most sinful of all sinners, yet you shall verily cross all sins by the raft of Knowledge.

यथैधांसि समिद्धोऽग्निर्भस्मसात्कुरुतेऽर्जुन ।
ज्ञानाग्निः सर्वकर्माणि भस्मसात्कुरुते तथा ।।३७।।

*yathaidhāṁsi samiddho'gnirbhasmasātkurute'rjuna,*
*jñānāgniḥ sarvakarmāṇi bhasmasātkurute tathā (37)*

As the blazing fire reduces fuel to ashes, O Arjuna, so does the fire of knowledge reduce all actions to ashes.

न हि ज्ञानेन सदृशं पवित्रमिह विद्यते ।
तत्स्वयं योगसंसिद्धः कालेनात्मनि विन्दति ।।३८।।

*na hi jñānena sadṛśaṁ pavitramiha vidyate,*
*tatsvayaṁ yogasaṁsiddhaḥ kālenātmani vindati.* (38)

Certainly, there is no purifier in this world like Knowledge. He, who is himself perfected in yoga finds it in the Self in time.

श्रद्धावाँल्लभते ज्ञानं तत्परः संयतेन्द्रियः ।
ज्ञानं लब्ध्वा परां शान्तिमचिरेणाधिगच्छति ।।३९।।

*śraddhāvāṁllabhate jñānaṁ tatparaḥ saṁyatendriyaḥ,*
*jñānaṁ labdhvā parāṁ śāntimacireṇādhigacchati.* (39)

The man who is full of faith, who is devoted to It, and who has subdued the senses, obtains (this) Knowledge; and having obtained knowledge, ere long he goes to the supreme peace.

अज्ञश्चाश्रद्दधानश्च संशयात्मा विनश्यति ।
नायं लोकोऽस्ति न परो न सुखं संशयात्मनः ।।४०।।

*ajñaścāśraddadhānaśca saṁśayātmā vinaśyati,*
*nāyaṁ loko'sti na paro na sukhaṁ saṁśayātmanaḥ.* (40)

The ignorant, the faithless, the doubting-self goes to destruction; there is neither this world, nor the other, nor happiness for the doubter.

योगसन्न्यस्तकर्माणं ज्ञानसंञ्छिन्नसंशयम् ।
आत्मवन्तं न कर्माणि निबध्नन्ति धनञ्जय ।।४१।।

*yogasannyastakarmāṇaṁ jñānasañchinnasaṁśayam,*
*ātmavantaṁ na karmāṇi nibadhnanti dhanañjaya. (41)*

He who has renounced actions by yoga, whose doubts are rent asunder by Knowledge, who is poised in the Self as the Self, actions do not bind him, O Dhanañjaya.

तस्मादज्ञानसम्भूतं हृत्स्थं ज्ञानासिनात्मनः ।
छित्त्वैनं संशयं योगमातिष्ठोत्तिष्ठ भारत ।।४२।।

*tasmādajñānasambhūtaṁ hṛtsthaṁ jñānāsinātmanaḥ,*
*chittvainaṁ saṁśayaṁ yogamātiṣṭhottiṣṭha bhārata. (42)*

Therefore, with the sword of Knowledge cut asunder the doubt of the Self, born of ignorance, residing in your heart, and take refuge in yoga. Arise, O Bhārata.

ॐ तत्सदिति श्रीमद्भगवद्गीतासूपनिषत्सु
ब्रह्मविद्यायां योगशास्त्रे श्रीकृष्णार्जुनसंवादे
ज्ञानकर्मसन्न्यासयोगो नाम चतुर्थोऽध्यायः

*om tatsaditi śrīmadbhagavadgītāsūpaniṣatsu*
*brahmavidyāyāṁ yogaśāstre śrīkṛṣṇārjunasaṁvāde*
*jñānakarmasannyāsayogo nāma caturtho'dhyāyaḥ*

Thus, in the Upaniṣad of the glorious Bhagavad-gītā, in the science of the eternal, in the scripture of yoga, in the dialogue between Śrī Kṛṣṇa and Arjuna, the fourth discourse ends entitled:

THE YOGA OF RENUNCIATION OF ACTION IN KNOWLEDGE

***

True Renunciation

# Chapter 5

## *Yoga of True Renunciation of Action*

अर्जुन उवाच
सन्न्यासं कर्मणां कृष्ण पुनर्योगं च शंससि ।
यच्छ्रेय एतयोरेकं तन्मे ब्रूहि सुनिश्चितम् ।।१।।

*arjuna uvāca*
*sannyāsaṁ karmaṇāṁ kṛṣṇa punaryogaṁ ca śaṁsasi,*
*yacchreya etayorekaṁ tanme brūhi suniścitam. (1)*

Arjuna said :

O Kṛṣṇa! you praise renunciation of action and again yoga - performance of action. Tell me conclusively that which is the better of the two.

श्रीभगवानुवाच
सन्न्यासः कर्मयोगश्च निःश्रेयसकरावुभौ ।
तयोस्तु कर्मसन्न्यासात्कर्मयोगो विशिष्यते ।।२।।

*śrībhagavānuvāca*
*sannyāsaḥ karmayogaśca niḥśreyasakarāvubhau,*
*tayostu karmasannyāsātkarmayogo viśiṣyate.* (2)

The Blessed Lord said:

Renunciation of action and yoga of action, both lead to the highest bliss; but of the two, yoga of action is superior to the renunciation of action.

ज्ञेयः स नित्यसन्न्यासी यो न द्वेष्टि न काङ्क्षति ।
निर्द्वन्द्वो हि महाबाहो सुखं बन्धात्प्रमुच्यते ।।३।।

*jñeyaḥ sa nityasannyāsī yo na dveṣṭi na kāṅkṣati,*
*nirdvandvo hi mahābāho sukhaṁ bandhātpramucyate.* (3)

He should be known as a perpetual sannyāsī who neither hates nor desires; for, free from the pairs of opposites, O mighty-armed, he is easily set free from bondage.

साङ्ख्ययोगौ पृथग्बालाः प्रवदन्ति न पण्डिताः।
एकमप्यास्थितः सम्यगुभयोर्विन्दते फलम् ।।४।।

*sāṅkhyayogau pṛthagbālāḥ pravadanti na paṇḍitāḥ,*
*ekamapyāsthitaḥ samyagubhayorvindate phalam. (4)*

Children, not the wise, speak of Sāṅkhya (Knowledge) and Yoga (yoga of action) as distinct; he who is truly established even in one, obtains the fruits of both.

यत्साङ्ख्यैः प्राप्यते स्थानं तद्योगैरपि गम्यते ।
एकं साङ्ख्यं च योगं च यः पश्यति स पश्यति ।।५।।

*yatsāṅkhyaiḥ prāpyate sthānaṁ tadyogairapi gamyate,*
*ekaṁ sāṅkhyaṁ ca yogaṁ ca yaḥ paśyati sa paśyati. (5)*

That place which is reached by the Sāṅkhyas (jñānīs) is also reached by the yogins (karma-yogins). He 'sees', who 'sees' sāṅkhya and yoga as one.

सन्न्यासस्तु महाबाहो दुःखमाप्तुमयोगतः।
योगयुक्तो मुनिर्ब्रह्म नचिरेणाधिगच्छति ।।६।।

*sannyāsastu mahābāho duḥkhamāptumayogataḥ,*
*yogayukto munirbrahma nacireṇādhigacchati. (6)*

But, renunciation, O mighty-armed, is hard to attain without yoga; the yoga-harmonised man of (steady) contemplation quickly goes to Brahman.

योगयुक्तो विशुद्धात्मा विजितात्मा जितेन्द्रियः।
सर्वभूतात्मभूतात्मा कुर्वन्नपि न लिप्यते ।।७।।

*yogayukto viśuddhātmā vijitātmā jitendriyaḥ,*
*sarvabhūtātmabhūtātmā kurvannapi na lipyate. (7)*

He, who is devoted to the path of action, whose mind is quite pure, who has conquered the Self, who has subdued his senses, who realises his Self as the Self in all beings, though acting, is not tainted.

नैव किञ्चित्करोमीति युक्तो मन्येत तत्त्ववित् ।
पश्यञ्शृण्वन्स्पृशञ्जिघ्रन्नश्नन्गच्छन्स्वपञ्श्वसन् ।।८।।

*naiva kiñcitkaromīti yukto manyeta tattvavit,*
*paśyañśṛṇvanspṛśañjighrannaśnangacchansvapañśvasan. (8)*

'I do nothing at all', thus would the harmonised knower of Truth think - seeing, hearing, touching, smelling, eating, going, sleeping, breathing....

प्रलपन्विसृजन्गृह्णन्नुन्मिषन्निमिषन्नपि ।
इन्द्रियाणीन्द्रियार्थेषु वर्तन्त इति धारयन् ।।९।।

*pralapanvisṛjangṛhṇannunmiṣannimiṣannapi,*
*indriyāṇīndriyārtheṣu vartanta iti dhārayan. (9)*

Speaking, letting go, seizing, opening and closing the eyes - convinced that the senses move among the sense objects.

ब्रह्मण्याधाय कर्माणि सङ्गं त्यक्त्वा करोति यः ।
लिप्यते न स पापेन पद्मपत्रमिवाम्भसा ।।१०।।

*brahmaṇyādhāya karmāṇi saṅgaṁ tyaktvā karoti yaḥ,*
*lipyate na sa pāpena padmapatramivāmbhasā. (10)*

He, who does actions, offering them to Brahman, abandoning attachment, is not tainted by sin, just as a lotus leaf remains unaffected by the water on it.

कायेन मनसा बुद्ध्या केवलैरिन्द्रियैरपि ।
योगिनः कर्म कुर्वन्ति सङ्गं त्यक्त्वात्मशुद्धये ।।११।।

*kāyena manasā buddhyā kevalairindriyairapi,*
*yoginaḥ karma kurvanti saṅgaṁ tyaktvātmaśuddhaye. (11)*

Yogīs, having abandoned attachment, perform actions merely by the body, mind, intellect and senses, for the purification of the self (ego).

युक्तः कर्मफलं त्यक्त्वा शान्तिमाप्नोति नैष्ठिकीम् ।
अयुक्तः कामकारेण फले सक्तो निबध्यते ।।१२।।

*yuktaḥ karmaphalaṁ tyaktvā śāntimāpnoti naiṣṭhikīm,*
*ayuktaḥ kāmakāreṇa phale sakto nibadhyate. (12)*

The united one (the well-poised or the harmonised), having abandoned the fruits of action, attains eternal peace; the non-united (the unsteady or the unbalanced), impelled by desire and attached to the fruit, is bound.

सर्वकर्माणि मनसा सन्न्यस्यास्ते सुखं वशी ।
नवद्वारे पुरे देही नैव कुर्वन्न कारयन् ।।१३।।

*sarvakarmāṇi manasā sannyasyāste sukhaṁ vaśī,*
*navadvāre pure dehī naive kurvanna kārayan. (13)*

Mentally renouncing all actions and fully self-controlled, the embodied one rests happily in the city of nine gates, neither acting nor causing others (body and senses) to act.

न कर्तृत्वं न कर्माणि लोकस्य सृजति प्रभुः ।
न कर्मफलसंयोगं स्वभावस्तु प्रवर्तते ।।१४।।

*na kartṛtvaṁ na karmāṇi lokasya sṛjati prabhuḥ,*
*na karmaphalasaṁyogaṁ svabhāvastu pravartate. (14)*

Neither agency nor actions does the Lord create for the world, nor union with the fruits of actions. But it is nature that acts.

नादत्ते कस्यचित्पापं न चैव सुकृतं विभुः ।
अज्ञानेनावृतं ज्ञानं तेन मुह्यन्ति जन्तवः ।।१५।।

*nādatte kasyacitpāpaṁ na caiva sukṛtaṁ vibhuḥ,*
*ajñānenāvṛtaṁ jñānaṁ tena muhyanti jantavaḥ. (15)*

The Lord takes neither the demerit nor even the merit of any; knowledge is enveloped by ignorance, thereby beings are deluded.

ज्ञानेन तु तदज्ञानं येषां नाशितमात्मनः ।
तेषामादित्यवज्ज्ञानं प्रकाशयति तत्परम् ।।१६।।

*jñānena tu tadajñānaṁ yeṣāṁ nāśitamātmanaḥ,*
*teṣāmādityavajjñānaṁ prakāśayati tatparam. (16)*

But to those whose ignorance is destroyed by the knowledge of the Self, like the sun, to them Knowledge reveals the Supreme (Brahman).

तद्बुद्धयस्तदात्मानस्तन्निष्ठास्तत्परायणाः ।
गच्छन्त्यपुनरावृत्तिं ज्ञाननिर्धूतकल्मषाः ।।१७।।

*tadbuddhayastadātmānastanniṣṭhāstatparāyaṇāḥ,*
*gacchantyapunarāvṛttiṁ jñānanirdhūtakalmaṣāḥ. (17)*

Intellect absorbed in That, their Self being That, established in That, with That for their supreme Goal, they go whence there is no return, their sins dispelled by Knowledge.

विद्याविनयसम्पन्ने ब्राह्मणे गवि हस्तिनि ।
शुनि चैव श्वपाके च पण्डिताः समदर्शिनः ।।१८।।

*vidyāvinayasampanne brāhmaṇe gavi hastini,*
*śuni caiva śvapāke ca pāṇḍitāḥ samadarśinaḥ. (18)*

Sages look with an equal eye upon a brāhmaṇa endowed with learning and humility, on a cow, on an elephant, and even on a dog and an outcaste.

इहैव तैर्जितः सर्गो येषां साम्ये स्थितं मनः ।
निर्दोषं हि समं ब्रह्म तस्माद्ब्रह्मणि ते स्थिताः ।।१९।।

*ihaiva tairjitaḥ sargo yeṣāṁ sāmye sthitaṁ manaḥ,*
*nirdoṣaṁ hi samaṁ brahma tasmādbrahmaṇi te sthitāḥ. (19)*

Even here (in this world), birth (everything) is overcome by those whose minds rest in equality; Brahman is spotless indeed and equal; therefore they are established in Brahman.

न प्रहृष्येत्प्रियं प्राप्य नोद्विजेत्प्राप्य चाप्रियम् ।
स्थिरबुद्धिरसम्मूढो ब्रह्मविद् ब्रह्मणि स्थितः ।।२०।।

*na prahṛṣyetpriyaṁ prāpya nodvijetprāpya cāpriyam,*
*sthirabuddhirasammūḍho brahmavid brahmaṇi sthitaḥ. (20)*

Resting in Brahman, with steady intellect and undeluded, the knower of Brahman, neither rejoices on obtaining what is pleasant, nor grieves on obtaining what is unpleasant.

बाह्यस्पर्शेष्वसक्तात्मा विन्दत्यात्मनि यत्सुखम् ।
स ब्रह्मयोगयुक्तात्मा सुखमक्षयमश्नुते ।।२१।।

*bāhyasparśeṣvasaktātmā vindatyātmani yatsukham,*
*sa brahmayogayuktātmā sukhamakṣayamaśnute. (21)*

With the self unattached to external contacts, he finds happiness in the Self; with the self engaged in the meditation of Brahman, he attains endless happiness.

ये हि संस्पर्शजा भोगा दुःखयोनय एव ते ।
आद्यन्तवन्तः कौन्तेय न तेषु रमते बुधः ।।२२।।

*ye hi saṁsparśajā bhogā duḥkhayonaya eva te,*
*ādyantavantaḥ kaunteya na teṣu ramate budhaḥ. (22)*

The enjoyments that are born of contacts are only generators of pain, for they have a beginning and an end. O son of Kuntī, the wise do not rejoice in them.

शक्नोतीहैव यः सोढुं प्राक्शरीरविमोक्षणात् ।
कामक्रोधोद्भवं वेगं स युक्तः स सुखी नरः ।।२३।।

*śaknotīhaiva yaḥ soḍhuṁ prākśarīravimokṣaṇāt,*
*kāmakrodhodbhavaṁ vegaṁ sa yuktaḥ sa sukhī naraḥ.* (23)

He who is able, while still here (in this world) to withstand, before the liberation from the body (death), the impulse born out of desire and anger, he is a yogī, he is a happy man.

योऽन्तःसुखोऽन्तरारामस्तथान्तर्ज्योतिरेव यः ।
स योगी ब्रह्मनिर्वाणं ब्रह्मभूतोऽधिगच्छति ।।२४।।

*yo'ntaḥsukho'ntarārāmastathāntarjyotireva yaḥ,*
*sa yogī brahmanirvāṇaṁ brahmabhūto'dhigacchati.* (24)

He, who is happy within, who rejoices within, who is illuminated within, that yogī attains absolute freedom or mokṣa, himself becoming Brahman.

लभन्ते ब्रह्मनिर्वाणमृषयः क्षीणकल्मषाः ।
छिन्नद्वैधा यतात्मानः सर्वभूतहिते रताः ।।२५।।

*labhante brahmanirvāṇamṛṣayaḥ kṣīṇakalmaṣāḥ,*
*chinnadvaidhā yatātmānaḥ sarvabhūtahite ratāḥ. (25)*

Those ṛṣis obtain absolute freedom or mokṣa, whose sins have been destroyed, whose dualities are torn asunder, who are self-controlled and intent on the welfare of all beings.

कामक्रोधवियुक्तानां यतीनां यतचेतसाम् ।
अभितो ब्रह्मनिर्वाणं वर्तते विदितात्मनाम् ।।२६।।

*kāmakrodhaviyuktānāṁ yatīnāṁ yatacetasām,*
*abhito brahmanirvāṇaṁ vartate viditātmanām. (26)*

Absolute freedom (or Brahmika bliss) exists on all sides for those self-controlled ascetics, who are free from desires and anger, who have controlled their thoughts and who have realised the Self.

स्पर्शान्कृत्वा बहिर्बाह्यांश्चक्षुश्चैवान्तरे भ्रुवोः ।
प्राणापानौ समौ कृत्वा नासाभ्यन्तरचारिणौ ।।२७।।

*sparśānkṛtvā bahirbāhyāṁścakṣuścaivāntare bhruvoḥ,*
*prāṇāpānau samau kṛtvā nāsābhyantaracāriṇau. (27)*

Shutting out (all) external contacts and fixing the gaze (as though) between the eyebrows, equalising the outgoing and incoming breath moving within the nostrils,

यतेन्द्रियमनोबुद्धिर्मुनिर्मोक्षपरायणः ।
विगतेच्छाभयक्रोधो यः सदा मुक्त एव सः ।।२८।।

*yatendriyamanobuddhirmunirmokṣaparāyaṇaḥ,*
*vigatecchābhayakrodho yaḥ sadā mukta eva saḥ. (28)*

With senses, mind and intellect (ever) controlled, having liberation as his supreme goal, free from desire, fear and anger, the Sage is verily liberated forever.

भोक्तारं यज्ञतपसां सर्वलोकमहेश्वरम् ।
सुहृदं सर्वभूतानां ज्ञात्वा मां शान्तिमृच्छति ।।२९।।

*bhoktāraṁ yajñatapasāṁ sarvalokamaheśvaram,*
*suhṛdaṁ sarvabhūtānāṁ jñātvā māṁ śāntimṛcchati. (29)*

Knowing Me as enjoyer of sacrifices and austerities, the great Lord of all worlds, the friend of all beings, he attains peace.

ॐ तत्सदिति श्रीमद्भगवद्गीतासूपनिषत्सु
ब्रह्मविद्यायां योगशास्त्रे श्रीकृष्णार्जुनसंवादे
कर्मसन्न्यासयोगो नाम पञ्चमोऽध्यायः

*om tatsaditi śrīmadbhagavadgītasūpaniṣatsu*
*brahmavidyāyāṁ yogaśāstre śrīkṛṣṇārjunasaṁvāde*
*karmasannyāsayogo nāma pañcamo'dhyāyaḥ*

Thus, in the Upaniṣad of the glorious Bhagawad-gītā, in the science of the eternal, in the scripture of yoga, in the dialogue between Śrī Kṛṣṇa and Arjuna, the fifth discourse ends entitled:

YOGA OF TRUE RENUNCIATION OF ACTION

***

Meditation

# Chapter 6

## *Yoga of Self-Control / Meditation*

श्रीभगवानुवाच

अनाश्रितः कर्मफलं कार्यं कर्म करोति यः ।
स सन्न्यासी च योगी च न निरग्निर्न चाक्रियः ।।१ ।।

*śrībhagavānuvāca:*

*anāśritaḥ karmaphalaṁ kāryaṁ karma karoti yaḥ,*
*sa sannyāsī ca yogī ca na niragnirna cākriyaḥ. (1)*

The Blessed Lord said :

He, who performs his bounden duty without depending on the fruits of actions, is a sannayāsī and a yogī; not he who (has renounced) is without fire and without actions.

यं सन्न्यासमिति प्राहुर्योगं तं विद्धि पाण्डव ।
न ह्यसन्न्यस्तसङ्कल्पो योगी भवति कश्चन ।।२।।

*yaṁ sannyāsamiti prāhuryogaṁ taṁ viddhi pāṇḍava,*
*na hyasannyastasaṅkalpo yogī bhavati kaścana. (2)*

O Pāṇḍava, please know yoga to be that which they call renunciation; no one verily, becomes a yogī who has not renounced thoughts.

आरुरुक्षोर्मुनेर्योगं कर्म कारणमुच्यते ।
योगारूढस्य तस्यैव शमः कारणमुच्यते ।।३।।

*ārurukṣormuneryogaṁ karma kāraṇamucyate,*
*yogārūḍhasya tasyaiva śamaḥ kāraṇamucyate. (3)*

For a Muni or Sage who wishes to attune to yoga, action is said to be the means; for the same Sage who has attuned to yoga, inaction (quiescence) is said to be the means.

यदा हि नेन्द्रियार्थेषु न कर्मस्वनुषज्जते ।
सर्वसङ्कल्पसन्न्यासी योगारूढस्तदोच्यते ।।४।।

*yadā hi nendriyārtheṣu na karmasvanuṣajjate,*
*sarvasaṅkalpasannyāsī yogārūḍhastadocyate. (4)*

When a man is not attached to sense objects or to actions, having renounced all thoughts, he is said to have attuned to yoga.

उद्धरेदात्मनात्मानं नात्मानमवसादयेत् ।
आत्मैव ह्यात्मनो बन्धुरात्मैव रिपुरात्मनः ।।५ ।।

*uddharedātmanātmānaṁ nātmānamavasādayet,*
*ātmaiva hyātmano bandhurātmaiva ripurātmanaḥ. (5)*

Let a man lift himself by his own Self alone and let him not lower himself; for, this Self alone is the friend of oneself and this Self is the enemy of oneself.

बन्धुरात्मात्मनस्तस्य येनात्मैवात्मना जितः ।
अनात्मनस्तु शत्रुत्वे वर्तेतात्मैव शत्रुवत् ।।६ ।।

*bandhurātmātmanastasya yenātmaivātmanā jitaḥ,*
*anātmanastu śatrutve vartetātmaiva śatruvat. (6)*

The Self is the friend of the self for him who has conquered himself by the Self; but to the unconquered self, the Self stands in the position of an enemy like the (external) foe.

जितात्मनः प्रशान्तस्य परमात्मा समाहितः ।
शीतोष्णसुखदुःखेषु तथा मानापमानयोः ।।७।।

*jitātmanaḥ praśāntasya paramātmā samāhitaḥ,*
*śītoṣṇasukhaduḥkheṣu tathā mānāpamānayoḥ. (7)*

The supreme Self of him who is self-controlled and peaceful, is balanced in cold and heat, pleasure and pain, as also in honour and dishonour.

ज्ञानविज्ञानतृप्तात्मा कूटस्थो विजितेन्द्रियः।
युक्त इत्युच्यते योगी समलोष्टाश्मकाञ्चनः।।८।।

*jñānavijñānatṛptātmā kūṭastho vijitendriyaḥ,*
*yukta ityucyate yogī samaloṣṭśmakāñcanaḥ. (8)*

The yogī, who is satisfied with knowledge and wisdom, who remains unshaken, who has conquered the senses, to whom a lump of earth, a stone and gold are the same, is said to be harmonised (i.e. is said to have attained nirvikalpa samādhi).

सुहृन्मित्रार्युदासीनमध्यस्थद्वेष्यबन्धुषु ।
साधुष्वपि च पापेषु समबुद्धिर्विशिष्यते ।।९।।

*suhṛnmitrāryudāsīnamadhyasthadveṣyabandhuṣu,*
*sādhuṣvapi ca pāpeṣu samabuddhirviśiṣyate.* (9)

He, who is of the same mind to the good-hearted, friends, relatives, enemies, the indifferent, the neutral, the hateful, the righteous and the unrighteous, excels.

योगी युञ्जीत सततमात्मानं रहसि स्थितः।
एकाकी यतचित्तात्मा निराशीरपरिग्रहः।।१०।।

*yogī yuñjīta satatamātmānaṁ rahasi sthitaḥ,*
*ekāki yatacittātmā nirāśīraparigrahaḥ.* (10)

Let the yogī try constantly to keep the mind steady, remaining in solitude, alone with the mind and body controlled, free from hope and greed.

शुचौ देशे प्रतिष्ठाप्य स्थिरमासनमात्मनः ।
नात्युच्छ्रितं नातिनीचं चैलाजिनकुशोत्तरम् ।।११।।

*śucau deśe pratiṣṭhāpya sthiramāsanamātmanaḥ,*
*nātyucchritaṁ nātinīcaṁ cailājinakuśottaram. (11)*

Having established a firm seat of his own in a clean spot, neither too high nor too low, made of a cloth, a skin and kuśa-grass, one over the other...

तत्रैकाग्रं मनः कृत्वा यतचित्तेन्द्रियक्रियः।
उपविश्यासने युञ्ज्याद्योगमात्मविशुद्धये ।।१२।।

*tatraikāgraṁ manaḥ kṛtvā yatacittendriyakriyaḥ,*
*upaviśyāsane yuñjyādyogamātmaviśuddhaye. (12)*

There, having made the mind single pointed, with the actions of the mind and the senses controlled, let him, seated on the seat, practise yoga for the purification of the self.

समं कायशिरोग्रीवं धारयन्नचलं स्थिरः ।
सम्प्रेक्ष्य नासिकाग्रं स्वं दिशश्चानवलोकयन् ।।१३।।

*samaṁ kāyaśirogrīvaṁ dhārayannacalaṁ sthiraḥ,*
*samprekṣya nāsikāgraṁ svaṁ diśaścānavalokayan.* (13)

Let him firmly hold his body, head and neck erect and still, gazing at the tip of the nose, without looking around.

प्रशान्तात्मा विगतभीर्ब्रह्मचारिव्रते स्थितः ।
मनः संयम्य मच्चित्तो युक्त आसीत मत्परः ।।१४।।

*praśāntātmā vigatabhīrbrahmacārivrate sthitaḥ,*
*manaḥ saṁyamya maccitto yukta āsīta matparaḥ.* (14)

Serene-minded, fearless, firm in the vow of Brahmacarya, having controlled the mind, meditating, thinking of Me and balanced, let him sit, having Me as the supreme goal.

युञ्जन्नेवं सदात्मानं योगी नियतमानसः ।
शान्तिं निर्वाणपरमां मत्संस्थामधिगच्छति ।।१५।।

*yuñjannevaṁ sadātmānaṁ yogī niyatamānasaḥ,*
*śāntiṁ nirvāṇaparamāṁ matsaṁsthāmadhigacchati.* (15)

Thus, always keeping the mind balanced, the yogī, with his mind controlled, attains the peace abiding in Me, which culminates in total liberation (nirvāṇa or mokṣa).

नात्यश्नतस्तु योगोऽस्ति न चैकान्तमनश्नतः ।
न चाति स्वप्नशीलस्य जाग्रतो नैव चार्जुन ।।१६।।

*nātyaśnatastu yogo'sti na caikāntamanaśnataḥ,*

*na cāti svapnaśīlasya jāgrato naiva cārjuna. (16)*

Verily, yoga is not possible for him who eats too much, nor for him who does not eat at all; nor for him who sleeps too much, nor for him who is (always) awake, O Arjuna.

युक्ताहारविहारस्य युक्तचेष्टस्य कर्मसु ।
युक्तस्वप्नावबोधस्य योगो भवति दुःखहा ।।१७।।

*yuktāhāravihārasya yuktaceṣṭasya karmasu*

*yuktasvapnāvabodhasya yogo bhavati duḥkhahā. (17)*

Yoga becomes the destroyer of pain for him who is moderate in eating and recreation, who is moderate in his exertion during his actions, who is moderate in sleep and wakefulness.

यदा विनियतं चित्तमात्मन्येवावतिष्ठते ।
निःस्पृहः सर्वकामेभ्यो युक्त इत्युच्यते तदा ।।१८।।

*yadā viniyataṁ cittamātmanyevāvatiṣṭhate,*
*niḥspṛhaḥ sarvakāmebhyo yukta ityucyate tadā. (18)*

When the perfectly controlled mind rests in the Self only, free from longing for all (objects of) desires, then it is said: 'He is united' (yuktaḥ).

यथा दीपो निवातस्थो नेङ्गते सोपमा स्मृता ।
योगिनो यतचित्तस्य युञ्जतो योगमात्मनः ।।१९।।

*yathā dīpo nivātastho neṅgate sopamā smṛtā,*
*yogino yatacittasya yuñjato yogamātmanaḥ. (19)*

'As a lamp placed in a windless place does not flicker', is a simile used to describe the yogī of controlled mind, practising yoga of the Self (or absorbed in the yoga of the Self).

यत्रोपरमते चित्तं निरुद्धं योगसेवया ।
यत्र चैवात्मनात्मानं पश्यन्नात्मनि तुष्यति ।।२०।।

*yatroparamate cittaṁ niruddaṁ yogasevayā,*
*yatra caivātmanātmānaṁ paśyannātmani tuṣyati. (20)*

When the mind, restrained by the practice of yoga, attains quietitude and seeing the Self by the self, he is satisfied in his own Self;

सुखमात्यन्तिकं यत्तद्बुद्धिग्राह्यमतीन्द्रियम् ।
वेत्ति यत्र न चैवायं स्थितश्चलति तत्त्वतः ।।२१।।

*sukhamātyantikaṁ yattadbuddhigrāhyamatīndriyam,*
*vetti yatra na caivayaṁ sthitaścalati tattvataḥ. (21)*

When, he (the yogī) feels that infinite Bliss, which can be grasped by the (pure) intellect and which transcends the senses - wherein established he never moves from the Reality;

यं लब्ध्वा चापरं लाभं मन्यते नाधिकं ततः ।
यस्मिन्स्थितो न दुःखेन गुरुणापि विचाल्यते ।।२२।।

*yaṁ labdhvā cāparaṁ lābhaṁ manyate nādhikaṁ tataḥ,*
*yasminsthito na duḥkhena guruṇāpi vicālyate.* (22)

Which having obtained, he thinks there is no other gain superior to it; wherein established, he is not moved even by heavy sorrow.

तं विद्याद् दुःखसंयोगवियोगं योगसञ्ज्ञितम् ।
स निश्चयेन योक्तव्यो योगोऽनिर्विण्णचेतसा ।। २३।।

*taṁ vidyād duḥkhasaṁyogaviyogaṁ yogasañjñitam,*
*sa niścayena yoktavyo yogo'nirviṇṇacetasā.* (23)

Let it be known; the severance from the union with pain is yoga. This yoga should be practised with determination and with a mind steady and undespairing.

सङ्कल्पप्रभवान्कामांस्त्यक्त्वा सर्वानशेषतः ।
मनसैवेन्द्रियग्रामं विनियम्य समन्ततः ।।२४।।

*saṅkalpaprabhavānkāmāṁstyaktvā sarvānaśeṣataḥ,*
*manasaivendriyagrāmaṁ viniyamya samantataḥ.* (24)

Abandoning, without reserve, all desires born of saṅkalpa, and completely restraining the whole group of senses by the mind from all sides....

शनैः शनैरुपरमेद्बुद्ध्या धृतिगृहीतया ।
आत्मसंस्थं मनः कृत्वा न किञ्चिदपि चिन्तयेत् ।।२५।।

*śanaiḥ śanairuparamedbuddhyā dhṛtigṛhītayā,*
*ātmasaṁsthaṁ manaḥ kṛtvā na kiñcidapi cintayet. (25)*

Little by little, let him attain quietude by his intellect held firm; having made the mind established in the Self, let him not think of anything.

यतो यतो निश्चरति मनश्चञ्चलमस्थिरम् ।
ततस्ततो नियम्यैतदात्मन्येव वशं नयेत् ।।२६।।

*yato yato niścarati manaścañcalamasthiram,*
*tatastato niyamyaitadātmanyeva vaśaṁ nayet. (26)*

From whatever cause the restless and the unsteady mind wanders away, from that let him restrain it and bring it back under the control of the Self alone.

प्रशान्तमनसं ह्येनं योगिनं सुखमुत्तमम् ।
उपैति शान्तरजसं ब्रह्मभूतमकल्मषम् ।।२७।।

*praśāntamanasaṁ hyenaṁ yoginaṁ sukhamuttamam,*
*upaiti śāntarajasaṁ brahmabhūtamakalmaṣam.* (27)

Supreme bliss verily comes to this yogī, whose mind is quite peaceful, whose passion is quietened, who is free from sin and who has become Brahman.

युञ्जन्नेवं सदात्मानं योगी विगतकल्मषः ।
सुखेन ब्रह्मसंस्पर्शमत्यन्तं सुखमश्नुते ।।२८।।

*yuñjannevaṁ sadātmānaṁ yogī vigatakalmaṣaḥ,*
*sukhena brahmasaṁsparśamatyantaṁ sukhamaśnute.* (28)

The yogī, always engaging the mind thus (in the practice of yoga), freed from sins, easily enjoys the infinite Bliss of 'Brahman-contact'.

सर्वभूतस्थमात्मानं सर्वभूतानि चात्मनि ।
ईक्षते योगयुक्तात्मा सर्वत्र समदर्शनः ।।२९।।

*sarvabhūtasthamātmānaṁ sarvabhūtāni cātmani,*
*īkṣate yogayuktātmā sarvatra samadarśanaḥ.* (29)

With the mind harmonised by yoga, he sees the Self abiding in all beings and all beings in the Self; he sees the same everywhere.

योो मां पश्यति सर्वत्र सर्वं च मयि पश्यति ।
तस्याहं न प्रणश्यामि स च मे न प्रणश्यति ।।३०।।

*yo māṁ paśyati sarvatra sarvaṁ ca mayi paśyati,*
*tasyāhaṁ na praṇaśyāmi sa ca me na praṇaśyati.* (30)

He, who sees Me everywhere and sees everything in Me, he never gets separated from Me nor do I get separated from him.

सर्वभूतस्थितं यो मां भजत्येकत्वमास्थितः ।
सर्वथा वर्तमानोऽपि स योगी मयि वर्तते ।।३१।।

*sarvabhūtasthitaṁ yo māṁ bhajatyekatvamāsthitaḥ,*
*sarvathā vartamāno'pi sa yogī mayi vartate.* (31)

He, who, being established in unity worships Me, dwelling in all beings, that yogī abides in Me whatever be his mode of living.

आत्मौपम्येन सर्वत्र समं पश्यति योऽर्जुन ।
सुखं वा यदि वा दुःखं स योगी परमो मतः ।।३२।।

*ātmaupamyena sarvatra samaṁ paśyati yorjuna,*
*sukhaṁ vā yadi vā duḥkhaṁ sa yogī paramo mataḥ. (32)*

He who, through the likeness (sameness) of the Self, O Arjuna, sees equality everywhere, be it pleasure or pain, is regarded as the highest yogī.

अर्जुन उवाच
योऽयं योगस्त्वया प्रोक्तः साम्येन मधुसूदन ।
एतस्याहं न पश्यामि चञ्चलत्वात्स्थितिं स्थिराम् ।।३३।।

*arjuna uvāca*

*yo'yaṁ yogastvayā proktaḥ sāmyena madhusūdana,*
*etasyāhaṁ na paśyāmi cañcalatvātsthitiṁ sthirām. (33)*

Arjuna said:

This 'yoga of equanimity', taught by Thee, O slayer of Madhu, I see not its enduring continuity because of the restlessness (of the mind).

चञ्चलं हि मनः कृष्ण प्रमाथि बलवद्दृढम् ।
तस्याहं निग्रहं मन्ये वायोरिव सुदुष्करम् ।।३४।।

*cañcalaṁ hi manaḥ kṛṣṇa pramāthi balavaddṛḍham,*
*tasyāhaṁ nigrahaṁ manye vāyoriva suduṣkaram.* (34)

The mind verily is, O Kṛṣṇa, restless, turbulent, strong and unyielding; I deem it quite (as) difficult to control as the wind.

श्रीभगवानुवाच
असंशयं महाबाहो मनो दुर्निग्रहं चलम् ।
अभ्यासेन तु कौन्तेय वैराग्येण च गृह्यते ।।३५।।

*śrībhagavānuvāca*

*asaṁśayaṁ mahābāho mano durnigrahaṁ calam,*
*abhyāsena tu kaunteya vairāgyeṇa ca gṛhyate.* (35)

The Blessed Lord said:

O mighty-armed one, undoubtedly, the mind is difficult to control and is restless; but, O son of Kuntī, by practice, and by dispassion, it is restrained.

असंयतात्मना योगो दुष्प्राप इति मे मतिः।
वश्यात्मना तु यतता शक्योऽवाप्तुमुपायतः।।३६।।

*asaṁyatāmanā yogo duṣprāpa iti me matiḥ,*
*vaśyātmanā tu yatatā śakyo'vāptumupāyataḥ.* (36)

Yoga, I think, is hard to be attained by one of uncontrolled self; but the self-controlled, striving, can obtain it by (proper) means.

अर्जुन उवाच
अयतिः श्रद्धयोपेतो योगाच्चलितमानसः ।
अप्राप्य योगसंसिद्धिं कां गतिं कृष्ण गच्छति ।।३७।।

*arjuna uvāca*

*ayatiḥ śradhayopeto yogāccalitamānasaḥ,*
*aparāpya yogasaṁsiddhiṁ kāṁ gatiṁ kṛṣṇa gacchati.* (37)

Arjuna said:

When a man, though possessed of faith, is unable to control himself, whose mind wanders away from yoga, to what end does he - having failed to attain perfection in yoga - go, O Kṛṣṇa?

कच्चिन्नोभयविभ्रष्टश्छिन्नाभ्रमिव नश्यति ।
अप्रतिष्ठो महाबाहो विमूढो ब्रह्मणः पथि ।।३८।।

*kaccinnobhayavībhraṣṭaśchinnābhramiva naśyati,*
*apratiṣṭho mahābāho vimūḍho brahmaṇaḥ pathi. (38)*

Fallen from both, does he not, O mighty-armed, perish like a rent cloud, supportless and deluded in the path of Brahman?

एतन्मे संशयं कृष्ण छेत्तुमर्हस्यशेषतः ।
त्वदन्यः संशयस्यास्य छेत्ता न ह्युपपद्यते ।।३९।।

*etanme saṁsayaṁ kṛṣṇa chettumarhasyaśeṣataḥ,*
*tvadanyaḥ saṁśayasyāsya chettā na hyupapadyate. (39)*

This doubt of mine, O Kṛṣṇa, please dispel completely; because it is not possible for any one but you to dispel this doubt.

श्रीभगवानुवाच
पार्थ नैवेह नामुत्र विनाशस्तस्य विद्यते ।
न हि कल्याणकृत्कश्चिद्दुर्गतिं तात गच्छति ।।४०।।

*śrībhagavānuvāca*

*pārtha naiveha nāmutra vīnāśastasya vidyate,*
*na hi kalyāṇakṛtkaściddurgatiṁ tāta gacchati. (40)*

The Blessed Lord said:

O Pārtha, neither in this world nor in the next world is there destruction for him; none, verily, who strives to be good, O my son, ever comes to grief.

प्राप्य पुण्यकृतां लोकानुषित्वा शाश्वतीः समाः ।
शुचीनां श्रीमतां गेहे योगभ्रष्टोऽभिजायते ।।४१।।

*prāpya puṇyakṛtāṁ lokānuṣitvā śāśvatīḥ samāḥ,*
*śucīnāṁ srīmatāṁ gehe yogabhraṣṭo'bhijāyate. (41)*

Having attained to the worlds of the righteous and having dwelt there for everlasting (long) years, he who had fallen from yoga, is born again in the house of the pure and the wealthy.

अथवा योगिनामेव कुले भवति धीमताम् ।
एतद्धि दुर्लभतरं लोके जन्म यदीदृशम् ।।४२।।

*athavā yogināmeva kule bhavati dhīmatām,*
*etaddhi durlabhataraṁ loke janma yadīdṛśam. (42)*

Or, he is even born in the family of the wise yogīs; verily, a birth like this is very difficult to obtain in this world.

तत्र तं बुद्धिसंयोगं लभते पौर्वदेहिकम् ।
यतते च ततो भूयः संसिद्धौ कुरुनन्दन ।।४३।।

*tatra taṁ buddhisaṁyogaṁ labhate paurvadehikam,*
*yatate ca tato bhūyaḥ saṁsiddhau kurunandana. (43)*

There, he comes to be united with the knowledge acquired in his former body and strives more than before for Perfection, O son of the Kurus.

पूर्वाभ्यासेन तेनैव ह्रियते ह्यवशोऽपि सः ।
जिज्ञासुरपि योगस्य शब्दब्रह्मातिवर्तते ।।४४।।

*pūrvābhyāsena tenaiva hriyate hyavaśo'pi saḥ,*
*jijñāsurapi yogasya śabdabrahmātivartate. (44)*

By that very former practice, he is borne on and gets attracted to the Highest inspite of himself. Even he, who merely wishes to know yoga, goes beyond the śabdabrahman.

प्रयत्नाद्यतमानस्तु योगी संशुद्धकिल्बिषः ।
अनेकजन्मसंसिद्धस्ततो याति परां गतिम् ।।४५।।

*prayatnādyatamānastu yogī saṁśuddhakilbiṣaḥ,*
*anekajanmasaṁsiddhastato yāti parāṁ gatim. (45)*

But the yogī, who strives with assiduity, purified from sins and perfected (gradually) through many births, then attains the highest goal.

तपस्विभ्योऽधिको योगी ज्ञानिभ्योऽपि मतोऽधिकः ।
कर्मिभ्यश्चाधिको योगी तस्माद्योगी भवार्जुन ।।४६।।

*tapasvibhyo'dhiko yogī jñānibhyo'pi mato'dhikaḥ,*
*karmibhyaścādhiko yogī tasmādyogī bhavārjuna. (46)*

The yogī is thought to be superior to the ascetics and even superior to men of knowledge (mere scholars); he is also superior to men of action; therefore (you strive to) be a yogī, O Arjuna.

योगिनामपि सर्वेषां मद्गतेनान्तरात्मना ।
श्रद्धावान्भजते यो मां स मे युक्ततमो मतः ।।४७।।

*yogināmapi saraveṣāṁ madgatenāntarātmanā,*
*śrāddḥāvānbhajate yo māṁ sa me yuktatamo mataḥ. (47)*

And among all yogīs, he who, full of faith, with his innerself merged in Me, worships Me, is, according to Me, the most devout.

ॐ तत्सदिति श्रीमद्भगवद्गीतासूपनिषत्सु
ब्रह्मविद्यायां योगशास्त्रे श्रीकृष्णार्जुनसंवादे
आत्मसंयमयोगो नाम षष्ठोऽध्यायः

*om tatsatditi srīmadbhagavadgītasūpaniṣatsu brahmavidyāyāṁ yogaśāstre śrīkṛṣṇārjunasaṁvāde ātmasaṁyamayogo nāma ṣaṣṭho'dhyāyaḥ.*

Thus, in the Upaniṣads of the glorious Bhagavad-gītā, in the science of the eternal, in the scripture of yoga, in the dialogue between Śrī Kṛṣṇa and Arjuna, the sixth discourse ends entitled.

THE YOGA OF SELF-CONTROL/MEDITATION

***

Knowledge and Wisdom

# Chapter 7

## *Yoga of Knowledge and Wisdom*

**श्रीभगवानुवाच**

**मय्यासक्तमनाः पार्थ योगं युञ्जन्मदाश्रयः ।**
**असंशयं समग्रं मां यथा ज्ञास्यसि तच्छृणु ।।१।।**

*śrībhagavānuvāca*

*mayyāsaktamanāḥ pārtha yogaṁ yuñjanmadāśrayaḥ,*
*asaṁśayaṁ samagraṁ māṁ yathā jñāsyasi tacchṛṇu. (1)*

The Blessed Lord said :

With the mind intent on Me, Pārtha, practising yoga and taking refuge in Me, how thou shalt, without doubt, know Me fully, that do thou listen.

ज्ञानं तेऽहं सविज्ञानमिदं वक्ष्याम्यशेषतः ।
यज्ज्ञात्वा नेह भूयोऽन्यज्ज्ञातव्यमवशिष्यते ।।२।।

*jñānaṁ te'haṁ savijñānamidaṁ vakṣyāmyaśeṣataḥ,*
*yajjñātva neha bhūyo'nyajjñātavyamavaśiṣyate.* (2)

I shall declare to thee, in full, this knowledge combined with Realisation, which being known, nothing more here remains to be known.

मनुष्याणां सहस्रेषु कश्चिद्यतति सिद्धये ।
यततामपि सिद्धानां कश्चिन्मां वेत्ति तत्त्वतः ।।३।।

*manuṣyāṇāṁ sahasreṣu kaṣcidyatati siddhaye,*
*yatatāmapi siddhānāṁ kaścinmāṁ vetti tattvataḥ.* (3)

Among thousands of men, one perchance strives for perfection; even among those successful strivers, only one perchance knows Me in essence.

भूमिरापोऽनलो वायुः खं मनो बुद्धिरेव च ।
अहङ्कार इतीयं मे भिन्ना प्रकृतिरष्टधा ।।४।।

*bhūmirāpo'nalo vāyuḥ khaṁ mano buddhireva ca,*
*ahaṅkāra itīyaṁ me bhinnā prakṛtiraṣṭadhā. (4)*

Earth, water, fire, air, ether, mind, intellect, egoism; these are My eightfold prakṛti.

अपरेयमितस्त्वन्यां प्रकृतिं विद्धि मे पराम् ।
जीवभूतां महाबाहो ययेदं धार्यते जगत् ।।५।।

*apareyamitastvanyāṁ prakṛtiṁ viddhi me parām,*
*jīvabhūtāṁ mahābāho yayedaṁ dhāryate jagat. (5)*

This is the lower prakṛti; different from it, know thou, O mighty-armed, My higher prakṛti, the very life element, by which this world is upheld.

एतद्योनीनि भूतानि सर्वाणीत्युपधारय ।
अहं कृत्स्नस्य जगतः प्रभवः प्रलयस्तथा ।।६।।

*etadyonīni bhūtāni sarvāṇītyupadhāraya,*
*ahaṁ kṛtsnasya jagataḥ prabhavaḥ pralayastathā. (6)*

Know that these (two prakṛtis), are the womb of all beings. So, I am the source and dissolution of the whole universe.

मत्तः परतरं नान्यत्किञ्चिदस्ति धनञ्जय ।
मयि सर्वमिदं प्रोतं सूत्रे मणिगणा इव ॥७॥

*mattaḥ parataraṁ nānyatkiñcidasti dhanañjaya,*
*mayi sarvamidaṁ protaṁ sūtre maṇigaṇā iva. (7)*

There is nothing whatsoever higher than Me, O Dhanañjaya. All this is strung in Me, as clusters of gems on a string.

रसोऽहमप्सु कौन्तेय प्रभास्मि शशिसूर्ययोः ।
प्रणवः सर्ववेदेषु शब्दः खे पौरुषं नृषु ॥८॥

*raso'hamapsu kaunteya prabhāsmi śaśisūryayoḥ,*
*praṇavaḥ sarvavedeṣu śabadaḥ khe pauruṣaṁ nṛṣu. (8)*

I am the sapidity in water, O son of Kuntī, I am the light in the moon and the sun; I am the syllable Om in all the Vedas, sound in ether and virility in men;

पुण्यो गन्धः पृथिव्यां च तेजश्चास्मि विभावसौ ।
जीवनं सर्वभूतेषु तपश्चास्मि तपस्विषु ॥९॥

*puṇyo gandhaḥ pṛthivyāṁ ca tejaścāsmi vibhāvasau,*
*jīvanaṁ sarvabhūteṣu tapaścasmi tapasviṣu. (9)*

I am the sweet fragrance in earth and the brilliance in fire, the life in all beings and I am austerity in the austere.

बीजं मां सर्वभूतानां विद्धि पार्थ सनातनम् ।
बुद्धिर्बुद्धिमतामस्मि तेजस्तेजस्विनामहम् ।।१०।।

*bījaṁ māṁ sarvabhūtānāṁ viddhi pārtha sanātanam,*
*buddhirbuddhimatāmasmi tejastejasvināmaham. (10)*

Know me, O Pārtha, as the eternal seed of all beings; I am the intelligence of the intelligent. The splendour of the splendid (things and beings), am I.

बलं बलवतां चाहं कामरागविवर्जितम् ।
धर्माविरुद्धो भूतेषु कामोऽस्मि भरतर्षभ ।।११।।

*balaṁ balavatāṁ cāhaṁ kāmarāgavivarjitam,*
*dharmāviruddho bhūteṣu kāmo'smi bharatarṣabha. (11)*

Of the strong, I am the strength devoid of desire and attachment and in (all) beings, I am the desire unopposed to dharma, O best among the Bhāratas.

ये चैव सात्त्विका भावा राजसास्तामसाश्च ये ।
मत्त एवेति तान्विद्धि न त्वहं तेषु ते मयि ।।१२।।

*ye caiva sāttvikā bhāvā rājasāstāmasāśca ye,*
*matta eveti tānviddhi na tvahaṁ teṣu te mayi.* (12)

Whatever beings (and objects) that are pure, active and inert, know them to proceed from Me; yet, I am not in them, they are in Me.

त्रिभिर्गुणमयैर्भावैरेभिः सर्वमिदं जगत् ।
मोहितं नाभिजानाति मामेभ्यः परमव्ययम् ।।१३।।

*tribhirguṇamayairbhāvairebhiḥ sarvamidaṁ jagat,*
*mohitaṁ nābhijānāti māmebhyaḥ paramavyayam.* (13)

Deluded by these natures (states or things) composed of the three guṇas (of prakṛti), all the world knows Me not as immutable and distinct from them.

दैवी ह्येषा गुणमयी मम माया दुरत्यया ।
मामेव ये प्रपद्यन्ते मायामेतां तरन्ति ते ।।१४।।

*daivī hyeṣā guṇamayī mama māyā duratyayā,*
*māmeva ye prapadyante māyāmetāṁ taranti te. (14)*

Verily, this divine illusion of Mine made up of guṇas (caused by the qualities) is difficult to cross over; those who take refuge in Me, they alone can cross over this illusion.

न मां दुष्कृतिनो मूढाः प्रपद्यन्ते नराधमाः ।
माययापहृतज्ञाना आसुरं भावमाश्रिताः ।।१५।।

*na māṁ duṣkṛtino mūḍhāḥ prapadyante narādhamāḥ,*
*māyayāpahṛtajñānā āsuraṁ bhāvamāśritāḥ. (15)*

The evil-doers, the deluded, the lowest of men do not seek Me; they, whose discrimination has been destroyed by their own delusions, follow the ways of the demons.

चतुर्विधा भजन्ते मां जनाः सुकृतिनोऽर्जुन ।
आर्तो जिज्ञासुरर्थार्थी ज्ञानी च भरतर्षभ ।।१६।।

*caturvidhā bhajante māṁ janāḥ sukṛtino'rjuna,*
*ārto jijñsurarthārthī jñānī ca bharatarṣabha. (16)*

Four kinds of virtuous people worship Me, O Arjuna, the dissatisfied, the seeker of (systematised) knowledge, the seeker of wealth and the wise, O best among the Bhāratas.

तेषां ज्ञानी नित्ययुक्त एकभक्तिर्विशिष्यते ।
प्रियो हि ज्ञानिनोऽत्यर्थमहं स च मम प्रियः ॥१७॥

*teṣāṁ jñānī nityayukta ekabhaktirviśiṣyate,*
*priyo hi jñānino'tyarthamahaṁ sa ca mama priyaḥ. (17)*

Of them, the wise ever steadfast and devoted to the One, excels; for, I am exceedingly dear to the wise and he is dear to Me.

उदाराः सर्व एवैते ज्ञानी त्वात्मैव मे मतम् ।
आस्थितः स हि युक्तात्मा मामेवानुत्तमां गतिम् ॥१८॥

*udārāḥ sarva evaite jñānī tvātmaiva me matam,*
*āsthitaḥ sa hi yuktātmā māmevānuttamāṁ gatim. (18)*

Noble indeed are all these, but the wise man, I deem, as My very Self; for steadfast in mind, he is established in Me alone as the supreme goal.

बहूनां जन्मनामन्ते ज्ञानवान्मां प्रपद्यते ।
वासुदेवः सर्वमिति स महात्मा सुदुर्लभः ।।१९।।

*bahūnāṁ janmanāmante jñānavānmāṁ prapadyate,*
*vāsudevaḥ sarvamiti sa mahātmā sudurlabhaḥ. (19)*

At the end of many births, the wise man comes to Me, realising that all this is Vāsudeva (the innermost Self); such a great soul (Mahātmā) is very hard to find.

कामैस्तैस्तैर्हृतज्ञानाः प्रपद्यन्तेऽन्यदेवताः ।
तं तं नियममास्थाय प्रकृत्या नियताः स्वया ।।२०।।

*kāmaistaistairhṛtajñānāḥ prapadyante'nyadevatāḥ,*
*taṁ taṁ niyamamāsthāya prakṛtyā niyatāḥ svayā. (20)*

Those, whose wisdom has been looted away by this or that desire, go to other gods, following this or that norm, led by their own nature.

यो यो यां यां तनुं भक्तः श्रद्धयार्चितुमिच्छति ।
तस्य तस्याचलां श्रद्धां तामेव विदधाम्यहम् ।।२१।।

*yo yo yāṁ yāṁ tanuṁ bhaktaḥ śraddhayārcitumicchati,*
*tasya tasyācalāṁ śraddhāṁ tāmeva vidadhāmyaham.* (21)

Whatsoever form any devotee desires to worship with faith, that (same) faith of his I make (firm and) unflinching.

स तया श्रद्धया युक्तस्तस्याराधनमीहते ।
लभते च ततः कामान्मयैव विहितान्हि तान् ।।२२।।

*sa tayā śraddhayā yuktastasyārādhanamīhate,*
*labhate ca tataḥ kāmānmayaiva vihitānhi tān.* (22)

Endowed with that faith, he engages in the worship of that devatā and from it, he obtains his desire fulfilments; all these being ordained by Me (alone).

अन्तवत्तु फलं तेषां तद्भवत्यल्पमेधसाम् ।
देवान्देवयजो यान्ति मद्भक्ता यान्ति मामपि ।।२३।।

*antavattu phalaṁ teṣāṁ tadbhavatyalpamedhasām,*
*devāndevayajo yānti madbhaktā yānti māmapi.* (23)

Verily, the fruit that accrues to those men of little intelligence is finite. The worshippers of the devas go to the devas but My devotees come to Me.

अव्यक्तं व्यक्तिमापन्नं मन्यन्ते मामबुद्धयः ।
परं भावमजानन्तो ममाव्ययमनुत्तमम् ।।२४।।

*avyaktaṁ vyaktimāpannaṁ manyante māmabuddhayaḥ,*
*paraṁ bhāvamajānanto mamāvyayamanuttamam.* (24)

The foolish think of Me, the Unmanifest, as having come to manifestation, not knowing My higher, immutable and peerless nature.

नाहं प्रकाशः सर्वस्य योगमायासमावृतः ।
मूढोऽयं नाभिजानाति लोको मामजमव्ययम् ।।२५।।

*nāhaṁ prakāśaḥ sarvasya yogamāyāsamāvṛtaḥ,*
*mūḍho'yaṁ nābhijānāti loko māmajamavyayam.* (25)

I am not manifest to all (in My real nature) veiled by divine Māyā. This deluded world knows not Me, the unborn, the imperishable.

वेदाहं समतीतानि वर्तमानानि चार्जुन ।
भविष्याणि च भूतानि मां तु वेद न कश्चन ।।२६।।

*vedāhaṁ samatītāni vartamānāni cārjuna,*
*bhaviṣyāṇi ca bhūtāni māṁ tu veda na kaścana.* (26)

I know, O Arjuna, the beings of the past, present and the future, but no one knows Me.

इच्छाद्वेषसमुत्थेन द्वन्द्वमोहेन भारत ।
सर्वभूतानि सम्मोहं सर्गे यान्ति परन्तप ।।२७।।

*icchādveṣasamutthena dvandvamohena bhārata,*
*sarvabhūtāni sammohaṁ sarge yānti parantapa.* (27)

By the delusion of the pairs of opposites, arising from desire and aversion, O Bhārata, all beings are subject to delusion at birth, O Parantapa (scorcher of foes).

येषां त्वन्तगतं पापं जनानां पुण्यकर्मणाम् ।
ते द्वन्द्वमोहनिर्मुक्ता भजन्ते मां दृढव्रताः ।।२८।।

*yeṣaṁ tvantagataṁ pāpaṁ janānāṁ puṇyakarmaṇām,*
*te dvandvamohanirmuktā bhajante māṁ dṛḍhavratāḥ.* (28)

But, those men of virtuous deeds whose sins have come to an end, who are freed from the delusion of the pairs of opposites and steadfast in vows, worship Me.

जरामरणमोक्षाय मामाश्रित्य यतन्ति ये ।
ते ब्रह्म तद्विदुः कृत्स्नमध्यात्मं कर्म चाखिलम् ।।२९।।

*jarāmaraṇamokṣāya māmāśritya yatanti ye,*
*te brahma tadviduḥ kṛtsnamadhyātmaṁ karma cākhilam.* (29)

Those who strive for liberation from old age and death, taking refuge in Me, they realise in full that Brahman, the whole knowledge of the Self and all action.

साधिभूताधिदैवं मां साधियज्ञं च ये विदुः ।
प्रयाणकालेऽपि च मां ते विदुर्युक्तचेतसः ।।३०।।

*sādhibhūtādhidaivaṁ māṁ sādhiyajñaṁ ca ye viduḥ,*
*prayāṇakāle'pi ca māṁ te viduryuktacetasaḥ.* (30)

Those who know Me with the Adhibhūta (pertaining to elements - the world of objects), Adhidaiva (pertaining to the gods - the sense-organs) and the Adhiyajña (pertaining to the sacrifice - all perceptions), even at the time of death, steadfast in mind, know Me.

ॐ तत्सदिति श्रीमद्भगवद्गीतासूपनिषत्सु
ब्रह्मविद्यायां योगशास्त्रे श्रीकृष्णार्जुनसंवादे
ज्ञानविज्ञानयोगो नाम सप्तमोऽध्यायः

*om tatsaditi śrīmadbhagavadgītāsūpaniṣatsu*
*brahmavidyāyāṁ yogaśāstre śrīkṛṣṇārjunasaṁvāde*
*jñānavijñānayogo nāma saptamo'dhyāyaḥ.*

Thus, in the Upaniṣads of the glorious Bhagavad-gītā, in the science of the eternal, in the scripture of yoga, in the dialogue between Śrī Kṛṣṇa and Arjuna, the seventh discourse ends entitled:

YOGA OF KNOWLEDGE AND WISDOM

***

Imperishable Brahman

# Chapter 8

## *Yoga of Imperishable Brahman*

अर्जुन उवाच

किं तद्ब्रह्म किमध्यात्मं किं कर्म पुरुषोत्तम ।
अधिभूतं च किं प्रोक्तमधिदैवं किमुच्यते ।।१।।

*arjuna uvāca*

*kiṁ tadbrahma kimadhyātmaṁ kiṁ karma puruṣottama,*
*adhibhūtaṁ ca kiṁ proktamadhidaivaṁ kimucyate.(1)*

Arjuna said :

What is that Brahman? What is the Adhyātma? What is action? O best among men, what is declared to be the Adhibhūta? And what is Adhidaiva said to be?

अधियज्ञः कथं कोऽत्र देहेऽस्मिन्मधुसूदन ।
प्रयाणकाले च कथं ज्ञेयोऽसि नियतात्मभिः ॥२॥

*adhiyajñaḥ kathaṁ ko'tra dehe'sminmadhusūdana,*
*prayāṇakāle ca kathaṁ jñeyo'si niyatātmabhiḥ. (2)*

Who and how is Adhiyajña here in this body, O destroyer of Madhu? And how, at the time of death, are you to be known by the self-controlled?

श्रीभगवानुवाच
अक्षरं ब्रह्म परमं स्वभावोऽध्यात्ममुच्यते ।
भूतभावोद्भवकरो विसर्गः कर्मसञ्ज्ञितः ॥३॥

*śrībhagavānuvāca*
*akṣaraṁ brahma paramaṁ svabhāvo'dhyātmamucyate,*
*bhūtabhāvodbhavakaro visargaḥ karmasañjñitaḥ. (3)*

The Blessed Lord said :
Brahman is Imperishable, the Supreme; His essential nature is called Self-knowledge, the creative force that causes beings to spring forth into manifestation is called 'work' (action).

अधिभूतं क्षरो भावः पुरुषश्चाधिदैवतम् ।
अधियज्ञोऽहमेवात्र देहे देहभृतां वर ।।४।।

*adhibhūtaṁ kṣaro bhāvaḥ puruṣaścādhidaivatam,*
*adhiyajño'hamevātra dehe dehabhṛtāṁ vara. (4)*

Adhibhūta, (or elememts) constitutes My perishable nature and the Indweller (or the essence) is the Adhidaiva; I alone am the Adhiyajña here, in this body, O best of the embodied.

अन्तकाले च मामेव स्मरन्मुक्त्वा कलेवरम् ।
यः प्रयाति स मद्भावं याति नास्त्यत्र संशयः ।।५।।

*antakāle ca māmeva smaranmuktvā kalevaram,*
*yaḥ prayāti sa madbhāvaṁ yāti nāstyatra saṁśayaḥ. (5)*

And whosoever, leaving the body, goes forth remembering Me alone, at the time of his death, he attains My being; there is no doubt about this.

यं यं वापि स्मरन्भावं त्यजत्यन्ते कलेवरम् ।
तं तमेवैति कौन्तेय सदा तद्भावभावितः ।।६।।

*yaṁ yaṁ vāpi smaranbhāvaṁ tyajatyante kalevaram,*
*taṁ tamevaiti kaunteya sadā tadbhāvabhāvitaḥ. (6)*

Whosoever, at the end, leaves the body, thinking of any being, to that being only he goes, O Kaunteya (O son of Kuntī), because of his constant thought of that being.

तस्मात्सर्वेषु कालेषु मामनुस्मर युध्य च ।
मय्यर्पितमनोबुद्धिर्मामेवैष्यस्यसंशयम् ।।७।।

*tasmātsarveṣu kāleṣu māmanusmara yudhya ca,*
*mayyarpitamanobuddhirmāmevaiṣyasyasaṁśayam. (7)*

Therefore, at all times, remember Me and fight, with mind and intellect fixed (or absorbed) in Me; you shall doubtless, come to Me alone.

अभ्यासयोगयुक्तेन चेतसा नान्यगामिना ।
परमं पुरुषं दिव्यं याति पार्थानुचिन्तयन् ।।८।।

*abhyāsayogayuktena cetasā nānyagāminā,*
*paramaṁ puruṣaṁ divyaṁ yāti pārthānucintayan. (8)*

With the mind not moving towards any other thing, made steadfast by the method of habitual meditation, and constantly meditating on the supreme Puruṣa, the Resplendent, O Pārtha, he goes (to Him).

कविं पुराणमनुशासितार-
मणोरणीयांसमनुस्मरेद्यः ।
सर्वस्य धातारमचिन्त्यरूप-
मादित्यवर्णं तमसः परस्तात् ।।९।।

*kaviṁ purāṇamanuśāsitāra–*
*maṇoraṇīyāṁsamanusmaredyaḥ,*
*sarvasya dhātāramacintyarūpa–*
*mādityavarṇaṁ tamasaḥ parastāt. (9)*

Whosoever, meditates upon the Omniscient, the Ancient, the Ruler (of the whole world), minuter than the atom, the nourisher (supporter) of all, of form inconceivable, effulgent like the Sun and beyond the darkness (of ignorance)...

प्रयाणकाले मनसाचलेन
भक्त्या युक्तो योगबलेन चैव ।
भ्रुवोर्मध्ये प्राणमावेश्य सम्यक्-
स तं परं पुरुषमुपैति दिव्यम् ।।१०।।

*prayāṇakāle manasācalena*
*bhaktyā yukto yogabalena caiva,*
*bhruvormadhye prāṇamāveśya samyak-*
*sa taṁ paraṁ puruṣamupaiti divyam. (10)*

At the time of death, with an unshaken mind full of devotion, by the power of yoga fixing the whole prāṇa (breath) between the two eyebrows, he (the seeker) reaches the supreme resplendent Puruṣa.

यदक्षरं वेदविदो वदन्ति
विशन्ति यद्यतयो वीतरागाः ।
यदिच्छन्तो ब्रह्मचर्यं चरन्ति
तत्ते पदं सङ्ग्रहेण प्रवक्ष्ये ।।११।।

*yadakṣaraṁ vedavido vadanti*
*viśanti yadyatayo vītarāgāḥ,*
*yadicchanto brahmacaryaṁ caranti*
*tatte padaṁ saṅgraheṇa pravakṣye. (11)*

That which is declared Imperishable by the Veda-knowers; That into which, the self-controlled and desire-freed enter; That desiring for which brahmcarya is practised - that goal I will declare to thee in brief.

सर्वद्वाराणि संयम्य मनो हृदि निरुध्य च ।
मूर्ध्न्याधायात्मनः प्राणमास्थितो योगधारणाम् ।।१२।।

*sarvadvārāṇi saṁyamya mano hṛdi nirudhya ca,*
*mūrdhnyādhāyātmanaḥ prāṇamāsthito yogadhāraṇām. (12)*

Having closed all the gates, having confined the mind in the heart, having fixed the life-breath in the head, engaged in the practice of concentration....

ओमित्येकाक्षरं ब्रह्म व्याहरन्मामनुस्मरन् ।
यः प्रयाति त्यजन्देहं स याति परमां गतिम् ।।१३।।

*omityekākṣaraṁ brahma vyāharanmāmanusmaran,*
*yaḥ prayāti tyajandehaṁ sa yāti paramāṁ gatim.* (13)

Uttering the one syllabled 'Om' – the (symbol of) Brahman – and remembering Me, he who departs, leaving the body, attains the supreme Goal.

अनन्यचेताः सततं यो मां स्मरति नित्यशः ।
तस्याहं सुलभः पार्थ नित्ययुक्तस्य योगिनः ।।१४।।

*ananyacetāḥ satataṁ yo māṁ smarati nityaśaḥ,*
*tasyāhaṁ sulabhaḥ pārtha nityayuktasya yoginaḥ.* (14)

I am easily attainable by that ever-steadfast yogī who constantly remembers Me daily, not thinking of anything else, O Pārtha.

मामुपेत्य पुनर्जन्म दुःखालयमशाश्वतम् ।
नाप्नुवन्ति महात्मानः संसिद्धिं परमां गताः ।।१५।।

*māmupetya punarjanma duḥkhālayamaśāśvatam,*
*nāpnuvanti mahātmānaḥ saṁsiddhiṁ paramāṁ gatāḥ.* (15)

Having attained Me, these Mahātmās (great souls) do not again take birth, which is the house of pain and is non-eternal, they having reached the highest perfection - mokṣa.

आब्रह्मभुवनाल्लोकाः पुनरावर्तिनोऽर्जुन ।
मामुपेत्य तु कौन्तेय पुनर्जन्म न विद्यते ।।१६।।

*ābrahmabhuvanāllokāḥ punarāvartino'rjuna,*
*māmupetya tu kaunteya punarjanma na vidyate.* (16)

Worlds upto the 'world of Brahmājī' are subject to rebirth, O Arjuna; but he who reaches Me, O Kaunteya, has no rebirth.

सहस्रयुगपर्यन्तमहर्यद्ब्रह्मणो विदुः ।
रात्रिं युगसहस्रान्तां तेऽहोरात्रविदो जनाः ।।१७।।

*sahasrayugaparyantamaharyadbrahmaṇo viduḥ,*
*rātriṁ yugasahasrāntāṁ te'horātravido janāḥ.* (17)

Those people, who know (the length of) the day of Brahmā which ends in a thousand yugas (aeons) and the night which (also) ends in a thousand yugas (aeons), they know day and night.

अव्यक्ताद्व्यक्तयः सर्वाः प्रभवन्त्यहरागमे ।
रात्र्यागमे प्रलीयन्ते तत्रैवाव्यक्तसञ्ज्ञके ।।१८।।

*avyaktādvyaktayaḥ sarvāḥ prabhavantyaharāgame,*
*rātryāgame pralīyante tatraivāvyaktasañjñake. (18)*

From the unmanifest, all the manifest proceed at the coming of the 'day'; at the coming of 'night', they dissolve verily in that alone, which is called the unmanifest.

भूतग्रामः स एवायं भूत्वा भूत्वा प्रलीयते ।
रात्र्यागमेऽवशः पार्थ प्रभवत्यहरागमे ।।१९।।

*bhūtagrāmaḥ sa evāyaṁ bhūtvā bhūtvā pralīyate,*
*rātryāgame'vaśaḥ pārtha praabhavatyaharāgame. (19)*

This same multiples of beings, are being born again and again and are dissolved (into the unmanifest); helplessly, O Pārtha, at the coming of 'night', and they come forth again at the coming of 'day'.

परस्तस्मात्तु भावोऽन्योऽव्यक्तोऽव्यक्तात्सनातनः ।
यः स सर्वेषु भूतेषु नश्यत्सु न विनश्यति ।।२०।।

*parastasmāttu bhāvo'nyo'vyakto'vyaktātsanātanaḥ,*
*yaḥ sa sarveṣu bhūteṣu naśyatsu na vinaśyati.* (20)

But verily, there exists, higher than that unmanifest (avyakta), another unmanifest, which is Eternal, which is not destroyed when all beings are destroyed.

अव्यक्तोऽक्षर इत्युक्तस्तमाहुः परमां गतिम् ।
यं प्राप्य न निवर्तन्ते तद्धाम परमं मम ।।२१।।

*avyakto'kṣara ityuktastamāhuḥ paramāṁ gatim,*
*yaṁ prāpya na nivartante taddhām paramaṁ mama.* (21)

That, which is called the Unmanifest and the Imperishable, they say is the highest Goal (path). They who reach it, never again return. That is My highest abode (state).

पुरुषः स परः पार्थ भक्त्या लभ्यस्त्वनन्यया ।
यस्यान्तःस्थानि भूतानि येन सर्वमिदं ततम् ।।२२।।

*puruṣaḥ sa paraḥ pārtha bhaktyā labyastvananyayā,*
*yasyāntaḥsthāni bhūtāni yena sarvamidaṁ tatam.* (22)

That highest Puruṣa, O Pārtha, is attainable by unswerving devotion to Him alone, within whom all beings dwell, by whom all this is pervaded.

यत्र काले त्वनावृत्तिमावृत्तिं चैव योगिनः ।
प्रयाता यान्ति तं कालं वक्ष्यामि भरतर्षभ ।।२३।।

*yatra kāle tvanāvṛttimāvṛttiṁ caiva yoginaḥ,*
*prayātā yānti taṁ kālaṁ vakṣyāmi bharatarṣabha.* (23)

Now at what time (path) departing, yogīs go , never to return, as also to return, that time (path), I will tell you, O chief of Bharata dynasty.

अग्निर्ज्योतिरहः शुक्लः षण्मासा उत्तरायणम् ।
तत्र प्रयाता गच्छन्ति ब्रह्म ब्रह्मविदो जनाः ।।२४।।

*agnirjyotirahaḥ śuklaḥ ṣaṇmāsā uttarāyaṇam,*
*tatra prayātā gacchanti brahma brahmavido janāḥ.* (24)

Fire, light, daytime, the bright fortnight, the six months of the northern solstice; following this path, men who know Brahman go to Brahman.

धूमो रात्रिस्तथा कृष्णः षण्मासा दक्षिणायनम् ।
तत्र चान्द्रमसं ज्योतिर्योगी प्राप्य निवर्तते ।।२५।।

*dhūmo rātristathā kṛṣṇaḥ ṣaṇmāsā dakṣiṇāyanam,*
*tatra cāndramasaṁ jyotiryogī prāpya nivartate.* (25)

Smoke, night-time, the dark fortnight, also months of the southern solstice, attaining by these to the moon, the lunar light, the yogī returns.

शुक्लकृष्णे गती ह्येते जगतः शाश्वते मते ।
एकया यात्यनावृत्तिमन्ययावर्तते पुनः ।।२६।।

*śuklakṛṣṇe gatī hyete jagataḥ śāśvate mate,*
*ekayā yātyanāvṛttimanyayāvartate punaḥ.* (26)

The path of light and the path of darkness available for the world are both verily thought to be eternal; by the one, the path of light, a man does not return and by the other, the path of darkness, he returns again.

नैते सृती पार्थ जानन्योगी मुह्यति कश्चन ।
तस्मात्सर्वेषु कालेषु योगयुक्तो भवार्जुन ।।२७।।

*naite sṛtī pārtha jānanyogī muhyati kaścana,*
*tasmātsarveṣu kāleṣu yogayukto bhavārjuna. (27)*

Knowing these paths, O Pārtha, no yogī is deluded; therefore, at all times, be steadfast in yoga, O Arjuna.

वेदेषु यज्ञेषु तपःसु चैव
दानेषु यत्पुण्यफलं प्रदिष्टम् ।
अत्येति तत्सर्वमिदं विदित्वा
योगी परं स्थानमुपैति चाद्यम् ।।२८।।

*vedeṣu yajñeṣu tapaḥsu caiva*
*dāneṣu yatpuṇyaphalaṁ pradiṣṭam,*
*atyeti tatsarvamidaṁ viditvā*
*yogī paraṁ sthānamupaiti cādyam. (28)*

Whatever fruit of merit is declared (in the scriptures) as springing up from study of the Vedas, from performance of sacrifices, from practice of austerities and from charity – beyond all these goes the yogī, who having known this (the two paths) attains to the supreme Primeval (essence).

ॐ तत्सदिति श्रीमद्भगवद्गीतासूपनिषत्सु
ब्रह्मविद्यायां योगशास्त्रे श्रीकृष्णार्जुनसंवादे
अक्षरब्रह्मयोगो नाम अष्टमोऽध्यायः

*om tatsaditi śrīmadbhagavadgītāsūpaniṣatsu*
*brahmavidyāyāṁ yogaśāstre śrīkṛṣṇārjunasaṁvāde*
*akṣarabrahmayogo nāma aṣṭamo'dhyāyaḥ*

Thus, in the Upaniṣads of the glorious Bhagavad-gītā, in the science of the eternal, in the scripture of yoga, in the dialogue betwen Śrī Kṛṣṇa and Arjuna, the eighth discourse ends entitled:

YOGA OF IMPERISHABLE BRAHMAN

***

Royal Knowledge and Royal Secret

# Chapter 9

## *Yoga of Royal Knowledge and Royal Secret*

श्रीभगवानुवाच

इदं तु ते गुह्यतमं प्रवक्ष्याम्यनसूयवे ।
ज्ञानं विज्ञानसहितं यज्ज्ञात्वा मोक्ष्यसेऽशुभात् ।।१।।

*śrībhagavānuvāca*

*idaṁ tu te guhyatamaṁ pravakṣyāmyanasūyave,*
*jñānaṁ vijñānasahitaṁ yajjñātvā mokṣyase'śubhāt.* (1)

The Blessed Lord said :

To you who do not cavil, I shall now declare this, the greatest secret, the most profound knowledge combined with experience (or Realisation); which having known, you shall be free from the sorrows of life.

राजविद्या राजगुह्यं पवित्रमिदमुत्तमम् ।
प्रत्यक्षावगमं धर्म्यं सुसुखं कर्तुमव्ययम् ।।२।।

*rājavidyā rājaguhyaṁ pavitramidamuttamam,*
*pratyakṣāvagamaṁ dharmyaṁ susukhaṁ kartumavyayam.* (2)

This royal science, royal secret, the supreme purifier, realisable by direct intuitive knowledge, according to the dharma, is very easy to perform and imperishable.

अश्रद्दधानाः पुरुषा धर्मस्यास्य परन्तप ।
अप्राप्य मां निवर्तन्ते मृत्युसंसारवर्त्मनि ।।३।।

*aśraddadhānāḥ puruṣā dharmasyāsya parantapa,*
*aprāpya māṁ nivartante mṛtyusaṁsāravartmani.* (3)

Persons without faith in this dharma (the divine Self), O Parantapa, without attaning Me return to the path of rebirth, fraught with death.

मया ततमिदं सर्वं जगदव्यक्तमूर्तिना ।
मत्स्थानि सर्वभूतानि न चाहं तेष्ववस्थितः ।।४।।

*mayā tatamidaṁ sarvaṁ jagadavyaktamūrtinā,*
*matsthāni sarvabhūtāni na cāhaṁ teṣvavasthitaḥ.* (4)

All this world (universe) is pervaded by Me in My unmanifest form (aspect); all beings exist in Me, but I do not dwell in them.

न च मत्स्थानि भूतानि पश्य मे योगमैश्वरम् ।
भूतभृन्न च भूतस्थो ममात्मा भूतभावनः ।।५।।

*na ca matsthāni bhūtāni paśya me yogamaiśvaram,*
*bhūtabhṛnna ca bhūtastho mamātmā bhūtabhāvanaḥ.* (5)

Nor do beings exist (in reality) in Me, behold My divine yoga supporting all beings, but not dwelling in them, I am My Self, the efficient cause of all beings.

यथाकाशस्थितो नित्यं वायुः सर्वत्रगो महान् ।
तथा सर्वाणि भूतानि मत्स्थानीत्युपधारय ।।६।।

*yathākāśasthito nityaṁ vāyuḥ sarvatrago mahān,*
*tathā sarvāṇi bhūtāni matsthānītyupadhāraya. (6)*

As the mighty wind moving everywhere rests always in space (the ākāśa), even so, know you, all beings rest in Me.

सर्वभूतानि कौन्तेय प्रकृतिं यान्ति मामिकाम् ।
कल्पक्षये पुनस्तानि कल्पादौ विसृजाम्यहम् ।।७।।

*sarvabhūtāni kaunteya prakṛtiṁ yānti māmikām,*
*kalpakṣaye punastāni kalpādau visṛjāmyaham. (7)*

All beings, O Kaunteya (O son of Kuntī), go into My prakṛti (nature) at the end of a kalpa; I send them forth again at the beginning of (the next) kalpa.

प्रकृतिं स्वामवष्टभ्य विसृजामि पुनः पुनः ।
भूतग्राममिमं कृत्स्नमवशं प्रकृतेर्वशात् ।।८।।

*prakṛtiṁ svāmavaṣṭabhya visṛjāmi punaḥ punaḥ,*
*bhūtagramamimaṁ kṛtsnamavaśaṁ prakṛtervaśāt. (8)*

Animating My prakṛti, I, again and again send forth all this helpless multitude of beings by the force of nature (prakṛti).

न च मां तानि कर्माणि निबध्नन्ति धनञ्जय ।
उदासीनवदासीनमसक्तं तेषु कर्मसु ।।९।।

*na ca māṁ tāni karmāṇi nibadhnanti dhanañjaya,*
*udāsīnavadāsīnamasaktaṁ teṣu karmasu. (9)*

Sitting like one indifferent and unattached to these acts, O Dhanañjaya, these acts do not bind Me.

मयाध्यक्षेण प्रकृतिः सूयते सचराचरम् ।
हेतुनानेन कौन्तेय जगद्विपरिवर्तते ।।१०।।

*mayādhyakṣeṇa prakṛtiḥ sūyate sacarācaram,*
*hetunānena kaunteya jagadviparivartate. (10)*

Under Me as her supervisor, prakṛti (nature) produces the moving and the unmoving; because of this, O Kaunteya, the world revolves?

अवजानन्ति मां मूढा मानुषीं तनुमाश्रितम् ।
परं भावमजानन्तो मम भूतमहेश्वरम् ।।११।।

*avajānanti māṁ mūḍhā mānuṣīṁ tanumāśritam,*
*paraṁ bhāvamajānanto mama bhūtamaheśvaram. (11)*

Fools disregard Me when I dwell in human form; they know not My higher being as the great Lord of all beings.

मोघाशा मोघकर्माणो मोघज्ञाना विचेतसः ।
राक्षसीमासुरीं चैव प्रकृतिं मोहिनीं श्रिताः ।।१२।।

*moghāśā moghakarmāṇo moghajñānā vicetasaḥ,*
*rākṣasīmāsurīṁ caiva prakṛtiṁ mohinīṁ śritāḥ. (12)*

Of vain hopes, of vain actions, of vain knowledge and senseless (devoid of discrimination), they verily are possessed of the delusive nature of rākṣasas and asuras.

महात्मानस्तु मां पार्थ दैवीं प्रकृतिमाश्रिताः ।
भजन्त्यनन्यमनसो ज्ञात्वा भूतादिमव्ययम् ।।१३।।

*mahātmānastu māṁ pārtha daivīṁ prakṛtimāśritāḥ,*
*bhajantyananyamanaso jñātvā bhūtādimavyayam.* (13)

But the Mahātmās (great souls), O Pārtha, partaking of My divine nature, worship Me with a single mind (with a mind devoted to nothing else), knowing Me as the imperishable source of all beings.

सततं कीर्तयन्तो मां यतन्तश्च दृढव्रताः ।
नमस्यन्तश्च मां भक्त्या नित्ययुक्ता उपासते ।।१४।।

*satataṁ kīrtayanto māṁ yatantaśca dṛḍhavratāḥ,*
*namasyantaśca māṁ bhaktyā nityayuktā upāsate.* (14)

Always glorifying Me, striving, firm in vows, prostrating before Me, and always steadfast, they worship Me with devotion.

ज्ञानयज्ञेन चाप्यन्ये यजन्तो मामुपासते ।
एकत्वेन पृथक्त्वेन बहुधा विश्वतोमुखम् ।।१५।।

*jñānayajñena cāpyanye yajanto māmupāsate,*
*ekatvena pṛthaktvena bahudhā viśvatomukham.* (15)

Others also, offering the 'wisdom sacrifice' worship Me, regarding Me as One, as distinct, as manifold Me, who in all forms, faces everywhere.

अहं क्रतुरहं यज्ञः स्वधाहमहमौषधम् ।
मन्त्रोऽहमहमेवाज्यमहमग्निरहं हुतम् ।।१६।।

*ahaṁ kraturahaṁ yajñaḥ svadhāhamahamauṣadham,*
*mantro'hamahamevājyamahamagnirahaṁ hutam. (16)*

I am the Kratu; I am the sacrifice; I am the offering (food) to pitṛs (ancestors); I am the medicinal herb, and all plants; I am the mantra; I am also the clarified butter; I am the fire; I am the oblation.

पिताहमस्य जगतो माता धाता पितामहः ।
वेद्यं पवित्रमोङ्कार ऋक्साम यजुरेव च ।।१७।।

*pitāhamasya jagato mātā dhātā pitāmahaḥ,*
*vedyaṁ pavitramoṅkāra ṛksāma yajureva ca. (17)*

I am the father of this world, the mother, the sustainer and the grandsire; the (one) thing to be known, the purifier, (the syllable) Om, and also the Ṛk, the Sāma and the Yajuḥ also.

गतिर्भर्ता प्रभुः साक्षी निवासः शरणं सुहृत् ।
प्रभवः प्रलयः स्थानं निधानं बीजमव्ययम् ।।१८।।

*gatirbhartā prabhuḥ sākṣī nivāsaḥ śaraṇaṁ suhṛt,*
*prabhavaḥ pralayaḥ sthānaṁ nidhānaṁ bījamavyayam. (18)*

I am the goal, the supporter, the Lord, the witness, the abode, the shelter, the friend, the origin, the dissolution, the foundation, the treasure-house and the seed imperishable.

तपाम्यहमहं वर्षं निगृह्णाम्युत्सृजामि च ।
अमृतं चैव मृत्युश्च सदसच्चाहमर्जुन ।।१९।।

*tapāmyahamahaṁ varṣaṁ nigṛhṇāmyutsṛjāmi ca,*
*amṛtaṁ caiva mṛtyuśca sadasaccāhamarjuna. (19)*

(As Sun) I give heat; I withhold and send forth the rain; I am immortality and also death, both existence and non-existence, O Arjuna.

त्रैविद्या मां सोमपाः पूतपापा-
यज्ञैरिष्ट्वा स्वर्गतिं प्रार्थयन्ते ।
ते पुण्यमासाद्य सुरेन्द्रलोक-
मश्नन्ति दिव्यान्दिवि देवभोगान् ।।२०।।

*traividyā māṁ somapāḥ pūtapāpā-*
*yajñairiṣṭvā svargatiṁ prārthayante,*
*te puṇyamāsādya surendraloka-*
*maśnanti divyāndivi devabhogān. (20)*

The knowers of the three Vedas, the drinkers of soma, purified from sin, worshipping Me by sacrifices, pray for the way to heaven; they reach the holy world of the Lord of the gods and enjoy in heaven the divine pleasures of the gods.

ते तं भुक्त्वा स्वर्गलोकं विशालं-
क्षीणे पुण्ये मर्त्यलोकं विशन्ति ।
एवं त्रयीधर्ममनुप्रपन्ना-
गतागतं कामकामा लभन्ते ।।२१।।

*te taṁ bhuktvā svargalokaṁ viśālaṁ-*
*kṣīṇe puṇye martyalokaṁ viśanti,*
*evaṁ trayīdharmamanuprapannā-*
*gatāgataṁ kāmakāmā labhante. (21)*

They, having enjoyed the vast heaven world, when their merits are exhausted, enter the world of the mortals; thus abiding by the injunctions of the three (Vedas), desiring (objects of) desires, they attain to the state of 'going and returning' (saṁsāra).

अनन्याश्चिन्तयन्तो मां ये जनाः पर्युपासते ।
तेषां नित्याभियुक्तानां योगक्षेमं वहाम्यहम् ।।२२।।

*ananyāścintayanto māṁ ye janāḥ paryupāsate,*
*teṣaṁ nityābhiyuktānāṁ yogakṣemaṁ vahāmyaham. (22)*

To those men who worship Me alone, thinking of no other, to those ever self-controlled, I secure for them that which is not already possessed (yoga) by them, and preserve for them what they already possess (kṣema).

येऽप्यन्यदेवता भक्ता यजन्ते श्रद्धयान्विताः ।
तेऽपि मामेव कौन्तेय यजन्त्यविधिपूर्वकम् ।।२३।।

*ye'pyanyadevata bhaktā yajante śraddhayānvitāḥ,*
*te'pi māmeva kaunteya yajantyavidhipūrvakam.* (23)

Even those devotees, who, endowed with faith, worship other gods, worship Me alone, O son of Kuntī, (but) by the wrong method.

अहं हि सर्वयज्ञानां भोक्ता च प्रभुरेव च ।
न तु मामभिजानन्ति तत्त्वेनातश्च्यवन्ति ते ।।२४।।

*ahaṁ hi sarvayajñānāṁ bhoktā ca prabhureva ca,*
*na tu māmabhijānanti tattvenātaścyavanti te.* (24)

(For) I alone am the enjoyer and the Lord of all sacrifices; but they do not know Me in essence, and hence they fall (return to this mortal world).

यान्ति देवव्रता देवान्पितृन्यान्ति पितृव्रताः ।
भूतानि यान्ति भूतेज्या यान्ति मद्याजिनोऽपि माम् ।।२५।।

*yānti devavratā devānpitṝnyānti pitṛvratāḥ,*
*bhūtāni yānti bhūtejyā yānti madyājino'pi mām.* (25)

The worshippers of the devas or gods go to the devas; the ancestor-worhippers go to the pitṛs or ancestors; worshippers of the bhūtas go to the bhūtas or the elements; but my worshippers come to Me.

पत्रं पुष्पं फलं तोयं यो मे भक्त्या प्रयच्छति ।
तदहं भक्त्युपहृतमश्नामि प्रयतात्मनः ।।२६।।

*patraṁ puṣpaṁ phalaṁ toyaṁ yo me bhaktyā prayacchati,*
*tadahaṁ bhaktyupahṛtamaśnāmi prayatātmanaḥ. (26)*

Whoever offers Me with devotion a leaf, a flower, a fruit, water, that I accept, offered by the pure-minded with devotion.

यत्करोषि यदश्नासि यज्जुहोषि ददासि यत् ।
यत्तपस्यसि कौन्तेय तत्कुरुष्व मदर्पणम् ।।२७।।

*yatkaroṣi yadaśnāsi yajjuhoṣi dadāsi yat,*
*yattapasyasi kaunteya tatkuruṣva madarpaṇam. (27)*

Whatever you do, whatever you eat, whatever you offer in sacrifice, whatever you give in charity, whatever you practise as austerity, O Kaunteya, do it as an offering to Me.

शुभाशुभफलैरेवं मोक्ष्यसे कर्मबन्धनैः ।
सन्न्यासयोगयुक्तात्मा विमुक्तो मामुपैष्यसि ।।२८।।

*śubhāśubhaphalairevaṁ mokṣyase karmabandhanaiḥ,*
*sannyāsayogayuktātmā vimukto māmupaiṣyasi. (28)*

Thus, shall you be freed from the bonds of actions yielding good and evil fruits; with the mind steadfast in the yoga of renunciation and liberated, you shall come unto Me.

समोऽहं सर्वभूतेषु न मे द्वेष्योऽस्ति न प्रियः ।
ये भजन्ति तु मां भक्त्या मयि ते तेषु चाप्यहम् ।।२९।।

*samo'haṁ sarvabhūteṣu na me dveṣyo'sti na priyaḥ,*
*ye bhajanti tu māṁ bhaktyā mayi te teṣu cāpyaham. (29)*

The same am I to all beings, to Me there is none hateful nor dear; but those who worship Me with devotion, are in Me and I am also in them.

अपि चेत्सुदुराचारो भजते मामनन्यभाक् ।
साधुरेव स मन्तव्यः सम्यग्व्यवसितो हि सः ।।३०।।

*api cetsudurācāro bhajate māmananyabhāk,*
*sādhureva sa mantavyaḥ samyagvyavasito hi saḥ. (30)*

Even if the most sinful worships Me, with devotion to none else, (or with single pointedness), he too, should indeed, be regarded as righteous, for, he has rightly resolved.

क्षिप्रं भवति धर्मात्मा शश्वच्छान्तिं निगच्छति ।
कौन्तेय प्रतिजानीहि न मे भक्तः प्रणश्यति ।।३१।।

*kṣipraṁ bhavati dharmātmā śaśvacchāntiṁ nigacchati,*
*kaunteya pratijānīhi na me bhaktaḥ praṇaśyati. (31)*

Soon, he becomes righteous and attains eternal peace, O Kaunteya, know for certain that My devotee is never destroyed.

मां हि पार्थ व्यपाश्रित्य येऽपि स्युः पापयोनयः ।
स्त्रियो वैश्यास्तथा शूद्रास्तेऽपि यान्ति परां गतिम् ।।३२।।

*māṁ hi pārtha vyapāśritya ye'pi syuḥ pāpayonayaḥ,*
*striyo vaiśyastathā śūdrāste'pi yānti parāṁ gatim. (32)*

For, taking refuge in Me, O Pārtha, they also – may be of a sinful birth, women, vaiśyas as well as śūdras – attain the supreme Goal.

किं पुनर्ब्राह्मणाः पुण्या भक्ता राजर्षयस्तथा ।
अनित्यमसुखं लोकमिमं प्राप्य भजस्व माम् ।।३३।।

*kiṁ punarbrāhmaṇāḥ puṇyā bhaktā rājarṣayastathā,*
*anityamasukhaṁ lokamimaṁ prāpya bhajasva mām. (33)*

How much more (easily) then the holy Brāhmaṇas and devoted royal saints (attain the goal)! Having reached (obtained) the impermanent and joyless world, do worship Me (devoutly).

मन्मना भव मद्भक्तो मद्याजी मां नमस्कुरु ।
मामेवैष्यसि युक्त्वैवमात्मानं मत्परायणः ।।३४।।

*manmanā bhava madbhakto madyājī māṁ namaskuru,*
*māmevaiṣyasi yuktvaivamātmānaṁ matparāyaṇaḥ. (34)*

Fix your mind on Me; be devoted to Me, sacrifice to Me, bow down to Me; having thus united your (whole) Self with Me, taking Me as the supreme goal, you shall come to Me.

ॐ तत्सदिति श्रीमद्भगवद्गीतासूपनिषत्सु
ब्रह्मविद्यायां योगशास्त्रे श्रीकृष्णार्जुनसंवादे
राजविद्याराजगुह्ययोगो नाम नवमोऽध्याय:

*om tatsaditi śrīmadbhagavadgītāsūpaniṣatsu*
*brahmavidyāyāṁ yogaśāstre śrīkṛṣṇārjunasaṁvāde*
*rājavidyārājaguhyayogo nāma navamo'dhyāyaḥ.*

Thus, in the Upaniṣads of the glorious Bhagavad-gītā, in the science of the eternal, in the scripture of yoga, in the dialouge between Śrī Kṛṣṇa and Arjuna, the ninth discourse ends entitled:

YOGA OF ROYAL KNOWLEDGE AND
ROYAL SECRET

***

Divine Glories

# Chapter 10

## *Yoga of Divine Glories*

**श्रीभगवानुवाच**

**भूय एव महाबाहो शृणु मे परमं वचः ।**
**यत्तेऽहं प्रीयमाणाय वक्ष्यामि हितकाम्यया ।।१।।**

*śrībhagavānuvāca*

*bhūya eva mahābāho śṛṇu me paramaṁ vacaḥ,*
*yatte'haṁ prīyamāṇāya vakṣyāmi hitakāmyayā. (1)*

The Blessed Lord said :

Again, O mighty-armed, listen to My supreme word; which I, wishing your welfare, will declare to you, who delight in hearing Me.

न मे विदुः सुरगणाः प्रभवं न महर्षयः ।
अहमादिर्हि देवानां महर्षीणां च सर्वशः ।।२।।

*na me viduḥ suragaṇāḥ prabhavaṁ na maharṣayaḥ,*
*ahamādirhi devānāṁ maharṣīṇāṁ ca sarvaśaḥ. (2)*

Neither the hosts of heaven nor great ṛṣis know My origin; for, in every way, I am the source of all the devas and the ṛṣis.

यो मामजमनादिं च वेत्ति लोकमहेश्वरम् ।
असम्मूढः स मर्त्येषु सर्वपापैः प्रमुच्यते ।।३।।

*yo māmajamanādiṁ ca vetti lokamaheśvaram,*
*asammūḍhaḥ sa martyeṣu sarvapāpaiḥ pramucyate. (3)*

He who amongst the mortals knows Me as unborn and beginningless, as the great Lord of the worlds, is undeluded and is liberated from all sins.

बुद्धिर्ज्ञानमसम्मोहः क्षमा सत्यं दमः शमः ।
सुखं दुःखं भवोऽभावो भयं चाभयमेव च ।।४।।

*buddhirjñānamasammohaḥ kṣamā satyaṁ damaḥ śamaḥ,*
*sukhaṁ duḥkhaṁ bhavo'bhāvo bhayaṁ cā'bhayameva ca. (4)*

Intellect, wisdom, non-illusion, forgiveness, truth, self-restraint, calmness, happiness, pain, birth or death, fear and also fearlessness....

अहिंसा समता तुष्टिस्तपो दानं यशोऽयशः ।
भवन्ति भावा भूतानां मत्त एव पृथग्विधाः ।।५।।

*ahiṁsā samatā tuṣṭistapo dānaṁ yaśo'yaśaḥ,*
*bhavanti bhāvā bhūtānāṁ matta eva pṛthagvidhāḥ. (5)*

Non-injury, equanimity, contentment, austerity, beneficence, fame, infamy – all these different kinds of qualities of beings arise from Me alone.

महर्षयः सप्त पूर्वे चत्वारो मनवस्तथा ।
मद्भावा मानसा जाता येषां लोक इमाः प्रजाः ।।६।।

*maharṣayaḥ sapta pūrve catvāro manavastathā,*
*madbhāvā mānasā jātā yeṣāṁ loka imāḥ prajāḥ. (6)*

The seven great ṛṣis, the ancient four and also the Manus, possessed of powers like Me, were born of

(My) mind; from them are these creatures in the world (originated and sustained).

एतां विभूतिं योगं च मम यो वेत्ति तत्त्वतः ।
सोऽविकम्पेन योगेन युज्यते नात्र संशयः ।।७।।

*etāṁ vibhūtiṁ yogaṁ ca mama yo vetti tattvataḥ,*
*so'vikampena yogena yujyate nātra saṁśayaḥ. (7)*

He, who in truth knows these manifold manifestations of My being (macrocosm) and (this) yoga-power of Mine (microcosm), becomes established in the 'tremorless-yoga'; there is no doubt about it.

अहं सर्वस्य प्रभवो मत्तः सर्वं प्रवर्तते ।
इति मत्वा भजन्ते मां बुधा भावसमन्विताः ।।८।।

*ahaṁ sarvasya prabhavo mattaḥ sarvaṁ pravartate,*
*iti matvā bhajante māṁ budhā bhāvasamanvitāḥ. (8)*

I am the source of all; from Me everything evolves; understanding thus, the wise endowed with loving consciousness worship Me.

मच्चित्ता मद्गतप्राणा बोधयन्तः परस्परम् ।
कथयन्तश्च मां नित्यं तुष्यन्ति च रमन्ति च ।।९।।

*maccittā madgataprāṇā bodhayantaḥ parasparaṁ,*
*kathayantaśca māṁ nityaṁ tuṣyanti ca ramanti ca.* (9)

With their minds wholly resting in Me, with their senses absorbed in Me, enlightening one another and ever speaking of Me, they are satisfied and delighted.

तेषां सततयुक्तानां भजतां प्रीतिपूर्वकम् ।
ददामि बुद्धियोगं तं येन मामुपयान्ति ते ।।१०।।

*teṣāṁ satatayuktānāṁ bhajatāṁ prītipūrvakam,*
*dadāmi buddhiyogaṁ taṁ yena māmupayānti te.* (10)

To the ever-steadfast, worshipping Me with love, I give the buddhi-yoga, by which they come to Me.

तेषामेवानुकम्पार्थमहमज्ञानजं तमः ।
नाशयाम्यात्मभावस्थो ज्ञानदीपेन भास्वता ।।११।।

*teṣāmevānukampārthamahamajñānajaṁ tamaḥ,*
*nāśayāmyātmabhāvastho jñānadīpena bhāsvatā.* (11)

Out of mere compassion for them, I, dwelling within their heart, destroy the darkness born of ignorance by the luminous lamp of Knowledge.

**अर्जुन उवाच**

**परं ब्रह्म परं धाम पवित्रं परमं भवान् ।**
**पुरुषं शाश्वतं दिव्यमादिदेवमजं विभुम् ।।१२।।**

*arjuna uvāca*

*paraṁ brahma paraṁ dhāma pavitraṁ paramaṁ bhavān,*
*puruṣaṁ śāśvataṁ divyamādidevamajaṁ vibhum.* (12)

Arjuna said:

You are the supreme Brahman, the supreme Abode, the supreme Purifier, eternal, divine Puruṣa, the God of all gods, unborn, omnipresent.

**आहुस्त्वामृषयः सर्वे देवर्षिर्नारदस्तथा ।**
**असितो देवलो व्यासः स्वयं चैव ब्रवीषि मे ।।१३।।**

*āhustvāmṛṣayaḥ sarve devarṣirnāradastathā,*
*asito devalo vyāsaḥ svayaṁ caiva bravīṣi me.* (13)

All the ṛṣis have thus declared You, as also the Devarṣi Nārada, so also, Asita, Devala and Vyāsa; and now the same You yourself say to me.

सर्वमेतदृतं मन्ये यन्मां वदसि केशव ।
न हि ते भगवन्व्यक्तिं विदुर्देवा न दानवाः ।।१४।।

*sarvametadṛtaṁ manye yanmāṁ vadasi keśava,*
*na hi te bhagavanvyaktiṁ vidurdevā na dānavāḥ. (14)*

I believe all this, that you say to me as true, O Keśava; verily, O Blessed Lord, neither the devas nor the dānavas know Your manifestation (identity).

स्वयमेवात्मनात्मानं वेत्थ त्वं पुरुषोत्तम ।
भूतभावन भूतेश देवदेव जगत्पते ।।१५।।

*svayamevātmanātmānaṁ vettha tvaṁ puruṣottama,*
*bhūtabhāvana bhūtesa devadeva jagatpate. (15)*

Verily, You yourself know yourself by yourself, O Puruṣottama, (supreme Puruṣa), O source of beings, O Lord of beings, O God of gods, O ruler of the world.

वक्तुमर्हस्यशेषेण दिव्या ह्यात्मविभूतयः ।
याभिर्विभूतिभिर्लोकानिमांस्त्वं व्याप्य तिष्ठसि ।।१६।।

*vaktumarhasyaśeṣeṇa divyā hyātmavibhūtayaḥ,*
*yābhirvibhūtibhirlokānimāṁstvaṁ vyāpya tiṣṭhasi.* (16)

You should indeed, without reserve, tell me of your divine glories by which You exist pervading all these worlds.

कथं विद्यामहं योगिंस्त्वां सदा परिचिन्तयन् ।
केषु केषु च भावेषु चिन्त्योऽसि भगवन्मया ।।१७।।

*kathaṁ vidyāmahaṁ yogiṁstvāṁ sadā paricintayan,*
*keṣu keṣu ca bhāveṣu cintyo'si bhagavanmayā.* (17)

How shall I, ever-meditating, know You, O yogin? In what aspects or things, O Blessed Lord, are You to be thought of by me?

विस्तरेणात्मनो योगं विभूतिं च जनार्दन ।
भूयः कथय तृप्तिर्हि शृण्वतो नास्ति मेऽमृतम् ।।१८।।

*vistareṇātmano yogaṁ vibhūtiṁ ca janārdana,*
*bhūyaḥ kathaya tṛptirhi śṛṇvato nāsti me'mṛtam.* (18)

Tell me again, in detail, O Janārdana, of your yoga-power and immanent glory; for I do not feel satisfied by hearing Your life giving and so nectar like speech.

श्रीभगवानुवाच

हन्त ते कथयिष्यामि दिव्या ह्यात्मविभूतयः ।
प्राधान्यतः कुरुश्रेष्ठ नास्त्यन्तो विस्तरस्य मे ।।१९।।

*śrībhagavānuvāca*

*hanta te kathayiṣyāmi divyā hyātmavibhūtayaḥ,*
*prādhānyataḥ kuruśreṣṭha nāstyanto vistarasya me. (19)*

The Blessed Lord said:

Alas! Now I will declare to you My divine glories, immanent in their prominence; O best of the Kurus, there is no end to the details of My extent.

अहमात्मा गुडाकेश सर्वभूताशयस्थितः ।
अहमादिश्च मध्यं च भूतानामन्त एव च ।।२०।।

*ahamātmā guḍākeśa sarvabhūtāśayasthitaḥ,*
*ahamādiśca madhyaṁ ca bhūtānāmanta eva ca. (20)*

I am the Self, O Guḍākeśa, seated in the hearts of all beings; I am the beginning, the middle and also the end of all beings.

आदित्यानामहं विष्णुर्ज्योतिषां रविरंशुमान् ।
मरीचिर्मरुतामस्मि नक्षत्राणामहं शशी ।।२१।।

*ādityānāmahaṁ viṣṇurjyotiṣāṁ raviraṁśumān,*
*maricirmarutāmasmi nakṣatrāṇāmahaṁ śaśī. (21)*

Among the (twelve) Ādityas I am Viṣṇu; among luminaries, the radiant Sun; I am Marici among the Maruts; among asterisms, the Moon am I.

वेदानां सामवेदोऽस्मि देवानामस्मि वासवः ।
इन्द्रियाणां मनश्चास्मि भूतानामस्मि चेतना ।।२२।।

*vedānāṁ sāmavedo'smi devānāmasmi vāsavaḥ,*
*indriyāṇāṁ manaścasmi bhūtānāmasmi cetanā. (22)*

Among the Vedas, I am the Sāma-veda; I am Vāsava among the gods; among the senses, I am the mind; and I am the intelligence among living beings.

रुद्राणां शङ्करश्चास्मि वित्तेशो यक्षरक्षसाम् ।
वसूनां पावकश्चास्मि मेरुः शिखरिणामहम् ।।२३।।

*rudrāṇāṁ śaṅkaraścāsmi vitteśo yakṣarakṣasām,*
*vasūnāṁ pāvakaścāsmi meruḥ śikhariṇāmaham. (23)*

And among the Rudras I am Śaṅkara; among the Yakṣas and Rākṣasas I am the Lord of wealth (Kubera); among the Vasus I am Pāvaka (Agni); and among the mountains I am the Meru.

पुरोधसां च मुख्यं मां विद्धि पार्थ बृहस्पतिम् ।
सेनानीनामहं स्कन्दः सरसामस्मि सागरः ।।२४।।

*purodhasāṁ ca mukhyaṁ māṁ viddhi pārtha bṛhaspatim,*
*senānīnāmahaṁ skandaḥ sarasāmasmi sāgaraḥ. (24)*

And among the household priests, O Pārtha, know Me to be the chief, Bṛhaspati; among generals, I am Skanda; among lakes, I am the ocean.

महर्षीणां भृगुरहं गिरामस्म्येकमक्षरम् ।
यज्ञानां जपयज्ञोऽस्मि स्थावराणां हिमालयः ।।२५।।

*maharṣīṇāṁ bhṛguraham girāmasmyekamakṣaram,*
*yajñānāṁ japayajño'smi sthāvarāṇāṁ himālayaḥ. (25)*

Among the great ṛṣīs, I am Bhṛgu; among words, I am the one-syllabled Om; among sacrifices, I am the sacrifice of silent repetition (japa-yajña); among immovable things, the Himālayas.

अश्वत्थः सर्ववृक्षाणां देवर्षीणां च नारदः ।
गन्धर्वाणां चित्ररथः सिद्धानां कपिलो मुनिः ।।२६।।

*aśvatthaḥ sarvavṛkṣāṇāṁ devarṣīṇāṁ ca nāradaḥ,*
*gandharvāṇāṁ citrarathaḥ siddhānāṁ kapilo muniḥ.(26)*

Among all trees (I am) the Aśvattha-tree; among divine ṛṣīs, Nārada; among Gandharvas, Citraratha; among perfected ones, the Muni Kapila.

उच्चैःश्रवसमश्वानां विद्धि माममृतोद्भवम् ।
ऐरावतं गजेन्द्राणां नराणां च नराधिपम् ।।२७।।

*uccaiḥśravasamaśvānāṁ viddhi māmamṛtodbhavam,*
*airāvataṁ gajendrāṇāṁ narāṇāṁ ca narādhipam. (27)*

Know Me among horses as Uccaiḥśravas, born of Amṛta; among lordly elephants, the Airāvata and among men, the king.

आयुधानामहं वज्रं धेनूनामस्मि कामधुक् ।
प्रजनश्चास्मि कन्दर्पः सर्पाणामस्मि वासुकिः ।।२८।।

*āyudhānāmahaṁ vajraṁ dhenunāmasmi kāmadhuk,*
*prajanaścāsmi kandarpaḥ sarpāṇāmasmi vāsukiḥ.* (28)

Among weapons, I am the thunderbolt; among cows, I am Kāmadhuk; I am Kandarpa, the cause for offspring; among serpents I am Vāsuki.

अनन्तश्चास्मि नागानां वरुणो यादसामहम् ।
पितॄणामर्यमा चास्मि यमः संयमतामहम् ।।२९।।

*anantaścāsmi nāgānāṁ varuṇo yādasāmaham,*
*pitṝṇāmaryamā cāsmi yamaḥ saṁyamatāmaham.* (29)

I am Ananta among Nāgas; I am Varuṇa among water deities; I am Aryamā among the ancestors; and I am Yama among controllers.

प्रह्लादश्चास्मि दैत्यानां कालः कलयतामहम् ।
मृगाणां च मृगेन्द्रोऽहं वैनतेयश्च पक्षिणाम् ।।३०।।

*prahlādaścāsmi daityānaṁ kālaḥ kalayatāmaham,*
*mṛgāṇāṁ ca mṛgendro'haṁ vainateyaśca pakṣiṇām. (30)*

I am Prahlāda among daityas; Time among reckoners; the Lord of beasts (lion) among animals, and Vainateya (garuḍa) among birds.

पवनः पवतामस्मि रामः शस्त्रभृतामहम् ।
झषाणां मकरश्चास्मि स्रोतसामस्मि जाह्नवी ।।३१।।

*pavanaḥ pavatāmasmi rāmaḥ śastrabhṛtāmaham,*
*jhaṣāṇāṁ makaraścāsmi srotasāmasmi jāhnavī. (31)*

Among purifiers, I am the wind; among warriors, I am Rāma; among fishes, I am the shark; among rivers, I am the Ganges.

सर्गाणामादिरन्तश्च मध्यं चैवाहमर्जुन ।
अध्यात्मविद्या विद्यानां वादः प्रवदतामहम् ।।३२।।

*sargāṇāmādirantaśca madhyaṁ caivāhamarjuna,*
*adhyātmavidyā vidyānāṁ vādaḥ pravadatāmaham. (32)*

Among creations, I am the beginning, the middle and also the end; O Arjuna, among sciences, I am the science of the Self and I am the logic in all arguments.

अक्षराणामकारोऽस्मि द्वन्द्वः सामासिकस्य च ।
अहमेवाक्षयः कालो धाताहं विश्वतोमुखः ।।३३।।

*akṣarāṇāmakāro'smi dvandvaḥ sāmāsikasya ca,*
*ahamevākṣayaḥ kālo dhātāhaṁ viśvatomukhaḥ. (33)*

Among letters I am the letter 'A'; among all compounds I am the dual (co-ordinates); I am verily the inexhaustible or the everlasting time; I am the (all-faced) dispenser (of fruits of actions), having faces in all directions.

मृत्युः सर्वहरश्चाहमुद्भवश्च भविष्यताम् ।
कीर्तिः श्रीर्वाक्च नारीणां स्मृतिर्मेधा धृतिः क्षमा ।।३४।।

*mṛtyuḥ sarvaharaścāhamudbhavaśca bhaviṣyatām,*
*kīrtiḥ śrīrvākca nārīṇāṁ smṛtirmedhā dhṛtiḥ kṣamā. (34)*

And I am all-devouring death and the prosperity of those who are to be prosperous; among the feminine qualities (I am) fame, prosperity, speech, memory, intelligence, firmness and forgiveness.

बृहत्साम तथा साम्नां गायत्री छन्दसामहम् ।
मासानां मार्गशीर्षोऽहमृतूनां कुसुमाकरः ।।३५।।

*bṛhatsāma tathā sāmnāṁ gāyatrī chandasāmaham,*
*māsānāṁ mārgaśīrṣo'hamṛtūnāṁ kusumākaraḥ. (35)*

Among hymns also, I am the Bṛhatsāma; among metres, Gāyatrī am I; among months, I am Mārgaśīrṣa (parts of December-Janauary); among seasons, I am the flowery spring.

द्यूतं छलयतामस्मि तेजस्तेजस्विनामहम् ।
जयोऽस्मि व्यवसायोऽस्मि सत्त्वं सत्त्ववतामहम् ।।३६।।

*dyūtaṁ chalayatāmasmi tejastejasvināmaham,*
*jayo'smi vyavasāyo'smi sattvaṁ sattvavatāmaham. (36)*

I am the gambling of the fraudulent; I am the splendour of the splendid; I am victory; I am the determination (in those who are determined); I am the goodness in the good.

वृष्णीनां वासुदेवोऽस्मि पाण्डवानां धनञ्जयः ।
मुनीनामप्यहं व्यासः कवीनामुशना कविः ।।३७।।

*vṛṣṇīnāṁ vāsudevo'smi pāṇḍavānāṁ dhanañjayaḥ,*
*munīnāmapyahaṁ vyāsaḥ kavīnāmuśanā kaviḥ. (37)*

Among the Vṛṣṇis I am Vāsudeva; among the Pāṇḍavas (I am) Dhanañjaya; also among the Munis I am Vyāsa; and among the poets, I am Uśanā, the great Seer.

दण्डो दमयतामस्मि नीतिरस्मि जिगीषताम् ।
मौनं चैवास्मि गुह्यानां ज्ञानं ज्ञानवतामहम् ।।३८।।

*daṇḍo damayatāmasmi nītirasmi jigīṣatām,*
*maunaṁ caivāsmi guhyānāṁ jñānaṁ jñānavatāmaham. (38)*

Among punishers, I am the sceptre; among those who seek victory, I am statemanship; and also among secrets, I am silence; and I am the knowledge among knowers.

यच्चापि सर्वभूतानां बीजं तदहमर्जुन ।
न तदस्ति विना यत्स्यान्मया भूतं चराचरम् ।।३९।।

*yaccāpi sarvabhūtānāṁ bījaṁ tadahamarjuna,*
*na tadasti vinā yatsyānmayā bhūtaṁ carācaram. (39)*

And whatsoever is the seed of all beings, that also am I, O Arjuna; there is no being, whether moving or unmoving that can exist without Me.

नान्तोऽस्ति मम दिव्यानां विभूतीनां परन्तप ।
एष तूद्देशतः प्रोक्तो विभूतेर्विस्तरो मया ।।४०।।

*nānto'sti mama divyānāṁ vibhūtīnāṁ parantapa,*
*eṣa tūddeśataḥ prokto vibhūtervistaro mayā. (40)*

There is no end to My divine glories, O Parantapa; but, this is just a brief statement by Me of the particulars of My divine glories.

यद्यद्विभूतिमत्सत्त्वं श्रीमदूर्जितमेव वा ।
तत्तदेवावगच्छ त्वं मम तेजोंऽशसम्भवम् ।।४१।।

*yadyadvibhūtimatsattvaṁ śrīmadūrjitameva vā,*
*tattadevāvagaccha tvaṁ mama tejoṁ'śasambhavam. (41)*

Whatever that is glorious, prosperous or powerful in any being, know that to be a manifestation of a part of My splendour.

अथवा बहुनैतेन किं ज्ञातेन तवार्जुन ।
विष्टभ्याहमिदं कृत्स्नमेकांशेन स्थितो जगत् ।।४२।।

*athavā bahunaitena kiṁ jñātena tavārjuna,*
*viṣṭabhyāhamidaṁ kṛtsnamekāṁśena sthito jagat. (42)*

But, of what avail to thee is the knowledge of all these details, O Arjuna? I exist, supporting this whole world by one part of Myself.

ॐ तत्सदिति श्रीमद्भगवद्गीतासूपनिषत्सु
ब्रह्मविद्यायां योगशास्त्रे श्रीकृष्णार्जुनसंवादे
विभूतियोगो नाम दशमोऽध्यायः

*om tatsaditi śrīmadbhagavadgītāsuūpaniṣatsu*
*brahmavidyāyāṁ yogaśāstre śrīkṛṣṇārjunasaṁvāde*
*vibhūtiyogo nāma daśamo'dhyāyaḥ*

Thus, in the Upaniṣads of the glorious Bhagavad-gītā, in the science of the eternal, in the scripure of yoga, in the dialogue between Śrī Kṛṣṇa and Arjuna, the tenth discourse ends entitled.

YOGA OF DIVINE GLORIES

***

Vision of the Universal Form

# Chapter 11

## *Yoga of Vision of the Divine Cosmic Form*

**अर्जुन उवाच**

**मदनुग्रहाय परमं गुह्यमध्यात्मसञ्ज्ञितम् ।**
**यत्त्वयोक्तं वचस्तेन मोहोऽयं विगतो मम ।।१।।**

*arjuna uvāca*

*madanugrahāya paramaṁ guhyamadhyātmasañjñitam,*
*yattvayoktaṁ vacastena moho'yaṁ vigato mama. (1)*

Arjuna said:

By this word of the highest secret concerning the Self, which You have spoken out of compassion towards me, my delusion is gone.

भवाप्ययौ हि भूतानां श्रुतौ विस्तरशो मया ।
त्वत्तः कमलपत्राक्ष माहात्म्यमपि चाव्ययम् ।।२।।

*bhavāpyayau hi bhūtānāṁ śrutau vistaraśo mayā,*
*tvattaḥ kamalapatrākṣa māhātmyamapi cāvyayam.* (2)

The origin and destruction of beings, verily, have been heard by me in detail from You, O lotus-eyed Kṛṣṇa, and also Your inexhaustible greatness.

एवमेतद्यथात्थ त्वमात्मानं परमेश्वर ।
द्रष्टुमिच्छामि ते रूपमैश्वरं पुरुषोत्तम ।।३।।

*evametadyathāttha tvamātmānaṁ parameśvara,*
*draṣṭumicchāmi te rūpamaiśvaraṁ puruṣottama.* (3)

(Now) O supreme Lord! As you have thus described Yourself, I wish to see (actually) Your form divine, O Puruṣottama.

मन्यसे यदि तच्छक्यं मया द्रष्टुमिति प्रभो ।
योगेश्वर ततो मे त्वं दर्शयात्मानमव्ययम् ।।४।।

*manyase yadi tacchakyaṁ mayā draṣṭumiti prabho,*
*yogeśvara tato me tvaṁ darśayātmānamavyayam.(4)*

If you, O Lord, think it possible for me to see it, if You please, then, O Lord of yoga, show me Your imperishable Self-form.

श्रीभगवानुवाच
पश्य मे पार्थ रूपाणि शतशोऽथ सहस्रशः ।
नानाविधानि दिव्यानि नानावर्णाकृतीनि च ।।५।।

*śrībhagavānuvāca*

*paśya me pārtha rūpāṇi śataśo'tha sahasraśaḥ,*
*nānāvidhāni divyāni nānāvarṇākṛtīni ca. (5)*

The Blessed Lord said:

Behold, O Pārtha, forms of Me, by hundreds and thousands of different sorts and divine, of various colours and shapes.

पश्यादित्यान्वसून्रुद्रानश्विनौ मरुतस्तथा ।
बहून्यदृष्टपूर्वाणि पश्याश्चर्याणि भारत ।।६।।

*paśyādityānvasūnrudrānaśvinau marutastathā,*
*bahūnyadṛṣṭapūrvāṇi pasyāścaryāṇi bhārata. (6)*

Behold the Ādityas, the Vasus, the Rudras, the (two) Aśvins and also the Maruts; behold many wonders never seen before, O Bhārata.

**इहैकस्थं जगत्कृत्स्नं पश्याद्य सचराचरम् ।**
**मम देहे गुडाकेश यच्चान्यद्द्रष्टुमिच्छसि ।।७।।**

*ihaikasthaṁ jagatkṛtsnaṁ paśyādya sacarācaram,*
*mama dehe guḍākeśa yaccānyaddraṣṭumicchasi. (7)*

Now behold, O Guḍākeśa, in this body, the whole universe centred in One - including the moving and the unmoving - and whatever else you desire to see.

**न तु मां शक्यसे द्रष्टुमनेनैव स्वचक्षुषा ।**
**दिव्यं ददामि ते चक्षुः पश्य मे योगमैश्वरम् ।।८।।**

*na tu māṁ śakyase draṣṭumanenaiva svacakṣuṣā,*
*divyaṁ dadāmi te cakṣuḥ paśya me yogamaiśvaram. (8)*

But you are not able to behold Me with these your own eyes; I give you the divine-eye; behold My Lordly Yoga.

**सञ्जय उवाच**

**एवमुक्त्वा ततो राजन्महायोगेश्वरो हरिः ।**
**दर्शयामास पार्थाय परमं रूपमैश्वरम् ।।९।।**

*sañjaya uvāca*

*evamuktvā tato rājanmahāyogeśvaro hariḥ,*
*darśayāmāsa pārthāya paramaṁ rūpamaiśvaram. (9)*

Sañjaya said:

Having thus spoken, O King, the great Lord of yoga, Hari, showed to Pārtha His supreme form as the Lord (of the universe).

**अनेकवक्त्रनयनमनेकाद्भुतदर्शनम् ।**
**अनेकदिव्याभरणं दिव्यानेकोद्यतायुधम् ।।१०।।**

*anekavaktranayanamanekādbhutadarśanam,*
*anekadivyābharaṇaṁ divyānekodyatāyudham. (10)*

With numerous mouths and eyes,with numerous wonderful sights, with numerous divine ornaments, with numerous divine weapons uplifted (such a form He showed).

दिव्यमाल्याम्बरधरं दिव्यगन्धानुलेपनम् ।
सर्वाश्चर्यमयं देवमनन्तं विश्वतोमुखम् ।।११।।

*divyamālyāmbaradharaṁ divyagandhānulepanam,*
*sarvāścaryamayaṁ devamanantaṁ viśvatomukham. (11)*

Wearing divine garlands (necklaces) and apparel, anointed with divine unguents (perfumes), the all-wonderful, resplendent, endless, facing all sides.

दिवि सूर्यसहस्रस्य भवेद्युगपदुत्थिता ।
यदि भाः सदृशी सा स्याद्भासस्तस्य महात्मनः ।।१२।।

*divi sūryasahasrasya bhavedyugapadutthitā,*
*yadi bhāḥ sadṛśī sā syādbhāsastasya mahātmanaḥ. (12)*

If the splendour of a thousand suns was to blaze all at once (simultaneously) in the sky, that would be like the splendour of that mighty being (great soul).

तत्रैकस्थं जगत्कृत्स्नं प्रविभक्तमनेकधा ।
अपश्यद्देवदेवस्य शरीरे पाण्डवस्तदा ।।१३।।

*tatraikasthaṁ jagatkṛtsnaṁ pravibhaktamanekadhā,*
*apaśyaddevadevasya śarīre pāṇḍavastadā.* (13)

There, in the body of the God of gods, the Pāṇḍava (son of Paṇḍu), then saw the whole universe resting in one, with all its infinite parts.

ततः स विस्मयाविष्टो हृष्टरोमा धनञ्जयः ।
प्रणम्य शिरसा देवं कृताञ्जलिरभाषत ।।१४।।

*tataḥ sa vismayāviṣṭo hṛṣṭaromā dhanañjayaḥ,*
*praṇamya śirasā devaṁ kṛtāñjalirabhāṣata.* (14)

Then, Dhanañjaya, filled with wonder, with his hair standing on end, bowed down his head to the God and spoke with joined palms.

अर्जुन उवाच

पश्यामि देवांस्तव देव देहे
सर्वांस्तथा भूतविशेषसङ्घान् ।
ब्रह्माणमीशं कमलासनस्थ-
मृषींश्च सर्वानुरगांश्च दिव्यान् ।।१५।।

*arjuna uvāca*

*paśyāmi devāṁstava deva dehe*
*sarvāṁstathā bhūtaviśeṣasaṅghān,*
*brahmāṇamīṣaṁ kamalāsanastha–*
*mṛṣīṁśca sarvānuragāṁśca divyān. (15)*

Arjuna said:

I see all the gods, O God, in your body and (also) hosts of various classes of beings, Bramhā the Lord of creation seated on a lotus, all the ṛṣis and celestial serpents.

अनेकबाहूदरवक्त्रनेत्रं-
पश्यामि त्वां सर्वतोऽनन्तरूपम् ।
नान्तं न मध्यं न पुनस्तवादिं-
पश्यामि विश्वेश्वर विश्वरूप ।।१६।।

*anekabāhūdaravaktranetraṁ-*
*paśyāmi tvāṁ sarvato'nantarūpam,*
*nāntaṁ na madhyaṁ na punastavādiṁ-*
*paśyāmi viśveśvara viśvarūpa. (16)*

I see Thee of boundless form on every side, with manifold arms, stomachs, mouths and eyes; neither the end, nor the middle, nor also the beginning do I see; O Lord of the universe, O cosmic form.

किरीटिनं गदिनं चक्रिणं च
तेजोराशिं सर्वतो दीप्तिमन्तम् ।
पश्यामि त्वां दुर्निरीक्ष्यं समन्ता-
द्दीप्तानलार्कद्युतिमप्रमेयम् ।।१७।।

*kirīṭinaṁ gadinaṁ cakriṇaṁ ca*
*tejorāśiṁ sarvato dīptimantam,*
*paśyāmi tvāṁ durnirīkṣyaṁ samantā-*
*ddīptānalārkadyutimaprameyam. (17)*

I see Thee with crown, club and discus; a mass of radiance shining everywhere, very hard to look at, all round blazing like burning fire and sun, and incomprehensible.

त्वमक्षरं परमं वेदितव्यं-
त्वमस्य विश्वस्य परं निधानम् ।
त्वमव्ययः शाश्वतधर्मगोप्ता
सनातनस्त्वं पुरुषो मतो मे ।।१८।।

*tvamakṣaraṁ paramaṁ veditavyaṁ-*
*tvamasya viśvasya paraṁ nidhānam,*
*tvamavyayaḥ śāśvatadharmagoptā*
*sanātanastvaṁ puruṣo mato me. (18)*

You are the imperishable, the supreme Being worthy to be known. You are the great treasure-house of this universe. You are the imperishable protector of the eternal dharma. In my opinion, you are the ancient Puruṣa.

**अनादिमध्यान्तमनन्तवीर्य-**
**मनन्तबाहुं शशिसूर्यनेत्रम् ।**
**पश्यामि त्वां दीप्तहुताशवक्त्रं-**
**स्वतेजसा विश्वमिदं तपन्तम् ।।१९।।**

*anādimadhyāntamanantavīrya-*
*manantabāhuṁ śaśisūryanetram,*
*paśyāmi tvāṁ dīptahutāśavaktraṁ-*
*svatejasā viśvamidaṁ tapantam. (19)*

I see You without beginning, middle or end, infinite in power, of endless arms, the sun and moon being Your eyes, the burning fire Your mouth, heating the whole universe with Your radiance.

द्यावापृथिव्योरिदमन्तरं हि
व्याप्तं त्वयैकेन दिशश्च सर्वाः ।
दृष्ट्वाद्भुतं रूपमुग्रं तवेदं-
लोकत्रयं प्रव्यथितं महात्मन् ।।२०।।

*dyāvāpṛthivyoridamantaraṁ hi*
*vyāptaṁ tvayaikena diśaśca sarvāḥ,*
*dṛṣṭvādbhutaṁ rūpamugraṁ tavedaṁ-*
*lokatrayaṁ pravyathitaṁ mahātman.* (20)

This space between earth and the heavens and all the quarters is filled by You alone; having seen this, Your wonderful and terrible form, the three worlds are trembling with fear, O great-souled Being.

अमी हि त्वां सुरसङ्घा विशन्ति
केचिद्भीताः प्राञ्जलयो गृणन्ति ।
स्वस्तीत्युक्त्वा महर्षिसिद्धसङ्घाः
स्तुवन्ति त्वां स्तुतिभिः पुष्कलाभिः ।।२१।।

*amī hi tvāṁ surasaṅghā viśanti*
*kecidbhītāḥ prāñjalayo gṛṇanti,*
*svastītyuktvā maharṣisiddhasaṅghāḥ*
*stuvanti tvāṁ stutibhiḥ puṣkalābhiḥ.* (21)

Verily, into You enter these hosts of devas; some extol You in fear with joined palms; 'May it be well' thus saying, bands of great ṛṣis and siddhas praise You with hymns sublime.

रुद्रादित्या वसवो ये च साध्या-
विश्वेऽश्विनौ मरुतश्चोष्मपाश्च ।
गन्धर्वयक्षासुरसिद्धसङ्घा-
वीक्षन्ते त्वां विस्मिताश्चैव सर्वे ।।२२।।

*rudrādityā vasavo ye ca sādhyā-*
*viśve'śvinau marutaścoṣmapāśca,*
*gandharvayakṣāsurasiddhasaṅghā-*
*vīkṣante tvāṁ vismitāścaiva sarve.* (22)

The Rudras, Ādityas, Vasus, Sādhyas, Viśvedevas, the two Aśvins, Maruts, Uṣmapas and hosts of Gandharvas, Yakṣas, Asuras and Siddhas – they are all looking at you, all quite astonished.

रूपं महत्ते बहुवक्त्रनेत्रं-
महाबाहो बहुबाहूरुपादम् ।
बहूदरं बहुदंष्ट्राकरालं-
दृष्ट्वा लोकाः प्रव्यथितास्तथाहम् ।।२३।।

*rūpaṁ mahatte bahuvaktranetraṁ-*
*mahābāho bahubāhūrupādam,*
*bahūdaraṁ bahudaṁṣṭrākarālaṁ-*
*dṛṣṭvā lokāḥ pravyathitāstathāham. (23)*

Having seen Your immeasurable form, with many mouths and eyes, O mighty-armed, with many arms, thighs and feet, with many stomachs and fearsome with many tusks, the worlds are terrified and so too, am I.

नभःस्पृशं दीप्तमनेकवर्णं
व्यात्ताननं दीप्तविशालनेत्रम् ।
दृष्ट्वा हि त्वां प्रव्यथितान्तरात्मा
धृतिं न विन्दामि शमं च विष्णो ।।२४।।

*nabhaḥspṛśaṁ dīptamanekavarṇaṁ*
*vyāttānanaṁ dīptaviśālanetram,*
*dṛṣṭvā hi tvāṁ pravyathitāntarātmā*
*dhṛtiṁ na vindāmi śamaṁ ca viṣṇo. (24)*

On seeing You (Your form) touching the sky, flaming in many colours, with mouths wide open, with large fiery eyes, I am terrified at heart, and I find neither courage nor peace, O Viṣṇu!

दंष्ट्राकरालानि च ते मुखानि
दृष्ट्वैव कालानलसन्निभानि ।
दिशो न जाने न लभे च शर्म
प्रसीद देवेश जगन्निवास ।।२५।।

*daṁṣṭrākarālāni ca te mukhāni*
*dṛṣṭvaiva kālānalasannibhāni,*
*diśo na jāne na labhe ca śarma*
*prasīda deveśa jagannivāsa.* (25)

Having seen your mouths fearsome with tusks (blazing) like pralaya-fires, I know not the four quarters, nor do I find peace; be gracious, O Lord of the devas, O Abode of the universe.

अमी च त्वां धृतराष्ट्रस्य पुत्राः
सर्वे सहैवावनिपालसङ्घैः ।
भीष्मो द्रोणः सूतपुत्रस्तथासौ
सहास्मदीयैरपि योधमुख्यैः ।।२६।।

*amī ca tvāṁ dhṛtarāṣṭrasya putrāḥ*
*sarve sahaivāvanipālasaṅghaiḥ,*
*bhīṣmo droṇaḥ sūtaputrastathāsau*
*sahāsmadīyairapi yodhamukhaiḥ. (26)*

All the sons of Dhṛtarāṣṭra with hosts of kings of the earth, Bhīṣma, Droṇa and the son of a charioteer, Karṇa, with the warrior chieftains of ours....

वक्त्राणि ते त्वरमाणा विशन्ति
दंष्ट्राकरालानि भयानकानि ।
केचिद्विलग्ना दशनान्तरेषु
सन्दृश्यन्ते चूर्णितैरुत्तमाङ्गैः ।।२७।।

*vaktrāṇi te tvaramāṇā viśanti*
*daṁṣṭrākarālāni bhayānakāni,*
*kecidvilagnā daśanāntareṣu*
*sandṛśyante cūrṇitairuttamāṅgaiḥ. (27)*

Into your mouths with terrible teeth and fearful to behold, they precipitately enter. Some are found sticking in the gaps between the teeth with their heads crushed into pulp.

यथा नदीनां बहवोऽम्बुवेगाः
समुद्रमेवाभिमुखा द्रवन्ति ।
तथा तवामी नरलोकवीरा-
विशन्ति वक्त्राण्यभिविज्वलन्ति ।।२८।।

*yathā nadīnāṁ bahavo'mbuvegāḥ*
*samudramevābhimukhā dravanti,*
*tathā tavāmī naralokavīrā-*
*viśanti vaktrāṇyabhivijvalanti. (28)*

Verily, as many torrents of rivers flow towards the ocean, so these heroes in the world of men enter Your flaming mouths.

यथा प्रदीप्तं ज्वलनं पतङ्गा-
विशन्ति नाशाय समृद्धवेगाः ।
तथैव नाशाय विशन्ति लोका-
स्तवापि वक्त्राणि समृद्धवेगाः ।।२९।।

*yathā pradīptaṁ jvalanaṁ pataṅgā-*
*viśanti nāśāya samṛddhavegāḥ,*
*tathaiva nāśāya viśanti lokā-*
*stavāpi vaktrāṇi samṛddhavegāḥ. (29)*

As moths rush hurriedly into a blazing fire for their own destruction, so also these creatures hastily rush into Your mouths of destruction.

लेलिह्यसे ग्रसमानः समन्ता-
ल्लोकान्समग्रान्वदनैर्ज्वलद्भिः।
तेजोभिरापूर्य जगत्समग्रं-
भासस्तवोग्राः प्रतपन्ति विष्णो ।।३०।।

*lelihyase grasamānaḥ samantā-*
*llokānsamagrānvadanairjvaladbhiḥ,*
*tejobhirāpūrya jagatsamagraṁ-*
*bhāsastavogrāḥ pratapanti viṣṇo. (30)*

Devouring all worlds on every side with Your flaming mouths, You are licking (in enjoyment). Your fierce rays, filling the whole world with radiance, are burning, O Viṣṇu.

आख्याहि मे को भवानुग्ररूपो-
नमोऽस्तु ते देववर प्रसीद।
विज्ञातुमिच्छामि भवन्तमाद्यं-
न हि प्रजानामि तव प्रवृत्तिम् ।।३१।।

*ākhyāhi me ko bhavānugrarūpo-*
*namo'stu te devavara prasīda,*
*vijñātumicchāmi bhavantamādyaṁ-*
*na hi prajānāmi tava pravṛttim. (31)*

Tell me, who You are, so fierce in form? Salutations to You, O God Supreme; have mercy. I desire to know You, the original Being, I know not indeed Your purpose.

श्रीभगवानुवाच
कालोऽस्मि लोकक्षयकृत्प्रवृद्धो
लोकान्समाहर्तुमिह प्रवृत्तः।
ऋतेऽपि त्वां न भविष्यन्ति सर्वे
येऽवस्थिताः प्रत्यनीकेषु योधाः ।।३२।।

*śrī bhagavānuvāca*

*kālo'smi lokakṣayakṛtpravṛddho*
*lokānsamāhartumiha pravṛttaḥ,*
*ṛte'pi tvāṁ na bhaviṣyanti sarve*
*ye'vasthitāḥ pratyanīkeṣu yodhāḥ. (32)*

The Blessed Lord said:

I am the mighty world-destroying Time, now engaged in destroying the worlds. Even without you, none of the warriors arrayed in hostile armies shall live.

तस्मात्त्वमुत्तिष्ठ यशो लभस्व
जित्वा शत्रून्भुङ्क्ष्व राज्यं समृद्धम् ।
मयैवैते निहताः पूर्वमेव
निमित्तमात्रं भव सव्यसाचिन् ।।३३।।

*tasmāttvamuttiṣṭha yaśo labhasva*
*jitvā śatrūnbhuṅkṣva rājyaṁ samṛddham,*
*mayaivaite nihatāḥ pūrvameva*
*nimittamātraṁ bhava savyasācin.* (33)

Therefore, stand up and obtain fame. Conquer the enemies and enjoy the flourishing kingdom. Verily, by Myself they have already been slain; be you a mere instrument, O left-handed archer.

द्रोणं च भीष्मं च जयद्रथं च
कर्णं तथान्यानपि योधवीरान् ।

मया हतांस्त्वं जहि मा व्यथिष्ठा-
युध्यस्व जेतासि रणे सपत्नान् ।।३४।।

*droṇaṁ ca bhīṣmaṁ ca jayadrathaṁ ca*
*karṇaṁ tathānyānapi yodhavīrān,*
*mayā hatāṁstvaṁ jahi mā vyathiṣṭhā-*
*yudhyasva jetāsi raṇe sapatnān. (34)*

Droṇa, Bhīṣma, Jayadratha, Karṇa and other brave warriors - those have already been slain by Me; you do kill; be not distressed with fear; fight and you shall conquer your enemies in battle.

सञ्जय उवाच
एतच्छ्रुत्वा वचनं केशवस्य
कृताञ्जलिर्वेपमानः किरीटी ।
नमस्कृत्वा भूय एवाह कृष्णं-
सगद्गदं भीतभीतः प्रणम्य ।।३५।।

*sañjaya uvāca*
*etacchrutvā vacanaṁ keśavasya*
*kṛtāñjalirvepamānaḥ kirīṭī,*
*namaskṛtvā bhūya evāha kṛṣṇaṁ–*
*sagadgadaṁ bhītabhītaḥ praṇamya. (35)*

Sañjaya said:

Having heard that speech of Keśava (Kṛṣṇa), the crowned-one (Arjuna), with joined palms, trembling and prostrating himself, again addressed Kṛṣṇa in a choked voice, bowing down, overwhelmed with fear.

अर्जुन उवाच

स्थाने हृषीकेश तव प्रकीर्त्या
जगत्प्रहृष्यत्यनुरज्यते च ।
रक्षांसि भीतानि दिशो द्रवन्ति
सर्वे नमस्यन्ति च सिद्धसङ्घाः ।।३६।।

*arjuna uvāca*

*sthāne hṛṣīkeśa tava prakīrtyā*
*jagatprahṛṣyatyanurajyate ca,*
*rakṣāṁsi bhītāni diśo dravanti*
*sarve namasyanti ca siddhasaṅghāḥ. (36)*

Arjuna said:

It is but apt, O Hṛṣīkeśa, (Kṛṣṇa) that the world delights and rejoices in Thy praise; Rākṣasas fly in fear to all quarters, and all hosts of Siddhas bow to Thee.

कस्माच्च ते न नमेरन्महात्मन्
गरीयसे ब्रह्मणोऽप्यादिकर्त्रे ।
अनन्त देवेश जगन्निवास
त्वमक्षरं सदसत्तत्परं यत् ।।३७।।

*kasmācca te na nameranmahātman*
*garīyase brahmaṇo'pyādikartre,*
*ananta deveśa jagannivāsa*
*tvamakṣaraṁ sadasattatparaṁ yat.* (37)

And why should they not, O great-souled One, bow to Thee, greater (than all else), the primal cause even of Brahmā, O infinite Being, O Lord of lords, O Abode of the universe, You are the imperishable, that which is beyond both the manifest and the unmanifest.

त्वमादिदेवः पुरुषः पुराण-
स्त्वमस्य विश्वस्य परं निधानम् ।
वेत्तासि वेद्यं च परं च धाम
त्वया ततं विश्वमनन्तरूप ।।३८।।

*tvamādidevaḥ puruṣaḥ purāṇa–*
*stvamasya viśvasya paraṁ nidhānam,*
*vettāsi vedyaṁ ca paraṁ ca dhāma*
*tvayā tataṁ viśvamanantarūpa. (38)*

You are the primal God, the ancient Puruṣa; You are the supreme refuge of this universe. You are the knower, the knowable, and the abode-supreme. By Thee is the universe pervaded, O Being of infinite forms.

वायुर्यमोऽग्निर्वरुणः शशाङ्कः
प्रजापतिस्त्वं प्रपितामहश्च ।
नमो नमस्तेऽस्तु सहस्रकृत्वः
पुनश्च भूयोऽपि नमो नमस्ते ।।३९।।

*vāyuryamo'gnirvaruṇaḥ śaśāṅkaḥ*
*prajāpatistvaṁ prapitāmahaśca,*
*namo namaste'stu sahasrakṛtvaḥ*
*punaśca bhūyo'pi namo namaste. (39)*

You are Vāyu, Yama, Agni, Varuṇa, the Moon Prajāpati, and the great-grandfather of all. Salutations!

Salutations unto You a thousand times, and again salutations unto You!

नमः पुरस्तादथ पृष्ठतस्ते
नमोऽस्तु ते सर्वत एव सर्व ।
अनन्तवीर्यामितविक्रमस्त्वं-
सर्वं समाप्नोषि ततोऽसि सर्वः ॥४०॥

*namaḥ purastādatha pṛṣṭhataste*
*namo'stu te sarvata eva sarva,*
*anantavīryāmitavikramastvaṁ-*
*sarvaṁ samāpnoṣi tato'si sarvaḥ. (40)*

Salutations to You, before and behind! Salutations to You on every side! O All! You, infinite in power and infinite in prowess, pervade all; wherefore You are the all.

सखेति मत्वा प्रसभं यदुक्तं-
हे कृष्ण हे यादव हे सखेति ।
अजानता महिमानं तवेदं-
मया प्रमादात्प्रणयेन वापि ॥४१॥

*sakheti matvā prasabhaṁ yaduktaṁ-*
*he kṛṣṇa he yādava he sakheti,*
*ajānatā mahimānaṁ tavedaṁ-*
*mayā pramādātpraṇayena vāpi. (41)*

Whatever I have rashly said, from carelessness or love, addressing You as "O Kṛṣṇa, O Yādava, O friend", and regarding You merely as a friend, unknowing of this greatness of Yours...

यच्चावहासार्थमसत्कृतोऽसि
विहारशय्यासनभोजनेषु ।
एकोऽथवाप्यच्युत तत्समक्षं-
तत्क्षामये त्वामहमप्रमेयम् ।।४२।।

*yaccāvahāsārthamasatkṛto'si*
*vihāraśayyāsanabhojaneṣu,*
*eko'thavāpyacyuta tatsamakṣaṁ-*
*tatkṣāmaye tvāmahamaprameyam. (42)*

In whatever way I may have insulted You for the sake of fun, while at play, reposing or sitting, or at meals, when alone (with You), O Acyuta, or in company, that, O immeasurable One, I implore You to forgive.

पितासि लोकस्य चराचरस्य
त्वमस्य पूज्यश्च गुरुर्गरीयान् ।
न त्वत्समोऽस्त्यभ्यधिकः कुतोऽन्यो-
लोकत्रयेऽप्यप्रतिमप्रभाव ।।४३।।

*pitāsi lokasya carācarasya*
*tvamasya pūjyaśca gururgarīyān,*
*na tvatsamo'styabhyadhikaḥ kuto'nyo-*
*lokatraye'pyapratimaprabhāva. (43)*

You are the father of this world, moving and unmoving. You are to be adored by this world. You are the greatest Guru , (for) there exists none who is equal to You; how can there be then another, superior to You in the three worlds, O Being of unequalled power?

तस्मात्प्रणम्य प्रणिधाय कायं-
प्रसादये त्वामहमीशमीड्यम् ।
पितेव पुत्रस्य सखेव सख्युः
प्रियः प्रियायार्हसि देव सोढुम् ।।४४।।

*tasmātpraṇamya praṇidhāya kāyaṁ-*
*prasādaye tvāmahamīśamīḍyam,*
*piteva putrasya sakheva sakhyuḥ*
*priyaḥ priyāyārhasi deva soḍhum. (44)*

Therefore, bowing down, prostrating my body, I crave Your forgiveness, O adorable Lord. As a father forgiveth his son, a friend his friend, a lover his beloved, even so should You forgive me, O Deva.

अदृष्टपूर्वं हृषितोऽस्मि दृष्ट्वा
भयेन च प्रव्यथितं मनो मे ।
तदेव मे दर्शय देवरूपं-
प्रसीद देवेश जगन्निवास ।।४५।।

*adṛṣṭapūrvaṁ hṛṣito'smi dṛṣṭvā*
*bhayena ca pravyathitaṁ mano me,*
*tadeva me darśaya devarūpaṁ-*
*prasīda deveśa jagannivāsa. (45)*

I am delighted, having seen what was never seen before; and (yet) my mind is distressed with fear. Show me Your previous form only, O God; have mercy, O God of gods, O Abode of the universe.

किरीटिनं गदिनं चक्रहस्त-
मिच्छामि त्वां द्रष्टुमहं तथैव ।
तेनैव रूपेण चतुर्भुजेन
सहस्रबाहो भव विश्वमूर्ते ।।४६।।

*kirīṭinaṁ gadinaṁ cakrahasta–*
*micchāmi tvāṁ draṣṭumahaṁ tathaiva,*
*tenaiva rūpeṇa caturbhujena*
*sahasrabāho bhava viśvamūrte. (46)*

I desire to see You as before, crowned, bearing a mace, with a discus in hand, in Your former form only, having four arms, O thousand-armed, O universal form.

श्रीभगवानुवाच
मया प्रसन्नेन तवार्जुनेदं-
रूपं परं दर्शितमात्मयोगात् ।
तेजोमयं विश्वमनन्तमाद्यं-
यन्मे त्वदन्येन न दृष्टपूर्वम् ।।४७।।

*śrībhagavānuvāca*

*mayā prasannena tavārjunedaṁ-*
*rūpaṁ paraṁ darṣitamātmayogāt,*
*tejomayaṁ viśvamanantamādyaṁ-*
*yanme tvadanyena na dṛṣṭapūrvam. (47)*

The Blessed Lord said:

Graciously by Me, O Arjuna, this supreme form has been shown to you by My own yoga-power, full of splendour, primeval, infinite, this universal form of Mine had never been seen by any one other than yourself.

न वेदयज्ञाध्ययनैर्न दानै-
र्न च क्रियाभिर्न तपोभिरुग्रैः ।
एवंरूपः शक्य अहं नृलोके
द्रष्टुं त्वदन्येन कुरुप्रवीर ॥४८॥

*na vedayajñādhyayanairna dānai–*
*rna ca kriyābhirna tapobhirugraiḥ,*
*evaṁrūpaḥ śakya ahaṁ nṛloke*
*draṣṭuṁ tvadanyena kurupravīra. (48)*

Neither by the study of the Vedas nor by sacrifices (yajñas), nor by gifts, nor by rituals, nor by severe austerities, can I be seen in this form in the world of men by any other than Yourself, O great hero among the Kurus.

मा ते व्यथा मा च विमूढभावो-
दृष्ट्वा रूपं घोरमीदृङ्ममेदम् ।
व्यपेतभीः प्रीतमनाः पुनस्त्वं-
तदेव मे रूपमिदं प्रपश्य ।।४९।।

*mā te vyathā mā ca vimūḍhabhāvo-*
*dṛṣṭvā rūpaṁ ghoramīdṛṅmamedam,*
*vyapetabhīḥ prītamanāḥ punastvaṁ-*
*tadeva me rūpamidaṁ prapaśya. (49)*

Be not afraid, nor bewildered on seeing such a terrible form of mine as this; with your fear dispelled and with gladdened heart, now behold again this form of Mine.

सञ्जय उवाच
इत्यर्जुनं वासुदेवस्तथोक्त्वा
स्वकं रूपं दर्शयामास भूयः ।
आश्वासयामास च भीतमेनं
भूत्वा पुनः सौम्यवपुर्महात्मा ॥५०॥

*sañjaya uvāca*

*ityarjunaṁ vāsudevastathoktvā*
*svakaṁ rūpaṁ darśayāmāsa bhūyaḥ,*
*āśvāsayāmāsa ca bhītamenaṁ*
*bhūtvā punaḥ saumyavapurmahātmā. (50)*

Sañjaya said:

Having thus spoken to Arjuna, Vāsudeva again showed His own form, and the great souled One, assuming His gentle form consoled him who was so terrified.

अर्जुन उवाच
दृष्ट्वेदं मानुषं रूपं तव सौम्यं जनार्दन ।
इदानीमस्मि संवृत्तः सचेताः प्रकृतिं गतः ॥५१॥

*arjuna uvāca*

*dṛṣṭvedaṁ mānuṣaṁ rūpaṁ tava saumyaṁ janārdana,*
*idānīmasmi saṁvṛttah sacetāḥ prakṛtiṁ gataḥ. (51)*

Arujuna said:
Having seen this, Thy gentle human form, O Janārdana, I am now composed and restored to my own nature.

**श्रीभगवानुवाच**
**सुदुर्दर्शमिदं रूपं दृष्टवानसि यन्मम ।**
**देवा अप्यस्य रूपस्य नित्यं दर्शनकाङ्क्षिणः ।।५२।।**

*śrībhagavānuvāca*

*sudurdarśamidaṁ rūpaṁ dṛṣṭavānasi yanmama,*
*devā apyasya rūpasya nityaṁ darśanakāṅkṣiṇaḥ.(52)*

The Blessed Lord said:

Very hard indeed, it is to see this form of Mine which you have seen. Even the gods are ever longing to behold this form.

नाहं वेदैर्न तपसा न दानेन न चेज्यया ।
शक्य एवंविधो द्रष्टुं दृष्टवानसि मां यथा ।।५३।।

*nāhaṁ vedairna tapasā na dānena na cejyayā,*
*śakya evaṁvidho draṣṭuṁ dṛṣṭavānasi māṁ yathā.* (53)

Neither by the Vedas, nor by austerity, nor by gift, nor by sacrifices can I be seen in this form as you have seen Me (in your present mental condition).

भक्त्या त्वनन्यया शक्य अहमेवंविधोऽर्जुन ।
ज्ञातुं द्रष्टुं च तत्त्वेन प्रवेष्टुं च परन्तप ।।५४।।

*bhaktyā tvananyayā śakya ahamevaṁvidho'rjuna,*
*jñātuṁ draṣṭuṁ ca tattvena praveṣṭuṁ ca parantapa.* (54)

But by single-minded devotion, can I, of this form, be known and seen in reality and also entered into, O Parantapa (O scorcher of your foes)!

मत्कर्मकृन्मत्परमो मद्भक्तः सङ्गवर्जितः ।
निर्वैरः सर्वभूतेषु यः स मामेति पाण्डव ।।५५।

*matkarmakṛnmatparamo madbhaktaḥ saṅgavarjitaḥ,*
*nirvairaḥ sarvabhūteṣu yaḥ sa māmeti pāṇḍava. (55)*

He who does actions for Me, who looks upon Me as the Supreme, who is devoted to Me, who is free from attachment, who bears enmity towards none, he comes to Me, O Pāṇḍava.

ॐ तत्सदिति श्रीमद्भगवद्गीतासूपनिषत्सु
ब्रह्मविद्यायां योगशास्त्रे श्रीकृष्णार्जुनसंवादे
विश्वरूपदर्शनयोगो नाम एकादशोऽध्यायः

*om tatsaditi śrīmadbhagavadgītāsūpaniṣatsu*
*brahmavidyāyāṁ yogaśāstre śrīkṛṣṇārjunasaṁvāde*
*viśvarūpadarśanayogo nāma ekādaśo'dhyāyaḥ.*

Thus, in the Upaniṣad of the glorious Bhagavad-gītā, in the science of the eternal, in the scripture of yoga, in the dialogue between Śrī Kṛṣṇa and Arjuna, the eleventh discource ends entitled:

YOGA OF VISION OF THE DIVINE COSMIC FORM

* * *

Path of Devotion

# Chapter 12

## *Yoga of Devotion*

**अर्जुन उवाच**

**एवं सततयुक्ता ये भक्तास्त्वां पर्युपासते ।**
**ये चाप्यक्षरमव्यक्तं तेषां के योगवित्तमाः ।।१।।**

*arjuna uvāca*

*evaṁ satatayuktā ye bhaktāstvāṁ paryupāsate,*
*ye cāpyakṣaramavyaktaṁ teṣāṁ ke yogavittamāḥ.* (1)

Arjuna said :

Those devotees who, ever steadfast, thus worship You, and also those who worship the Imperishable, the unmanifested, which of them are better versed in yoga?

श्रीभगवानुवाच
मय्यावेश्य मनो ये मां नित्ययुक्ता उपासते ।
श्रद्धया परयोपेतास्ते मे युक्ततमा मताः ।।२।।

*śrībhagavānuvāca*

*mayyāveśya mano ye māṁ nityayuktā upāsate,*
*śraddhayā parayopetāste me yuktatamā matāḥ.* (2)

The Blessed Lord said:

Those who, fixing their mind on Me, worship Me, ever steadfast and endowed with supreme faith, these, in My opinion, are the best in yoga.

ये त्वक्षरमनिर्देश्यमव्यक्तं पर्युपासते ।
सर्वत्रगमचिन्त्यं च कूटस्थमचलं ध्रुवम् ।।३।।

*ye tvakṣaramanirdeśyamavyaktaṁ paryupāsate,*
*sarvatragamacintyaṁ ca kūṭasthamacalaṁ dhruvam.* (3)

Those who worship the imperishable, the indefinable, the unmanifest, the omnipresent, the unthinkable, the unchangeable, the immovable and the eternal, ...

सन्नियम्येन्द्रियग्रामं सर्वत्र समबुद्धयः ।
ते प्राप्नुवन्ति मामेव सर्वभूतहिते रताः ।।४।।

*sanniyamyendriyagrāmaṁ sarvatra samabuddhayaḥ,*
*te prāpnuvanti māmeva sarvabhūtahite ratāḥ.* (4)

Having restrained all the senses, even-minded everywhere, rejoicing ever in the welfare of all beings, verily, they also come unto Me.

क्लेशोऽधिकतरस्तेषामव्यक्तासक्तचेतसाम् ।
अव्यक्ता हि गतिर्दुःखं देहवद्भिरवाप्यते ।।५।।

*kleśo'dhikatarasteṣāmavyaktāsaktacetasām,*
*avyaktā hi gatirduḥkhaṁ dehavadbhiravāpyate.* (5)

Greater is their trouble whose minds are set on the unmanifest; for the goal, the unmanifest, is very hard for the embodied to reach.

ये तु सर्वाणि कर्माणि मयि सन्न्यस्य मत्पराः ।
अनन्येनैव योगेन मां ध्यायन्त उपासते ।।६।।

*ye tu sarvāṇi karmāṇi mayi sannyasya matparāḥ,*
*ananyenaiva yogena māṁ dhyāyanta upāsate. (6)*

But, those who worship Me, renouncing all actions in Me, regarding Me as the supreme goal, meditating on Me with single-minded devotion (yoga)...

तेषामहं समुद्धर्ता मृत्युसंसारसागरात् ।
भवामि नचिरात्पार्थ मय्यावेशितचेतसाम् ।।७।।

*teṣāmahaṁ samuddhartā mṛtyusaṁsārasāgarāt,*
*bhavāmi nacirātpārtha mayyāveśitacetasām. (7)*

For them, whose minds are set on Me, verily, I become, ere-long, O Pārtha, the saviour, (to save them) out of the ocean of finite experiences; the saṁsāra.

मय्येव मन आधत्स्व मयि बुद्धिं निवेशय ।
निवसिष्यसि मय्येव अत ऊर्ध्वं न संशयः ।।८।।

*mayyeva mana ādhatsva mayi buddhiṁ niveśaya,*
*nivasiṣyasi mayyeva ata ūrdhvaṁ na saṁśayaḥ. (8)*

Fix your mind on Me only, place your intellect in Me; then, (thereafter) you shall, no doubt, live in Me alone.

अथ चित्तं समाधातुं न शक्नोषि मयि स्थिरम् ।
अभ्यासयोगेन ततो मामिच्छाप्तुं धनञ्जय ।।९।।

*atha cittaṁ samādhātuṁ na śaknoṣi mayi sthiram,*
*abhyāsayogena tato māmicchāptuṁ dhanañjaya. (9)*

If you are unable to fix your mind steadily upon Me, then by the yoga of constant practice, seek to reach Me, O Dhanañjaya.

अभ्यासेऽप्यसमर्थोऽसि मत्कर्मपरमो भव ।
मदर्थमपि कर्माणि कुर्वन्सिद्धिमवाप्स्यसि ।।१०।।

*abhyāse'pyasamartho'si matkarmaparamo bhava,*
*madarthamapi karmāṇi kurvansiddhimavāpsyasi. (10)*

If you are unable even to practise abhyāsa-yoga, be you intent on performing actions for My sake; even by doing actions for My sake, you shall attain perfection.

अथैतदप्यशक्तोऽसि कर्तुं मद्योगमाश्रितः ।
सर्वकर्मफलत्यागं ततः कुरु यतात्मवान् ।।११।।

*athaitadapyaśakto'si kartuṁ madyogamāśritaḥ,*
*sarvakarmaphalatyāgaṁ tataḥ kuru yatātmavān. (11)*

If you are unable to do even this, then taking refuge in Me, self-controlled, renounce the fruits of all actions.

श्रेयो हि ज्ञानमभ्यासाज्ज्ञानाद्ध्यानं विशिष्यते ।
ध्यानात्कर्मफलत्यागस्त्यागाच्छान्तिरनन्तरम् ।।१२।।

*śreyo hi jñānamabhyāsājjñānāddhyānaṁ viśiṣyate,*
*dhyānātkarmaphalatyāgastyāgācchāntiranantaram. (12)*

Knowledge is indeed better than practice; meditation is better than knowledge ; renunciation of the fruits of actions is better than meditation; peace immediately follows renunciation.

अद्वेष्टा सर्वभूतानां मैत्रः करुण एव च ।
निर्ममो निरहङ्कारः समदुःखसुखः क्षमी ।।१३।।

*adveṣṭā sarvabhūtānāṁ maitraḥ karuṇa eva ca,*
*nirmamo nirahaṅkāraḥ samaduḥkhasukhaḥ kṣamī. (13)*

He who hates no creature, who is friendly and compassionate to all, who is free from attachment and egoism, balanced in pleasure and pain and forgiving....

सन्तुष्टः सततं योगी यतात्मा दृढनिश्चयः।
मय्यर्पितमनोबुद्धिर्यो मद्भक्तः स मे प्रियः ॥१४॥

*santuṣṭaḥ satataṁ yogī yatātmā dṛḍhaniścayaḥ,*
*mayyarpitamanobuddhiryo madbhaktaḥ sa me priyaḥ. (14)*

Ever content, steady in meditation, self-controlled, possessed of firm conviction, with mind and intellect dedicated to Me, he, My devotee, is dear to Me.

यस्मान्नोद्विजते लोको लोकान्नोद्विजते च यः।
हर्षामर्षभयोद्वेगैर्मुक्तो यः स च मे प्रियः ॥१५॥

*yasmānnodvijate loko lokānnodvijate ca yaḥ,*
*harṣāmarṣabhayodvegairmukto yaḥ sa ca me priyaḥ. (15)*

He, by whom the world is not agitated (affected), and who cannot be agitated by the world, who is freed from joy, envy, fear and anxiety - he is dear to Me.

अनपेक्षः शुचिर्दक्ष उदासीनो गतव्यथः ।
सर्वारम्भपरित्यागी यो मद्भक्तः स मे प्रियः ।।१६।।

*anapekṣaḥ śucirdakṣa udāsīno gatavyathaḥ,*
*sarvārambhaparityāgī yo madbhaktaḥ sa me priyaḥ. (16)*

He, who is free from wants, pure, alert, unconcerned, untroubled, renouncing all undertakings (or commencements) – he, who is (thus) devoted to Me, is dear to Me.

यो न हृष्यति न द्वेष्टि न शोचति न काङ्क्षति ।
शुभाशुभपरित्यागी भक्तिमान्यः स मे प्रियः ।।१७।।

*yo na hṛṣyati na dveṣṭi na śocati na kāṅkṣati,*
*śubhāśubhaparityāgī bhaktimānyaḥ sa me priyaḥ. (17)*

He who neither rejoices, nor hates, nor grieves, nor desires, renouncing good and evil, full of devotion, is dear to Me.

समः शत्रौ च मित्रे च तथा मानापमानयोः ।
शीतोष्णसुखदुःखेषु समः सङ्गविवर्जितः ।।१८।।

*samaḥ śatrau ca mitre ca tathā mānāpamānayoḥ,*
*śītoṣṇasukhaduḥkeṣu samaḥ saṅgavivarjitaḥ. (18)*

He, who is the same to foe and friend and also in honour and dishonour, who is the same in cold and heat and in pleasure and pain, who is free from attachment...

तुल्यनिन्दास्तुतिर्मौनी सन्तुष्टो येन केनचित् ।
अनिकेतः स्थिरमतिर्भक्तिमान्मे प्रियो नरः ।।१९।।

*tulyanindāstutirmaunī santuṣṭo yena kenacit,*
*aniketaḥ sthiramatirbhaktimānme priyo naraḥ. (19)*

To whom censure and praise are equal, who is silent, content with anything, homeless, steady-minded, full of devotion – that man is dear to Me.

ये तु धर्म्यामृतमिदं यथोक्तं पर्युपासते ।
श्रद्दधाना मत्परमा भक्तास्तेऽतीव मे प्रियाः ।।२०।।

*ye tu dharmyāmṛtamidaṁ yathoktaṁ paryupāsate,*
*śraddadhānā matparamā bhaktāste'tīva me priyāḥ. (20)*

They indeed, who follow this immortal dharma (law of life) as described above, endowed with faith, regarding Me as their supreme goal - such devotees are exceedingly dear to Me.

ॐ तत्सदिति श्रीमद्भगवद्गीतासूपनिषत्सु
ब्रह्मविद्यायां योगशास्त्रे श्रीकृष्णार्जुनसंवादे
भक्तियोगो नाम द्वादशोऽध्यायः

*om tatsaditi śrīmadbhagavadgītāsūpaniṣatsu*
*brahmavidyāyāṁ yogaśāstre śrīkṛṣṇārjunasaṁvāde*
*bhaktiyogo nāma dvādaśo'dhyāyaḥ.*

Thus, in the Upaniṣads of the glorious Bhagavad-gītā, in the science of the eternal, in the scripture of yoga, in the dialogue between Śrī Kṛṣṇa and Arjuna, the twelfth discourse ends entitled:

THE YOGA OF DEVOTION

***

Field and its Knower

# Chapter 13

## *Yoga of Distinction between Field and its Knower*

अर्जुन उवाच

प्रकृतिं पुरुषं चैव क्षेत्रं क्षेत्रज्ञमेव च ।
एतद्वेदितुमिच्छामि ज्ञानं ज्ञेयं च केशव ।।१।।

*arjuna uvāca*

*prakṛtiṁ puruṣaṁ caiva kṣetraṁ kṣetrajñamevaca,*
*etatveditumicchāmi jñānaṁ jñeyaṁ ca keśava. (1)*

Arjuna said :

Prakṛti (matter) and Puruṣa (spirit), also the kṣetra (the field) and Kṣetrajña (the Knower of the field), knowledge and that which ought to be known – these, I wish to learn, O Keśava.

श्रीभगवानुवाच
इदं शरीरं कौन्तेय क्षेत्रमित्यभिधीयते ।
एतद्यो वेत्ति तं प्राहुः क्षेत्रज्ञ इति तद्विदः ।।२।।

*śrībhagavānuvāca*

*idaṁ śarīraṁ kaunteya kṣetramityabhidhīyate,*
*etadyo vetti taṁ prāhuḥ kṣetrajña iti tadvidaḥ.* (2)

The Blessed Lord said:

This body, O Kaunteya, is called kṣetra (the field) and he who knows it is called Kṣetrajña (the Knower of the field) by those who know them (kṣetra and Kṣetrajña), i.e., by the Sages.

क्षेत्रज्ञं चापि मां विद्धि सर्वक्षेत्रेषु भारत ।
क्षेत्रक्षेत्रज्ञयोर्ज्ञानं यत्तज्ज्ञानं मतं मम ।।३।।

*kṣetrajñaṁ cāpi māṁ viddhi sarvakṣetreṣu bhārata,*
*kṣetrakṣetrajñayorjñānaṁ yattajjñānaṁ mataṁ mama.* (3)

Know Me as the Knower of the field in all fields, O Bhārata. Knowledge of the field as also of the Knower of the field is considered by Me to be My Knowledge.

तत्क्षेत्रं यच्च यादृक्च यद्विकारि यतश्च यत् ।
स च यो यत्प्रभावश्च तत्समासेन मे शृणु ।।४।।

*tatkṣetraṁ yacca yādṛkca yadvikāri yataśca yat,*
*sa ca yo yatprabhāvaśca tatsamāsena me śṛṇu. (4)*

What that field is; of what nature it is; what are its modifications; whence it is; and also who He is; and what His powers are – these hear from Me, in brief.

ऋषिभिर्बहुधा गीतं छन्दोभिर्विविधैः पृथक् ।
ब्रह्मसूत्रपदैश्चैव हेतुमद्भिर्विनिश्चितैः ।।५।।

*ṛṣibhirbahudhā gītaṁ chandobhirvividhaiḥ pṛthak,*
*brahmasūtrapadaiścaiva hetumadbhirviniścitaiḥ. (5)*

Ṛṣis have sung (about the field and the Knower of the field) in many ways, in various distinctive chants and also in the suggestive words indicative of Brahman, full of reason and decision.

महाभूतान्यहङ्कारो बुद्धिरव्यक्तमेव च ।
इन्द्रियाणि दशैकं च पञ्च चेन्द्रियगोचराः ।।६।।

*mahābhūtānyahaṅkāro buddhiravyaktameva ca,*
*indriyāṇi daśaikaṁ ca pañca cendriyagocarāḥ. (6)*

The great elements, egoism, intellect and also the unmanifested (mūla prakṛti), the ten senses and the one (the mind) and the five objects of the senses . . .

इच्छा द्वेषः सुखं दुःखं सङ्घातश्चेतना धृतिः ।
एतत्क्षेत्रं समासेन सविकारमुदाहृतम् ।।७।।

*icchā dveṣaḥ sukhaṁ duḥkhaṁ saṅghātaścetanā dhṛtiḥ,*
*etatkṣetraṁ samāsena savikāramudāhṛtam. (7)*

Desire, hatred, pleasure, pain, aggregate (body), intelligence, fortitude – this kṣetra has been thus, briefly described with its modifications.

अमानित्वमदम्भित्वमहिंसा क्षान्तिरार्जवम् ।
आचार्योपासनं शौचं स्थैर्यमात्मविनिग्रहः ॥८॥

*amānitvamadambhitvamahiṁsā kṣāntirārjavam,*
*ācāryopāsanaṁ śaucaṁ sthairyamātmavinigrahaḥ. (8)*

Humility, unpretentiousness, non-injury, forgiveness, uprightness, service to the teacher, purity, steadfastness self-control...

इन्द्रियार्थेषु वैराग्यमनहङ्कार एव च ।
जन्ममृत्युजराव्याधिदुःखदोषानुदर्शनम् ॥९॥

*indriyārtheṣu vairāgyamanahaṅkāra eva ca,*
*janmamṛtyujarāvyādhiduḥkhadoṣānudarśanam. (9)*

Indifference to the objects of the senses and also, absence of egoism, perception of (or reflection upon) evils in birth, death, old age, sickness and pain.....

असक्तिरनभिष्वङ्गः पुत्रदारगृहादिषु ।
नित्यं च समचित्तत्वमिष्टानिष्टोपपत्तिषु ॥१०॥

*asaktiranabhiṣvaṅgaḥ putradāragṛhādiṣu,*
*nityaṁ ca samacittatvamiṣṭāniṣṭopapattiṣu.* (10)

Non-attachment; non-identification of Self with son, wife, home and the rest; and constant even-mindedness on the attainment of the desirable and the undesirable...

मयि चानन्ययोगेन भक्तिरव्यभिचारिणी ।
विविक्तदेशसेवित्वमरतिर्जनसंसदि ।।११।।

*mayi cānanyayogena bhaktiravyabhicāriṇī,*
*viviktadeśasevitvamaratirjanasaṁsadi.* (11)

Unswerving devotion unto Me, by the yoga of non-separation, resorting to solitary places, distaste for the society of men...

अध्यात्मज्ञाननित्यत्वं तत्त्वज्ञानार्थदर्शनम् ।
एतज्ज्ञानमिति प्रोक्तमज्ञानं यदतोऽन्यथा ।।१२।।

*adhyātmajñānanityatvaṁ tattvajñānārthadarśanam,*
*etajjñānamiti proktamajñānaṁ yadato'nyathā.* (12)

Constancy in Self-knowledge, perception of the end of true knowledge – this is declared to be Knowledge and what is opposed to it is ignorance.

ज्ञेयं यत्तत्प्रवक्ष्यामि यज्ज्ञात्वामृतमश्नुते ।
अनादिमत्परं ब्रह्म न सत्तन्नासदुच्यते ।।१३।।

*jñeyaṁ yattatpravakṣyāmi yajjñātvāmṛtamaśnute,*
*anādimatparaṁ brahma na sattannāsaducyate. (13)*

I will declare that, which has to be known, knowing which one attains to immortality – the beginningless supreme Brahman, called neither being nor non-being.

सर्वतःपाणिपादं तत्सर्वतोऽक्षिशिरोमुखम् ।
सर्वतःश्रुतिमल्लोके सर्वमावृत्य तिष्ठति ।।१४।।

*sarvataḥpāṇipādaṁ tatsarvato'kṣiśiromukham,*
*sarvataḥśrutimalloke sarvamāvṛtya tiṣṭhati. (14)*

With hands and feet everywhere, with eyes, heads and mouths everywhere, with ears everywhere, He exists in the world, enveloping all.

सर्वेन्द्रियगुणाभासं सर्वेन्द्रियविवर्जितम् ।
असक्तं सर्वभृच्चैव निर्गुणं गुणभोक्तृ च ।।१५।।

*sarvendriyaguṇābhāsaṁ sarvendriyavivarjitam,*
*asaktaṁ sarvabhṛccaiva nirguṇaṁ guṇabhoktṛ ca.* (15)

Shining by the functions of all the senses, yet without the senses; unattached, yet supporting all; devoid of qualities, yet their experiencer...

बहिरन्तश्च भूतानामचरं चरमेव च ।
सूक्ष्मत्वात्तदविज्ञेयं दूरस्थं चान्तिके च तत् ।।१६।।

*bahirantaśca bhūtānāmacaraṁ carameva ca,*
*sūkṣmatvāttadavijñeyaṁ dūrasthaṁ cāntike ca tat.* (16)

Without and within (all) beings, the unmoving and also the moving; because of its subtlety unknowable; and near and far away - is That.

अविभक्तं च भूतेषु विभक्तमिव च स्थितम् ।
भूतभर्तृ च तज्ज्ञेयं ग्रसिष्णु प्रभविष्णु च ।।१७।।

*avibhaktaṁ ca bhūteṣu vibhaktamiva ca sthitam,*
*bhūtabhartṛ ca tajjñeyaṁ grasiṣṇu prabhaviṣṇu ca. (17)*

And undivided, yet He exists as if divided in beings; That is to be known as the supporter of beings; He devours and He generates.

ज्योतिषामपि तज्ज्योतिस्तमसः परमुच्यते ।
ज्ञानं ज्ञेयं ज्ञानगम्यं हृदि सर्वस्य विष्ठितम् ।।१८।।

*jyotiṣāmapi tajjyotistamasaḥ paramucyate,*
*jñānaṁ jñeyaṁ jñānagamyaṁ hṛdi sarvasya viṣṭhitam. (18)*

That (Brahman), the 'light of all lights', is said to be beyond darkness; (It is) Knowledge, the object of Knowledge, seated in the hearts of all, to be reached by Knowledge.

इति क्षेत्रं तथा ज्ञानं ज्ञेयं चोक्तं समासतः ।
मद्भक्त एतद्विज्ञाय मद्भावायोपपद्यते ।।१९।।

*iti kṣetraṁ tatha jñānaṁ jñeyaṁ coktaṁ samāsataḥ,*
*madbhakta etadvijñāya madbhāvāyopapadyate. (19)*

Thus the field, as well as the knowlege and the knowable have been briefly stated. Knowing this, My devotee enters into My being.

प्रकृतिं पुरुषं चैव विद्ध्यनादी उभावपि ।
विकारांश्च गुणांश्चैव विद्धि प्रकृतिसम्भवान् ।।२०।।

*prakṛtiṁ puruṣaṁ caiva viddhyanādī ubhāvapi,*
*vikārāṁśca guṇaṁścaiva viddhi prakṛtisambhavān. (20)*

Know you, that matter (prakṛti) and spirit (Puruṣa) are both beginningless; and know you also that all modifications and qualities are born of prakṛti.

कार्यकरणकर्तृत्वे हेतुः प्रकृतिरुच्यते ।
पुरुषः सुखदुःखानां भोक्तृत्वे हेतुरुच्यते ।।२१।।

*kāryakaraṇakartṛtve hetuḥ prakṛtirucyate,*
*puruṣaḥ sukhaduḥkānāṁ bhoktṛtve heturucyate. (21)*

In the production of effect (kārya) & cause (kāraṇa) Prakṛti is said to be the cause; and in the experience of pleasure (sukha) & pain (duḥkha) Puruṣa is said to be the cause.

पुरुषः प्रकृतिस्थो हि भुङ्क्ते प्रकृतिजान्गुणान् ।
कारणं गुणसङ्गोऽस्य सदसद्योनिजन्मसु ।।२२।।

*puruṣaḥ prakṛtistho hi bhuṅkte prakṛtijānguṇān,*
*kāraṇaṁ guṇasaṅgo'sya sadasadyonijanmasu.* (22)

The Puruṣa, seated in prakṛti, experiences the qualities born of prakṛti; attachment to the qualities is the cause of his birth in good and evil wombs.

उपद्रष्टानुमन्ता च भर्ता भोक्ता महेश्वरः ।
परमात्मेति चाप्युक्तो देहेऽस्मिन्पुरुषः परः ।।२३।।

*upadraṣṭānumantā ca bhartā bhoktā maheśvaraḥ,*
*paramātmeti cāpyukto dehe'sminpuruṣaḥ paraḥ.* (23)

The supreme Puruṣa in this body is also called the spectator, the permitter, the supporter, the enjoyer, the great Lord and the supreme Self.

य एवं वेत्ति पुरुषं प्रकृतिं च गुणैः सह ।
सर्वथा वर्तमानोऽपि न स भूयोऽभिजायते ।।२४।।

*ya evaṁ vetti puruṣaṁ prakṛtiṁ ca guṇaiḥ saha,*
*sarvathā vartamāno'pi na sa bhūyo'bhijāyate. (24)*

He who thus knows the Puruṣa and prakṛti together with the qualities, in whatsoever condition he may be, he is not born again.

ध्यानेनात्मनि पश्यन्ति केचिदात्मानमात्मना ।
अन्ये साङ्ख्येन योगेन कर्मयोगेन चापरे ।। २५ ।।

*dhyānenātmani paśyanti kecidātmānamātmanā,*
*anye sāṅkhyena yogena karmayogena cāpare. (25)*

Some, by meditation, behold the Self in the self by the self; others by the yoga of Knowledge (by sāṅkhya-yoga); and others by karma-yoga.

अन्ये त्वेवमजानन्तः श्रुत्वान्येभ्य उपासते ।
तेऽपि चातितरन्त्येव मृत्युं श्रुतिपरायणाः ।।२६ ।।

*anye tvevamajānantaḥ śrutvānyebhya upāsate,*
*te'pi cātitarantyeva mṛtyuṁ śrutiparāyaṇāḥ. (26)*

Others also, not knowing this, worship, having heard of it from others; they too, cross beyond death, if they would regard what they have heard as their supreme refuge.

यावत्सञ्जायते किंञ्चित्सत्त्वं स्थावरजङ्गमम् ।
क्षेत्रक्षेत्रज्ञसंयोगात्तद्विद्धि भरतर्षभ ।।२७।।

*yāvatsañjāyate kiñcitsattvaṁ sthāvarajaṅgamam,*
*kṣetrakṣetrajñasaṁyogāttadviddhi bharatarṣabha. (27)*

Whenever any being is born, the unmoving or the moving, know you, O best of the Bharatas, that it is from the union between the field and the Knower of the field.

समं सर्वेषु भूतेषु तिष्ठन्तं परमेश्वरम् ।
विनश्यत्स्वविनश्यन्तं यः पश्यति स पश्यति ।।२८।।

*samaṁ sarveṣu bhūteṣu tiṣṭhantaṁ parameśvaram,*
*vinaśyatsvavinaśyantaṁ yaḥ paśyati sa paśyati. (28)*

He sees, who sees the supreme Lord existing equally in all beings, the unperishing within the perishing.

समं पश्यन्हि सर्वत्र समवस्थितमीश्वरम् ।
न हिनस्त्यात्मनात्मानं ततो याति परां गतिम् ।।२९।।

*samaṁ paśyanhi sarvatra samavasthitamīśvaram,*
*na hinastyātmanātmānaṁ tato yāti parāṁ gatim. (29)*

Indeed, he who sees the same Lord everywhere equally dwelling, destroys not the Self by the Self; therefore, he goes to the highest goal.

प्रकृत्यैव च कर्माणि क्रियमाणानि सर्वशः ।
यः पश्यति तथात्मानमकर्तारं स पश्यति ।।३०।।

*prakṛtyaiva ca karmāṇi kriyamāṇāni sarvaśaḥ,*
*yaḥ paśyati tathātmānamakartāraṁ sa paśyati. (30)*

He sees, who sees that all actions are performed by prakṛti alone, and that the Self is actionless.

यदा भूतपृथग्भावमेकस्थमनुपश्यति ।
तत एव च विस्तारं ब्रह्म सम्पद्यते तदा ।।३१।।

*yadā bhūtapṛthagbhāvamekasthamanupaśyati,*
*tata eva ca vistāraṁ brahma sampadyate tadā. (31)*

When he (man) sees the whole variety of beings, as resting in the 'One', and spreading forth from That (One) alone, he then, becomes Brahman.

अनादित्वान्निर्गुणत्वात्परमात्मायमव्ययः ।
शरीरस्थोऽपि कौन्तेय न करोति न लिप्यते ।।३२।।

*anāditvānnirguṇatvātparamātmāyamavyayaḥ,*
*śarīrastho'pi kaunteya na karoti na lipyate. (32)*

Being without beginning, and being devoid of qualities, the supreme Self, the imperishable though dwelling in the body, O Kaunteya, neither acts, nor is tainted.

यथा सर्वगतं सौक्ष्म्यादाकाशं नोपलिप्यते ।
सर्वत्रावस्थितो देहे तथात्मा नोपलिप्यते ।।३३।।

*yathā sarvagataṁ saukṣmyādākāśaṁ nopalipyate,*
*sarvatrāvasthito dehe tathātmā nopalipyate. (33)*

As the all-pervading ether is not tainted, because of its subtlety, so too the Self, seated everywhere in the body, is not tainted.

यथा प्रकाशयत्येकः कृत्स्नं लोकमिमं रविः ।
क्षेत्रं क्षेत्री तथा कृत्स्नं प्रकाशयति भारत ।।३४।।

*yathā prakāśayatyekaḥ kṛtsnaṁ lokamimaṁ raviḥ,*
*kṣetraṁ kṣetrī tathā kṛtsnaṁ prakāśyati bhārata. (34)*

Just as the one Sun illumines the whole world, so also the Lord of the field (Paramātman) illumines the whole field, O Bhārata.

क्षेत्रक्षेत्रज्ञयोरेवमन्तरं ज्ञानचक्षुषा ।
भूतप्रकृतिमोक्षं च ये विदुर्यान्ति ते परम् ।।३५।।

*kṣetrakṣetrajñayorevamantaraṁ jñānacakṣuṣā,*
*bhūtaprakṛtimokṣaṁ ca ye viduryānti te param. (35)*

They who, with their eye of wisdom come to know the distinction between the field and the Knower of the field, and of the liberation from the prakṛti of the being, go to the Supreme.

ॐ तत्सदिति श्रीमद्भगवद्गीतासूपनिषत्सु
ब्रह्मविद्यायां योगशास्त्रे श्रीकृष्णार्जुनसंवादे
क्षेत्रक्षेत्रज्ञविभागयोगो नाम त्रयोदशोऽध्यायः

*om tatsaditi śrīmadbhagavadgītāsūpaniṣatsu*
*brahmavidyāyāṁ yogaśāstre śrīkṛṣṇārjunasaṁvāde*
*kṣetrakṣetrajñavibhāgayogo nāma trayodaśo'dhyāyaḥ*

Thus, in the Upaniṣads of the glorious Bhagavad-gītā, in the science of the eternal, in the scripture of yoga, in the dialogue between Śrī Kṛṣṇa and Arjuna, the thirteenth discourse ends entitled:

YOGA OF DISTINCTION BETWEEN FIELD
AND ITS KNOWER

* * *

Three Guṇas

# Chapter 14

## *Yoga of Three Guṇas*

श्रीभगवानुवाच

परं भूयः प्रवक्ष्यामि ज्ञानानां ज्ञानमुत्तमम् ।
यज्ज्ञात्वा मुनयः सर्वे परां सिद्धिमितो गताः ।।१।।

*śrībhagavānuvāca*

*paraṁ bhūyaḥ pravakṣyāmi jñānānāṁ jñānamuttamam,*
*yajjñātvā munayaḥ sarve parāṁ siddhimito gatāḥ.* (1)

The Blessed Lord said :

I will again declare (to you) that supreme Knowledge, the best of all knowledges, having known which, all the sages have attained supreme perfection after this life.

**इदं ज्ञानमुपाश्रित्य मम साधर्म्यमागताः ।**
**सर्गेऽपि नोपजायन्ते प्रलये न व्यथन्ति च ।।२।।**

*idaṁ jñānamupāśritya mama sādharmyamāgatāḥ,*
*sarge'pi nopajāyante pralaye na vyathanti ca.* (2)

They who, having refuge in this Knowledge have attained to My being, are neither born at the time of creation, nor are they disturbed at the time of dissolution.

**मम योनिर्महद्ब्रह्म तस्मिन्गर्भं दधाम्यहम् ।**
**सम्भवः सर्वभूतानां ततो भवति भारत ।।३।।**

*mama yonirmahadbrahma tasmingarbhaṁ dadhāmyaham,*
*sambhavaḥ sarvabhūtānāṁ tato bhavati bhārata.* (3)

My womb is the great Brahman (mūla prakṛti); in that I place the germ; from which, O Bhārata, is the birth of all beings.

**सर्वयोनिषु कौन्तेय मूर्तयः सम्भवन्ति याः ।**
**तासां ब्रह्म महद्योनिरहं बीजप्रदः पिता ।।४।।**

*sarvayoniṣu kaunteya mūrtayaḥ sambhavanti yāḥ,*
*tāsāṁ brahma mahadyoniraham̐ bījapradaḥ pitā.* (4)

Whatever forms are produced, O Kaunteya, in all the wombs whatsoever, the great Brahman (mūla prakṛti) is their womb, and I am the seed-giving father.

सत्त्वं रजस्तम इति गुणाः प्रकृतिसम्भवाः ।
निबध्नन्ति महाबाहो देहे देहिनमव्ययम् ॥५॥

*sattvaṁ rajastama iti guṇāḥ prakṛtisambhavāḥ,*
*nibadhnanti mahābāho dehe dehinamavyayam. (5)*

Purity, passion, and inertia – these qualities (guṇas), O! mighty-armed, born of prakṛti, bind the indestructible embodied one, fast in the body.

तत्र सत्त्वं निर्मलत्वात्प्रकाशकमनामयम् ।
सुखसङ्गेन बध्नाति ज्ञानसङ्गेन चानघ ॥६॥

*tatra sattvaṁ nirmalatvātprakāśakamanāmayam,*
*sukhasaṅgena badhnāti jñānasaṅgena cānagha. (6)*

Of these, sattva, because of its stainlessness, is luminous and healthy (unobstructive). It binds by (creating) attachment to happiness and attachment to knowledge, O sinless one.

रजो रागात्मकं विद्धि तृष्णासङ्गसमुद्भवम् ।
तन्निबध्नाति कौन्तेय कर्मसङ्गेन देहिनम् ।।७।।

*rajo rāgātmakaṁ viddhi tṛṣṇāsaṅgasamudbhavam,*
*tannibadhnāti kaunteya karmasaṅgena dehinam.* (7)

Know thou, rajas (to be) of the nature of passion, the source of thirst and attachment; it binds fast, O Kaunteya, the embodied one, by attachment to action.

तमस्त्वज्ञानजं विद्धि मोहनं सर्वदेहिनाम् ।
प्रमादालस्यनिद्राभिस्तन्निबध्नाति भारत ।।८।।

*tamastvajñānajaṁ viddhi mohanaṁ sarvadehinām,*
*pramādālasyanidrābhistannibadhnāti bhārata.* (8)

But, know thou, tamas is born of ignorance, deluding all embodied beings, it binds fast, O Bhārata, by heedlessness, indolence and sleep.

सत्त्वं सुखे सञ्जयति रजः कर्मणि भारत ।
ज्ञानमावृत्य तु तमः प्रमादे सञ्जयत्युत ।।९।।

*sattvaṁ sukhe sañjayati rajaḥ karmaṇi bhārata,*
*jñānamāvṛtya tu tamaḥ pramāde sañjayatyuta.* (9)

Sattva attaches to happiness, rajas to action, O Bhārata, while tamas verily, shrouding knowledge, attaches to heedlessness.

रजस्तमश्चाभिभूय सत्त्वं भवति भारत ।
रजः सत्त्वं तमश्चैव तमः सत्त्वं रजस्तथा ॥१०॥

*rajastamaścābhibhūya sattvaṁ bhavati bhārata,*
*rajaḥ sattvaṁ tamaścaiva tamaḥ sattvaṁ rajastathā. (10)*

Now sattva rises (prevails), O Bhārata, having overpowered rajas and inertia (tamas); now rajas having overpowered sattva and inertia; and inertia (tamas), having overpowered sattva and rajas.

सर्वद्वारेषु देहेऽस्मिन्प्रकाश उपजायते ।
ज्ञानं यदा तदा विद्याद्विवृद्धं सत्त्वमित्युत ॥११॥

*sarvadvāreṣu dehe'sminprakāśa upajāyate,*
*jñānaṁ yadā tadā vidyādvivṛddhaṁ sattvamityuta. (11)*

When, through every gate (sense) of this body, the light of intelligence shines, then, it may be known that sattva is predominant.

**लोभः प्रवृत्तिरारम्भः कर्मणामशमः स्पृहा ।**
**रजस्येतानि जायन्ते विवृद्धे भरतर्षभ ।।१२।।**

*lobhaḥ pravṛttirārambhaḥ karmaṇāmaśamaḥ spṛhā,*
*rajasyetāni jāyante vivṛddhe bharatarṣabha. (12)*

Greed, activity, undertaking of actions, restlessness, longing – these arise when rajas is predominant, O best in the Bharata family.

**अप्रकाशोऽप्रवृत्तिश्च प्रमादो मोह एव च ।**
**तमस्येतानि जायन्ते विवृद्धे कुरुनन्दन ।।१३।।**

*aprakāśo'pravṛttisca pramādo moha eva ca,*
*tamasyetāni jāyante vivṛddhe kurunandana. (13)*

Darkness, inertness, heedlessness and delusion – these arise when tamas is predominant, O descendant of Kuru.

**यदा सत्त्वे प्रवृद्धे तु प्रलयं याति देहभृत् ।**
**तदोत्तमविदां लोकानमलान्प्रतिपद्यते ।।१४।।**

*yadā sattve pravṛddhe tu pralayaṁ yāti dehabhṛt,*
*tadottamavidāṁ lokānamalānpratipadyate. (14)*

If the embodied one meets with death when sattva is predominant, then he attains to the spotless worlds of the knowers of the highest.

रजसि प्रलयं गत्वा कर्मसङ्गिषु जायते ।
तथा प्रलीनस्तमसि मूढयोनिषु जायते ।।१५।।

*rajasi pralayaṁ gatvā karmasaṅgiṣu jāyate,*
*tathā pralīnastamasi mūḍhayoniṣu jāyate. (15)*

Meeting death in rajas, he is born among those attached to action; and dying in tamas, he is born in the womb of the senseless.

कर्मणः सुकृतस्याहुः सात्त्विकं निर्मलं फलम् ।
रजसस्तु फलं दुःखमज्ञानं तमसः फलम् ।।१६।।

*karmaṇaḥ sukṛtasyāhuḥ sāttvikaṁ nirmalaṁ phalam,*
*rajasastu phalaṁ duḥkamajñānaṁ tamasaḥ phalam. (16)*

The fruit of good action, they say, is sāttvika and pure; verily the fruit of rajas is pain, and the fruit of tamas is ignorance.

सत्त्वात्सञ्जायते ज्ञानं रजसो लोभ एव च ।
प्रमादमोहौ तमसो भवतोऽज्ञानमेव च ।।१७।।

*sattvātsañjāyate jñānaṁ rajaso lobha eva ca,*
*pramādamohau tamaso bhavato'jñānameva ca.* (17)

Knowledge arises from sattva, greed from rajas, heedlessness, delusion and also ignorance arise from tamas.

ऊर्ध्वं गच्छन्ति सत्त्वस्था मध्ये तिष्ठन्ति राजसाः ।
जघन्यगुणवृत्तिस्था अधो गच्छन्ति तामसाः ।।१८।।

*ūrdhvaṁ gacchanti sattvasthā madhye tiṣṭhanti rājasāḥ,*
*jaghanyaguṇavṛttisthā adho gacchanti tāmasāḥ.* (18)

Those who are abiding in sattva go upwards; the rājasika dwell in the middle; and the tāmasika, abiding in the function of the lowest guṇa, go downwards.

नान्यं गुणेभ्यः कर्तारं यदा द्रष्टानुपश्यति ।
गुणेभ्यश्च परं वेत्ति मद्भावं सोऽधिगच्छति ।।१९।।

*nānyaṁ guṇebhyaḥ kartāraṁ yadā draṣṭānupaśyati,*
*guṇebhyaśca paraṁ vetti madbhāvaṁ so'dhigacchati.* (19)

When the Seer, beholds no agent other than the guṇas and knows him who is higher than the guṇas, he attains to My being.

गुणानेतानतीत्य त्रीन्देही देहसमुद्भवान् ।
जन्ममृत्युजरादुःखैर्विमुक्तोऽमृतमश्नुते ।।२०।।

*guṇānetānatītya trīndehī dehasamudbhavān,*
*janmamṛtyujarāduḥkhairvimukto'mṛtamaśnute.* (20)

The embodied-one, having crossed beyond these three guṇas, out of which the body is evolved, is freed from birth, death, decay and pain and attains to immortality.

अर्जुन उवाच
कैर्लिङ्गैस्त्रीन्गुणानेतानतीतो भवति प्रभो ।
किमाचारः कथं चैतांस्त्रीन्गुणानतिवर्तते ।।२१।।

*arjuna uvāca*

*kairliṅgaistrīnguṇānetānatīto bhavati prabho,*
*kimācāraḥ kathaṁ caitāṁstrīnguṇānativartate.* (21)

Arjuna said:

What are the marks of him, who has crossed over the three guṇas, O Lord? What is his conduct, and how does he go beyond these three guṇas?

श्रीभगवानुवाच

प्रकाशं च प्रवृत्तिं च मोहमेव च पाण्डव ।
न द्वेष्टि सम्प्रवृत्तानि न निवृत्तानि काङ्क्षति ।।२२।।

*śrībhagavānuvāca*

*prakāśaṁ ca pravṛttim ca mohameva ca pāṇḍava,*
*na dveṣṭi sampravṛttāni na nivṛttāni kāṅkṣati. (22)*

The Blessed Lord said:

Light, activity and delusion, when present, O Pāṇḍava, he hates not, nor longs for them when absent.

उदासीनवदासीनो गुणैर्यो न विचाल्यते ।
गुणा वर्तन्त इत्येव योऽवतिष्ठति नेङ्गते ।।२३।।

*udāsīnavadāsīno guṇairyo na vicālyate,*
*guṇā vartanta ityeva yo'vatiṣṭhati neṅgate. (23)*

He who, seated like one unconcerned, is not moved by the guṇas who, knowing that the guṇas operate, is self-centred and swerves not.......

समदुःखसुखः स्वस्थः समलोष्टाश्मकाञ्चनः ।
तुल्यप्रियाप्रियो धीरस्तुल्यनिन्दात्मसंस्तुतिः ।।२४।।

*samaduḥkhasukhaḥ svasthaḥ samaloṣṭāśmakāñcanaḥ,*
*tulyapriyāpriyo dhīrastulyanindātmasaṁstutiḥ.* (24)

Alike in pleasure and pain; who dwells in the Self; to whom a clod of earth, a precious stone and gold are alike; to whom the dear and the not-dear are the same; firm; the same in censure and self-praise.......

मानापमानयोस्तुल्यस्तुल्यो मित्रारिपक्षयोः ।
सर्वारम्भपरित्यागी गुणातीतः स उच्यते ।।२५।।

*mānāpamānayostulyastulyo mitrāripakṣayoḥ,*
*sarvārambhaparityāgī guṇātītaḥ sa ucyate.* (25)

The same in honour and dishonour; the same to friend and foe; abandoning all undertakings – he is said to have crossed beyond the guṇas.

मां च योऽव्यभिचारेण भक्तियोगेन सेवते ।
स गुणान्समतीत्यैतान्ब्रह्मभूयाय कल्पते ।।२६।।

*māṁ ca yo'vyabhicāreṇa bhaktiyogena sevate,*
*sa guṇānsamatītyaitānbrahmabhūyāya kalpate.* (26)

And he, serving Me with unswerving devotion, and crossing beyond the guṇas, is fit to become Brahman.

ब्रह्मणो हि प्रतिष्ठाहममृतस्याव्ययस्य च ।
शाश्वतस्य च धर्मस्य सुखस्यैकान्तिकस्य च ।।२७।।

*brahmaṇo hi pratiṣṭhāhamamṛtasyāvyayasya ca,*
*śāśvatasya ca dharmasya sukhasyaikāntikasya ca.* (27)

For, I am the abode of Brahman, the immortal and the immutable, of everlasting dharma and of absolute bliss.

ॐ तत्सदिति श्रीमद्भगवद्गीतासूपनिषत्सु
ब्रह्मविद्यायां योगशास्त्रे श्रीकृष्णार्जुनसंवादे
गुणत्रयविभागयोगो नाम चतुर्दशोऽध्यायः

*om tatsaditi śrīmadbhagavadgītāsūpaniṣatsu*
*brahmavidyāyāṁ yogaśāstre śrīkṛṣṇārjunasaṁvāde*
*guṇatrayavibhāgayogo nāma caturdaśo'dhyāyaḥ.*

Thus, in the Upaniṣads of the glorious Bhagavad-gītā, in the science of the eternal, in the scipture of yoga, in the dialogue between Śrī Kṛṣṇa and Arjuna, the fourteenth discourse ends entitled:

YOGA OF THREE GUṆAS

***

Supreme Spirit

# Chapter 15

## *Yoga of Supreme Spirit*

**श्रीभगवानुवाच**

**ऊर्ध्वमूलमधःशाखमश्वत्थं प्राहुरव्ययम् ।**
**छन्दांसि यस्य पर्णानि यस्तं वेद स वेदवित् ।।१।।**

*śrībhagavānuvāca*

*ūrdhvamūlamadhaḥśākhamaśvatthaṁ prāhuravyayam,*
*chandāṁsi yasya parṇāni yastaṁ veda sa vedavit. (1)*

The Blessed Lord said :

They (wise people) speak of the indestructible Aśvattha tree, having its roots above and branches below, whose leaves are the Vedas; he who knows it, is alone a Veda-knower.

अधश्चोर्ध्वं प्रसृतास्तस्य शाखा
गुणप्रवृद्धा विषयप्रवालाः ।
अधश्च मूलान्यनुसन्ततानि
कर्मानुबन्धीनि मनुष्यलोके ।।२।।

*adhaścordhvaṁ prasṛtāstasya śākhā*
*guṇapravṛddhā viṣayapravālāḥ,*
*adhaśca mūlānyanusantatāni*
*karmānubandhīni manuṣyaloke. (2)*

Below and above are spread its branches, nourished by the guṇas; sense objects are its buds; and below, in the world of men, stretch forth the roots, originating in action.

न रूपमस्येह तथोपलभ्यते
नान्तो न चादिर्न च सम्प्रतिष्ठा ।
अश्वत्थमेनं सुविरूढमूल-
मसङ्गशस्त्रेण दृढेन छित्त्वा ।।३।।

*na rūpamasyeha tathopalabhyate*
*nānto na cādirna ca sampratiṣṭhā,*
*aśvatthamenaṁ suvirūḍhamūla–*
*masaṅgaśastreṇa dṛḍhena chittvā. (3)*

Its form is not perceived here as such, neither its end, or its foundation, nor its resting place; having cut asunder this firm-rooted Aśvattha-tree with the strong axe of non-attachment.....

ततः पदं तत्परिमार्गितव्यं–
यस्मिन्गता न निवर्तन्ति भूयः ।
तमेव चाद्यं पुरुषं प्रपद्ये
यतः प्रवृत्तिः प्रसृता पुराणी ।।४।।

*tataḥ padaṁ tatparimārgitavyaṁ-*
*yasmingatā na nivartanti bhuyah,*
*tameva cādyaṁ puruṣaṁ prapadye*
*yataḥ pravṛttiḥ prasṛtā purāṇī. (4)*

Then, that goal should be sought after, where having gone, none returns again. I seek refuge in that primeval Puruṣa from which streamed forth all activity (or energy).

निर्मानमोहा जितसङ्गदोषा-
अध्यात्मनित्या विनिवृत्तकामाः ।
द्वन्द्वैर्विमुक्ताः सुखदुःखसञ्ज्ञै-
र्गच्छन्त्यमूढाः पदमव्ययं तत् ।।५।।

*nirmānamohā jitasaṅgadoṣā-*
*adhyātmanityā vinivṛttakāmāḥ,*
*dvandvairvimuktāḥ sukhaduḥkhasañjñai-*
*rgacchantyamūḍhāḥ padamavyayaṁ tat. (5)*

Free from pride and delusion, victorious over the evil of attachment, dwelling constantly in the Self, their desires having completely retired, freed from the pairs of opposites, such as pleasure and pain, the undeluded reach that goal eternal.

न तद्भासयते सूर्यो न शशाङ्को न पावकः ।
यद्गत्वा न निवर्तन्ते तद्धाम परमं मम ।।६।।

*na tadbhāsayate sūryo na śaśāṅko na pāvakaḥ,*
*yadgatvā na nivartante taddhāma paramaṁ mama. (6)*

Neither does the sun shine there, nor the moon, nor fire; to which having gone they return not; that is My supreme Abode.

ममैवांशो जीवलोके जीवभूतः सनातनः ।
मनःषष्ठानीन्द्रियाणि प्रकृतिस्थानि कर्षति ॥७॥

*mamaivāṁśo jīvaloke jīvabhūtaḥ sanātanah,*
*manaḥṣaṣṭhānīndriyāṇi prakṛtisthāni karṣati. (7)*

An eternal portion of Myself, having become a living soul in the world of life, abiding in prakṛti, draws (to itself) the(five) senses, with mind as the sixth.

शरीरं यदवाप्नोति यच्चाप्युत्क्रामतीश्वरः ।
गृहीत्वैतानि संयाति वायुर्गन्धानिवाशयात् ॥८॥

*śarīraṁ yadavāpnoti yaccāpyutkrāmatīśvaraḥ,*
*gṛhītvaitāni saṁyāti vāyurgandhānivāśayāt. (8)*

When the Lord obtains a body and when He leaves it, He takes these and goes (with them) as the wind takes the scents from their seats (the flowers).

श्रोत्रं चक्षुः स्पर्शनं च रसनं घ्राणमेव च ।
अधिष्ठाय मनश्चायं विषयानुपसेवते ।।९।।

*śrotraṁ cakṣuḥ sparśanaṁ ca rasanaṁ ghrāṇameva ca,*
*adhiṣṭhāya manaścāyaṁ viṣayānupasevate. (9)*

Presiding over the ear, the eye, the touch, the taste and the smell, so also the mind, He enjoys the sense objects.

उत्क्रामन्तं स्थितं वापि भुञ्जानं वा गुणान्वितम् ।
विमूढा नानुपश्यन्ति पश्यन्ति ज्ञानचक्षुषः ।।१०।।

*utkrāmantaṁ sthitaṁ vāpi bhuñjānaṁ vā guṇānvitam,*
*vimūḍhā nānupaśyanti paśyanti jñānacakṣuṣaḥ. (10)*

Him, who departs, stays and enjoys, who is united with guṇas, the deluded do not see; but they, do behold Him, who posseses the 'eye of knowledge'.

यतन्तो योगिनश्चैनं पश्यन्त्यात्मन्यवस्थितम् ।
यतन्तोऽप्यकृतात्मानो नैनं पश्यन्त्यचेतसः ।।११।।

*yatanto yoginaścainaṁ paśyantyātmanyavasthitam,*
*yatanto'pyakṛtātmāno nainaṁ paśyantyacetasaḥ.* (11)

The seekers striving (for perfection), behold Him dwelling in the Self; but, the unrefined and unintelligent, even though striving, see Him not.

यदादित्यगतं तेजो जगद्भासयतेऽखिलम् ।
यच्चन्द्रमसि यच्चाग्नौ तत्तेजो विद्धि मामकम् ।।१२।।

*yadādityagataṁ tejo jagadbhāsayate'khilam,*
*yaccandramasi yaccāgnau tattejo viddhi māmakam.* (12)

That light, which is residing in the sun and which illumines the whole world, and that which is in the moon and in the fire – know that, light to be Mine.

गामाविश्य च भूतानि धारयाम्यहमोजसा ।
पुष्णामि चौषधीः सर्वाः सोमो भूत्वा रसात्मकः ।।१३।।

*gāmāviśya ca bhūtāni dhārayāmyahamojasā,*
*puṣṇāmi cauṣadhīḥ sarvāḥ somo bhūtvā rasātmakaḥ.* (13)

Permeating the earth, I support all beings by (My) energy; and having become the liquid moon, I nourish all herbs.

अहं वैश्वानरो भूत्वा प्राणिनां देहमाश्रितः ।
प्राणापानसमायुक्तः पचाम्यन्नं चतुर्विधम् ॥१४॥

*ahaṁ vaisvānaro bhūtvā prāṇināṁ dehamāśritaḥ,*
*prāṇāpānasamāyuktaḥ pacāmyannaṁ caturvidham. (14)*

Having become (the fire) Vaiśvānara, I abide in the body of beings and associated with prāṇa and apāna, digest the fourfold food.

सर्वस्य चाहं हृदि सन्निविष्टो-
मत्तः स्मृतिर्ज्ञानमपोहनं च ।
वेदैश्च सर्वैरहमेव वेद्यो-
वेदान्तकृद्वेदविदेव चाहम् ॥१५॥

*sarvasya cāham hṛdi sanniviṣṭo-*
*mattaḥ smṛtirjñānamapohanaṁ ca,*
*vedaiśca sarvairahameva vedyo-*
*vedāntakṛdvedavideva cāham. (15)*

And I am seated in the heart in the hearts of all, from Me are memory, knowledge as well as their absence. I am verily that which has to be known in all the Vedas; I am indeed the author of Vedānta and the Knower of the Vedas am I.

द्वाविमौ पुरुषौ लोके क्षरश्चाक्षर एव च ।
क्षरः सर्वाणि भूतानि कूटस्थोऽक्षर उच्यते ।।१६।।

*dvāvimau puruṣau loke kṣaraścākṣara eva ca,*
*kṣaraḥ sarvāṇi bhūtāni kūṭastho'kṣara ucyate. (16)*

Two Puruṣas are there in this world, the perishable and the Imperishable. All beings are the perishable and the Kūṭastha is called the Imperishable.

उत्तमः पुरुषस्त्वन्यः परमात्मेत्युदाहृतः ।
यो लोकत्रयमाविश्य बिभर्त्यव्यय ईश्वरः ।।१७।।

*uttamaḥ puruṣastvanyaḥ paramātmetyudāhṛtaḥ,*
*yo lokatrayamāviśya bibhartyavyaya īśvaraḥ. (17)*

But, distinct is the supreme Puruṣa called the highest Self, the indestructible Lord, who, pervading the three worlds (waking, dream and deep sleep), sustains them.

**यस्मात्क्षरमतीतोऽहमक्षरादपि चोत्तमः ।**
**अतोऽस्मि लोके वेदे च प्रथितः पुरुषोत्तमः ।।१८।।**

*yasmātkṣaramatīto'hamakṣarādapi cottamaḥ,*
*ato'smi loke vede ca prathitaḥ puruṣottamaḥ. (18)*

As I transcend the perishable and I am even Higher than the Imperishable, I am declared as the Puruṣottama (the highest Puruṣa), in the world and in the Vedas.

**यो मामेवमसम्मूढो जानाति पुरुषोत्तमम् ।**
**स सर्वविद्भजति मां सर्वभावेन भारत ।।१९।।**

*yo māmevamasammūḍho jānāti puruṣottamam,*
*sa sarvavidbhajati māṁ sarvabhāvena bhārata. (19)*

He who, undeluded, thus knows Me, the supreme Puruṣa, he, all-knowing, worships Me with his whole being, O Bhārata.

इति गुह्यतमं शास्त्रमिदमुक्तं मयानघ ।
एतद्बुद्ध्वा बुद्धिमान्स्यात्कृतकृत्यश्च भारत ।।२०।।

*ti guhyatamaṁ śāstramidamuktaṁ mayānagha,*
*etadbuddhvā buddhimānsyātkṛtakṛtyaśca bhārata. (20)*

Thus, this most secret science (teaching) has been taught by Me, O sinless one. On knowing this a man becomes wise and all his duties are accomplished, O Bhārata.

ॐ तत्सदिति श्रीमद्भगवद्गीतासूपनिषत्सु
ब्रह्मविद्यायां योगशास्त्रे श्रीकृष्णार्जुनसंवादे
पुरुषोत्तमयोगो नाम पञ्चदशोऽध्यायः

*om tatsaditi śrīmadbhagavadgītāsūpaniṣatsu*
*brahmavidyāyāṁ yogaśāstre śrīkṛṣṇārjunasaṁvāde*
*puruṣottamayogo nāma pañcadaśo'dhyāyaḥ.*

Thus, in the Upaniṣads of the glorious Bhagavad-gītā, in the science of the eternal, in the scripture of yoga, in the dialogue between Śrī Kṛṣṇa and Arjuna, the fifteenth discourse ends entitled:

YOGA OF SUPREME SPIRIT

* * *

Divine and Devilish Estates

# Chapter 16

## *Yoga of Divine And Devilish Estates*

श्रीभगवानुवाच
अभयं सत्त्वसंशुद्धिर्ज्ञानयोगव्यवस्थितिः ।
दानं दमश्च यज्ञश्च स्वाध्यायस्तप आर्जवम् ।।१।।

*śrībhagavānuvāca*

*abhayaṁ satvasaṁśuddhirjñānayogavyavasthitiḥ,*
*dānaṁ damaśca yajñaśca svādhyāyastapa ārjavam.* (1)

The Blessed Lord said :

Fearlessness, purity of heart, steadfastness in the yoga of knowledge, alms-giving, control of the senses, sacrifice, study of the śāstras and straightforwardness....

अहिंसा सत्यमक्रोधस्त्यागः शान्तिरपैशुनम् ।
दया भूतेष्वलोलुप्त्वं मार्दवं ह्रीरचापलम् ।।२।।

*ahiṁsā satyamakrodhastyāgaḥ śāntirapaiśunam,*
*dayā bhūteṣvaloluptvaṁ mārdavaṁ hrīracāpalam.* (2)

Harmlessness, truth, absence of anger, renunciation, peacefulness, absence of crookedness, compassion to beings, non-covetousness, gentleness, modesty, absence of fickleness....

तेजः क्षमा धृतिः शौचमद्रोहो नातिमानिता ।
भवन्ति सम्पदं दैवीमभिजातस्य भारत ।।३।।

*tejaḥ kṣamā dhṛtiḥ śaucamadroho nātimānitā,*
*bhavanti sampadaṁ daivīmabhijātasya bhārata.* (3)

Vigour, forgiveness, fortitude, purity, absence of hatred, absence of pride – these belong to the one, born for the divine estate, O Bhārata.

दम्भो दर्पोऽभिमानश्च क्रोधः पारुष्यमेव च ।
अज्ञानं चाभिजातस्य पार्थ सम्पदमासुरीम् ।।४।।

*dambho darpo'bhimānaśca krodhaḥ pāruṣyameva ca,*
*ajñānaṁ cābhijātasya pārtha sampadamāsurīm. (4)*

Hypocrisy, arrogance and self-conceit, anger and also harshness and ignorance belong to one who is born, O Pārtha, for a demoniac estate.

दैवी सम्पद्विमोक्षाय निबन्धायासुरी मता ।
मा शुचः सम्पदं दैवीमभिजातोऽसि पाण्डव ।।५।।

*daivī sampadvimokṣāya nibandhāyāsurī matā,*
*mā śucah sampadaṁ daivīmabhijāto'si pāṇḍava. (5)*

The divine nature is deemed for liberation, the demoniacal for bondage; grieve not, O Pāṇḍava, you are born with divine qualities.

द्वौ भूतसर्गौ लोकेऽस्मिन्दैव आसुर एव च ।
दैवो विस्तरशः प्रोक्त आसुरं पार्थ मे शृणु ।।६।।

*dvau bhūtasargau loke'smindaiva āsura eva ca,*
*daivo vistaraśaḥ prokta āsuraṁ pārtha me śṛṇu. (6)*

There are two types of beings in this world, the divine and the demoniacal; the divine have been described at length; hear from Me, O Pārtha, of the demoniacal.

**प्रवृत्तिं च निवृत्तिं च जना न विदुरासुराः ।**
**न शौचं नापि चाचारो न सत्यं तेषु विद्यते ।।७।।**

*pravṛttiṁ ca nivṛttiṁ ca janā na vidurāsurāḥ,*
*na śaucaṁ nāpi cācāro na satyaṁ teṣu vidyate. (7)*

The demoniac know not what to do and what to refrain from; neither purity, nor right conduct, nor truth is found in them.

**असत्यमप्रतिष्ठं ते जगदाहुरनीश्वरम् ।**
**अपरस्परसम्भूतं किमन्यत्कामहैतुकम् ।।८।।**

*asatyamapratiṣṭhaṁ te jagadāhuranīśvaram,*
*aparasparasambhūtaṁ kimanyatkāmahaitukam. (8)*

They say, 'The universe is without truth, without (moral) basis, without God; not brought about by any regular causal sequence, with lust for its cause, what else?'

एतां दृष्टिमवष्टभ्य नष्टात्मानोऽल्पबुद्धयः ।
प्रभवन्त्युग्रकर्माणः क्षयाय जगतोऽहिताः ।।९।।

*etām dṛṣṭimavaṣṭabhya naṣṭātmāno'lpabuddhayaḥ,*
*prabhavantyugrakarmāṇaḥ kṣayāyā jagato'hitāḥ.* (9)

Holding this view, these ruined souls of small intellect and fierce deeds come forth as the enemies of the world for its destruction.

काममाश्रित्य दुष्पूरं दम्भमानमदान्विताः ।
मोहाद्गृहीत्वासद्ग्राहान्प्रवर्तन्तेऽशुचिव्रताः ।।१०।।

*kāmamāśritya duṣpūraṁ dambhamānamadānvitāḥ,*
*mohādgṛhītvāsadgrāhānpravartante'śucivratāḥ.* (10)

Filled with insatiable desires, full of hypocrisy, pride and arrogance, holding evil ideas through delusion, they work with impure resolves.

चिन्तामपरिमेयां च प्रलयान्तामुपाश्रिताः ।
कामोपभोगपरमा एतावदिति निश्चिताः ।।११।।

*cintāmaparimeyāṁ ca pralayāntāmupāśritāḥ,*
*kāmopabhogaparamā etāvaditi niścitāḥ. (11)*

Giving themselves over to immeasurable cares ending only with death, regarding gratification of lust as their highest aim, and feeling sure that, that is all (that matters).

आशापाशशतैर्बद्धाः कामक्रोधपरायणाः ।
ईहन्ते कामभोगार्थमन्यायेनार्थसञ्चयान् ।।१२।।

*āśāpāśaśatairbaddhāḥ kāmakrodhaparāyaṇāh,*
*īhante kāmabhogārthamanyāyenārthasañcayān. (12)*

Bound by a hundred ties of hope, given to lust and anger, they do strive to obtain, by unlawful means, hoards of wealth for sensual enjoyments.

इदमद्य मया लब्धमिमं प्राप्स्ये मनोरथम् ।
इदमस्तीदमपि मे भविष्यति पुनर्धनम् ।।१३।।

*idamadya mayā labdhamimam prāpsye manoratham,*
*idamastīdamapi me bhaviṣyati punardhanam. (13)*

"This has today been gained by me, this desire I shall obtain, this is mine, and this wealth shall also be mine in future".

असौ मया हतः शत्रुर्हनिष्ये चापरानपि ।
ईश्वरोऽहमहं भोगी सिद्धोऽहं बलवान्सुखी ।।१४।।

*asau mayā hataḥ śatrurhaniṣye cāparānapi,*

*īśvaro'hamahaṁ bhogī siddho'haṁ balavānsukhi.* (14)

"That enemy has been slain by me and others also shall I destroy, I am the Lord, I am the enjoyer, I am perfect, powerful and happy".

आढ्योऽभिजनवानस्मि कोऽन्योऽस्ति सदृशो मया ।
यक्ष्ये दास्यामि मोदिष्य इत्यज्ञानविमोहिताः ।।१५।।

*āḍhyo'bhijanavānasmi ko'nyo'sti sadṛśo mayā,*

*yakṣye dāsyāmi modiṣya ityajñānavimohitāh.* (15)

"I am rich and well-born; who else is equal to me?' – 'I will give (alms, money), I will rejoice". Thus are they deluded by ignorance.

अनेकचित्तविभ्रान्ता मोहजालसमावृताः ।
प्रसक्ताः कामभोगेषु पतन्ति नरकेऽशुचौ ।।१६।।

*anekacittavibhrāntā mohajālasamāvṛtāḥ,*
*prasaktāḥ kāmabhogeṣu patanti narake'śucau. (16)*

Bewildered by many a fancy, entangled in the snare of delusion, addicted to the gratification of lust, they fall into a foul hell.

आत्मसम्भाविताः स्तब्धा धनमानमदान्विताः ।
यजन्ते नामयज्ञैस्ते दम्भेनाविधिपूर्वकम् ।।१७।।

*ātmasambhāvitāḥ stabdhā dhanamānamadānvitāḥ,*
*yajante nāmayajñaiste dambhenāvidhipūrvakam. (17)*

Self-conceited, stubborn, filled with pride and drunk with wealth, they perform sacrifices in name (only) out of ostentation, contrary to scriptural ordinance.

अहङ्कारं बलं दर्पं कामं क्रोधं च संश्रिताः ।
मामात्मपरदेहेषु प्रद्विषन्तोऽभ्यसूयकाः ।।१८।।

*ahaṅkāraṁ balaṁ darpaṁ kāmaṁ krodhaṁ ca saṁśritāḥ,*
*māmātmaparaḍeheṣu pradviṣanto'bhyasūyakāḥ.* (18)

Given to egoism, power, haughtiness, lust and anger, these malicious people hate Me in their own bodies and in those of others.

तानहं द्विषतः क्रूरान्संसारेषु नराधमान् ।
क्षिपाम्यजस्रमशुभानासुरीष्वेव योनिषु ।।१९।।

*tānahaṁ dviṣataḥ krūrānsaṁsāreṣu narādhamān,*
*kṣipāmyajasramaśubhānāsurīṣveva yoniṣu.* (19)

These cruel haters, worst among men in the world, I hurl these evil-doers forever, into the wombs of the demons only.

आसुरीं योनिमापन्ना मूढा जन्मनि जन्मनि ।
मामप्राप्यैव कौन्तेय ततो यान्त्यधमां गतिम् ।।२०।।

*āsurīṁ yonimāpannā mūḍhā janmani janmani,*
*māmaprāpyaiva kaunteya tato yāntyadhamāṁ gatim.* (20)

Entering into demoniacal wombs and deluded, not attaining to Me, birth after birth, they thus fall, O Kaunteya, into a condition still lower than that.

त्रिविधं नरकस्येदं द्वारं नाशनमात्मनः ।
कामः क्रोधस्तथा लोभस्तस्मादेतत्त्रयं त्यजेत् ।।२१।।

*trividhaṁ narakasyedaṁ dvāraṁ nāśanamātmanaḥ,*
*kāmaḥ krodhastathā lobhastasmādetattrayaṁ tyajet.* (21)

These three are gates of hell, destructive of the Self – lust, anger and greed; therefore, one should abandon these three.

एतैर्विमुक्तः कौन्तेय तमोद्वारैस्त्रिभिर्नरः ।
आचरत्यात्मनः श्रेयस्ततो याति परां गतिम् ।।२२।।

*etairvimuktaḥ kaunteya tamodvāraistribhirnaraḥ,*
*ācaratyātmanaḥ śreyastato yāti parāṁ gatim.* (22)

A man who is liberated from these three gates to darkness, O Kaunteya, practises what is good for him and thus goes to the supreme goal.

यः शास्त्रविधिमुत्सृज्य वर्तते कामकारतः ।
न स सिद्धिमवाप्नोति न सुखं न परां गतिम् ।।२३।।

*yaḥ śāstravidhimutsṛjya vartate kāmakārataḥ,*
*na sa siddhimavāpnoti na sukhaṁ na parāṁ gatim. (23)*

He who, having cast aside the ordinances of the scriptures, acts under the impulse of desire, attains neither perfection, nor happiness, nor the supreme goal.

तस्माच्छास्त्रं प्रमाणं ते कार्याकार्यव्यवस्थितौ ।
ज्ञात्वा शास्त्रविधानोक्तं कर्म कर्तुमिहार्हसि ।।२४।।

*tasmācchāstraṁ pramāṇaṁ te kāryākāryavyavasthitau,*
*jñātvā śāstravidhānoktaṁ karma kartumihārhasi. (24)*

Therefore, let the scriptures be your authority in determining what ought to be done and what ought not to be done. Having known what is said in the commandments of the scripture, you should act here (in this world).

ॐ तत्सदिति श्रीमद्भगवद्गीतासूपनिषत्सु
ब्रह्मविद्यायां योगशास्त्रे श्रीकृष्णार्जुनसंवादे
दैवासुरसम्पद्विभागयोगो नाम षोडशोऽध्यायः

*om tatsaditi śrīmadbhagavadgītāsūpaniṣatsu*
*brahmavidyāyāṁ yogaśāstre śrīkṛṣṇārjunasaṁvāde*
*daivāsurasampadvibhāgayogo nāma ṣodaśo'dhyayaḥ*

Thus, in the Upaniṣads of the glorious Bhagavad-gītā, in the science of the eternal, in the scipture of yoga, in the dialogue between Śrī Kṛṣṇa and Arjuna, the sixteenth discourse ends entitled:

YOGA OF DIVINE AND DEVILISH ESTATES

***

Threefold Faith

# Chapter 17

## *Yoga of Threefold Faith*

अर्जुन उवाच

ये शास्त्रविधिमुत्सृज्य यजन्ते श्रद्धयान्विताः ।
तेषां निष्ठा तु का कृष्ण सत्त्वमाहो रजस्तमः ।।१।।

*arjuna uvāca*

*ye śāstravidhimutsṛjya yajante śraddhayānvitāḥ,*
*teṣāṁ niṣṭhā tu kā kṛṣṇa sattvamāho rajastamaḥ. (1)*

Arjuna said :

Those who, setting aside the ordinances of the scriptures, perform sacrifice with faith, what is their condition, O Kṛṣṇa? Is it sattva, rajas, or tamas?

**श्रीभगवानुवाच**
**त्रिविधा भवति श्रद्धा देहिनां सा स्वभावजा ।**
**सात्त्विकी राजसी चैव तामसी चेति तां शृणु ।।२।।**

*śrībhagavānuvāca*

*trividhā bhavati śraddhā dehināṁ sā svabhāvajā,*
*sāttvikī rājasī caiva tāmasī ceti tāṁ śṛṇu. (2)*

The Blessed Lord said:

Threefold is the faith of the embodied which is inherent in their nature – the sāttvika (pure), the rājasika (passionate) and the tāmasika (dull, dark). Thus, thou hear of it.

**सत्त्वानुरूपा सर्वस्य श्रद्धा भवति भारत ।**
**श्रद्धामयोऽयं पुरुषो यो यच्छ्रद्धः स एव सः ।।३।।**

*sattvānurūpā sarvasya śraddhā bhavati bhārata,*
*śraddhāmayo'yaṁ puruṣo yo yacchraddhaḥ sa eva saḥ. (3)*

The faith of each is in accordance with his nature, O Bhārata. Man consists of his faith; as a man's faith is, so is he.

**यजन्ते सात्त्विका देवान्यक्षरक्षांसि राजसाः ।**
**प्रेतान्भूतगणांश्चान्ये यजन्ते तामसा जनाः ।।४।।**

*yajante sāttvikā devānyakṣarakṣāṁsi rājasāḥ,*
*pretānbhūtagaṇāṁscānye yajante tāmasā janāḥ. (4)*

The sāttvika or pure men, worship the gods (devas); the rājasika or the passionate, the yakṣas and the rākṣasās; the others - tāmasika people or the dark or dull folk, worship the ghosts (pretas) and the hosts of bhūtas (ghosts) or the nature or spirits.

**अशास्त्रविहितं घोरं तप्यन्ते ये तपो जनाः ।**
**दम्भाहङ्कारसंयुक्ताः कामरागबलान्विताः ।।५।।**

*aśāstravihitaṁ ghoraṁ tapyante ye tapo janāḥ,*
*dambhāhaṅkārasaṁyuktāḥ kāmarāgabalānvitāḥ. (5)*

Those men who practise terrible austerities not enjoined by the scriptures, given to hypocrisy and egoism, impelled by the force of lust attachment....

कर्शयन्तः शरीरस्थं भूतग्राममचेतसः ।
मां चैवान्तःशरीरस्थं तान्विद्ध्यासुरनिश्चयान् ।।६।।

*karṣayantaḥ śarīrasthaṁ bhūtagrāmamacetasaḥ,*
*māṁ caivāntaḥ śarīrasthaṁ tānviddhyāsuraniścayān. (6)*

Senselessly torturing all the elements in the body and Me also, who dwells within the body - you may know these to be of demoniacal resolves.

आहारस्त्वपि सर्वस्य त्रिविधो भवति प्रियः ।
यज्ञस्तपस्तथा दानं तेषां भेदमिमं शृणु ।।७।।

*āhārastvapi sarvasya trividho bhavati priyaḥ,*
*yajñastapastathā dānaṁ teṣāṁ bhedamimaṁ śṛṇu. (7)*

The food which is dear to each one is also threefold, as also sacrifice, austerity and alms-giving. You may now hear the distinction of these.

आयुःसत्त्वबलारोग्यसुखप्रीतिविवर्धनाः ।
रस्याः स्निग्धाः स्थिरा हृद्या आहाराः सात्त्विकप्रियाः ।।८।।

*āyuḥsattvabalārogyasukhaprītivivardhanāḥ,*
*rasyāḥ snigdhāḥ sthirā hṛdyā āhārāḥ sāttvikapriyāḥ.* (8)

The foods which increase life, purity, strength, health, joy and cheerfulness (good appetite), which are savoury and oleaginous, substantial and agreeable are dear to the sāttvika (pure).

कट्वम्ललवणात्युष्णतीक्ष्णरूक्षविदाहिनः ।
आहारा राजसस्येष्टा दुःखशोकामयप्रदाः ।।९।।

*kaṭvamlalavaṇātyuṣṇatīkṣṇarūkṣavidāhinaḥ,*
*āhārā rājasasyeṣṭā duḥkhaśokāmayapradaḥ.* (9)

The foods that are bitter, sour, saline, excessively hot, pungent, dry and burning are liked by the rājasika, and are productive of pain, grief and disease.

यातयामं गतरसं पूति पर्युषितं च यत् ।
उच्छिष्टमपि चामेध्यं भोजनं तामसप्रियम् ।।१०।।

*yātayāmaṁ gatarasaṁ pūti paryuṣitaṁ ca yat,*
*ucchiṣṭamapi cāmedhyaṁ bhojanaṁ tāmasapriyam.* (10)

That which is stale, tasteless, putrid and rotten, refuse and impure, is the food liked by the tāmasika.

अफलाकाङ्क्षिभिर्यज्ञो विधिदृष्टो य इज्यते ।
यष्टव्यमेवेति मनः समाधाय स सात्त्विकः ।।११।।

*aphalākāṅkṣibhiryajño vidhidṛṣṭo ya ijyate,*
*yaṣṭavyameveti manaḥ samādhāya sa sāttvikaḥ.* (11)

That sacrifice which is offered by men without desire for fruit, and as enjoined by ordinance, with a firm faith that sacrifice is a duty, is sāttvika or pure.

अभिसन्धाय तु फलं दम्भार्थमपि चैव यत् ।
इज्यते भरतश्रेष्ठ तं यज्ञं विद्धि राजसम् ।।१२।।

*abhisandhāya tu phalaṁ dambhārthamapi caiva yat,*
*ijyate bharataśreṣṭha taṁ yajñaṁ viddhi rājasam.* (12)

The sacrifice which is offered, O best of the Bharatas, seeking fruit and for ostentation, you may know that to be a rājasika-yajña.

**विधिहीनमसृष्टान्नं मन्त्रहीनमदक्षिणम् ।**
**श्रद्धाविरहितं यज्ञं तामसं परिचक्षते ।।१३।।**

*vidhihīnamasṛṣṭānnaṁ mantrahīnamadakṣiṇam,*
*śraddhāvirahitaṁ yajñaṁ tāmasaṁ paricakṣate.* (13)

They declare that sacifice to be tāmasika, which is contrary to the ordinances, in which no food is distributed, which is devoid of mantras and gifts, and which is devoid of faith.

**देवद्विजगुरुप्राज्ञपूजनं शौचमार्जवम् ।**
**ब्रह्मचर्यमहिंसा च शारीरं तप उच्यते ।।१४।।**

*devadvijagurupräjñapūjanaṁ śaucamārjavam,*
*brahmacaryamahiṁsā ca śārīraṁ tapa ucyate.* (14)

Worship of the gods, the twice-born, the teachers and the wise; purity, straightforwardness, celibacy and non-injury - these are called the 'austerity of the body'.

**अनुद्वेगकरं वाक्यं सत्यं प्रियहितं च यत् ।**
**स्वाध्यायाभ्यसनं चैव वाङ्मयं तप उच्यते ।।१५।।**

*anudvegakaraṁ vākyaṁ satyaṁ priyahitaṁ ca yat,*
*svādhyāyābhyasanaṁ caive vāṅmayaṁ tapa ucyate.* (15)

Speech which causes no excitement and is truthful, pleasant and beneficial, and the practice of the study of the Vedas - these consitute the austerity of speech.

मनःप्रसादः सौम्यत्वं मौनमात्मविनिग्रहः ।
भावसंशुद्धिरित्येतत्तपो मानसमुच्यते ।।१६।।

*manaḥprasādaḥ saumyatvaṁ maunamātmavinigrahaḥ,*
*bhāvasaṁśuddhirityetattapo mānasamucyate.* (16)

Serenity of mind, good-heartedness, silence, self-control, purity of nature - these together are called the mental austerity.

श्रद्धया परया तप्तं तपस्तत्त्रिविधं नरैः ।
अफलाकाङ्क्षिभिर्युक्तैः सात्त्विकं परिचक्षते ।।१७।।

*śraddhayā parayā taptaṁ tapastattrividhaṁ naraiḥ,*
*aphalākāṅkṣibhiryuktaiḥ sāttvikaṁ paricakṣate.* (17)

This threefold austerity practised by steadfast men with the utmost faith, desiring no fruit, they call sāttvika.

सत्कारमानपूजार्थं तपो दम्भेन चैव यत् ।
क्रियते तदिह प्रोक्तं राजसं चलमध्रुवम् ।।१८।।

*satkaramānapujārthaṁ tapo dambhena caiva yat,*
*kriyate tadiha proktaṁ rājasaṁ calamadhruvam. (18)*

The austerity which is practised with the object of gaining good reception, honour and worship and with hypocrisy is here said to be rājasika, unstable and transitory.

मूढग्राहेणात्मनो यत्पीडया क्रियते तपः ।
परस्योत्सादनार्थं वा तत्तामसमुदाहृतम् ।।१९।।

*mūḍhagrāheṇātmano yatpīḍayā kriyate tapaḥ,*
*parasyotsādanārthaṁ vā tattāmasamudāhṛtam. (19)*

That austerity which is practised with self-torture, out of some foolish notion for the purpose of destroying another is declared to be tāmasika.

दातव्यमिति यद्दानं दीयतेऽनुपकारिणे ।
देशे काले च पात्रे च तद्दानं सात्त्विकं स्मृतम् ।।२०।।

*dātavyamiti yaddānaṁ dīyate'nupakāriṇe,*
*deśe kāle ca pātre ca taddānaṁ sāttvikaṁ smṛtam. (20)*

That gift which is given knowing it to be a duty, in a fit time and place, to a worthy person, from whom we expect nothing in return, is held to be sāttvika.

यत्तु प्रत्युपकारार्थं फलमुद्दिश्य वा पुनः ।
दीयते च परिक्लिष्टं तद्दानं राजसं स्मृतम् ।।२१।।

*yattu pratyupakārārthaṁ phalamuddiśya vā punaḥ,*
*dīyate ca parikliṣṭaṁ taddānaṁ rājasaṁ smṛtam. (21)*

And that gift which is given with a view to receiving in return or looking for fruit again, or reluctantly, is held to be rājasika.

अदेशकाले यद्दानमपात्रेभ्यश्च दीयते ।
असत्कृतमवज्ञातं तत्तामसमुदाहृतम् ।।२२।।

*adeśakāle yaddānamapātrebhyaśca dīyate,*

*asatkṛtamavajñātaṁ tattāmasamudāhṛtam. (22)*

The gift that is given at a wrong place and time, to unworthy persons, without respect or with insult, is declared to be tāmasika.

ॐ तत्सदिति निर्देशो ब्रह्मणस्त्रिविधः स्मृतः ।
ब्राह्मणास्तेन वेदाश्च यज्ञाश्च विहिताः पुरा ।।२३।।

*om tatsaditi nirdeśo brahmaṇastrividhaḥ smṛtaḥ,*

*brāhmaṇāstena vedāśca yajñāśca vihitāḥ purā. (23)*

'Om tat sat' – this has been declared to be the triple designation of Brahman. By that were created formerly, the Brāhmaṇas, Vedas and Yagñas (sacrifices).

तस्मादोमित्युदाहृत्य यज्ञदानतपःक्रियाः ।
प्रवर्तन्ते विधानोक्ताः सततं ब्रह्मवादिनाम् ।।२४।।

*tasmādomityudāhṛtya yajñadānatapaḥkriyāḥ,*

*pravartante vidhānoktāḥ satataṁ brahmavādinām. (24)*

Therefore, with the utterance of 'Om' are begun the acts of sacrifice, gifts and austerity as enjoined in the scriptures, always by the students of Brahman.

तदित्यनभिसन्धाय फलं यज्ञतपःक्रियाः ।
दानक्रियाश्च विविधाः क्रियन्ते मोक्षकाङ्क्षिभिः ॥२५॥

*tadityanabhisandhāya phalaṁ yajñatapaḥkriyāḥ,*
*dānakriyāśca vividhāḥ kriyante mokṣakāṅkṣibhiḥ.* (25)

Uttering 'Tat' without aiming at the fruits are the acts of sacrifice and austerity and the various acts of gift performed by the seekers of liberation.

सद्भावे साधुभावे च सदित्येतत्प्रयुज्यते ।
प्रशस्ते कर्मणि तथा सच्छब्दः पार्थ युज्यते ॥२६॥

*sadbhāve sādhubhāve ca sadityetatprayujyate,*
*praśaste karmaṇi tathā sacchabdaḥ pārtha yujyate.* (26)

The word 'Sat' is used in the sense of Reality and of goodness; and also, O Pārtha, the word 'Sat' is used in the sense of an auspicious act.

यज्ञे तपसि दाने च स्थितिः सदिति चोच्यते ।
कर्म चैव तदर्थीयं सदित्येवाभिधीयते ।।२७।।

*yajñe tapasi dāne ca sthitiḥ saditi cocyate,*
*karma caiva tadarthīyaṁ sadityevābhidhīyate. (27)*

Steadfastness in sacrifice, austerity and gift is also called 'Sat' and also, action in connection with these (for the sake of the Supreme) is called 'Sat'.

अश्रद्धया हुतं दत्तं तपस्तप्तं कृतं च यत् ।
असदित्युच्यते पार्थ न च तत्प्रेत्य नो इह ।।२८।।

*aśraddhayā hutaṁ dattaṁ tapastaptaṁ kṛtaṁ ca yat,*
*asadityucyate pārtha na ca tatpretya no iha. (28)*

Whatever is sacrificed, given or performed and whatever austerity is practised without faith, it is called 'asat', O Pārtha, it is not for here or hereafter (after death).

ॐ तत्सदिति श्रीमद्भगवद्गीतासूपनिषत्सु
ब्रह्मविद्यायां योगशास्त्रे श्रीकृष्णार्जुनसंवादे
श्रद्धात्रयविभागयोगो नाम सप्तदशोऽध्याय:

*om tatsaditi śrīmadbhagavadgītāsūpaniṣatsu*
*brahmavidyāyāṁ yogaśāstre śrīkṛṣṇārjunasaṁvāde*
*śraddhātrayavibhāgayago nāma saptadaśo'dhyāyaḥ.*

Thus, in the Upaniṣad of the glorious Bhagavad-gītā, in the science of the eternal, in the scripture of yoga, in the dialogue between Śrī Kṛṣṇa and Arjuna, the seventeenth discourse ends entitled:

YOGA OF THREEFOLD FAITH

***

Liberation Through Renunciation

# Chapter 18

## *Yoga of Liberation Through Renunciation*

अर्जुन उवाच

सन्न्यासस्य महाबाहो तत्त्वमिच्छामि वेदितुम् ।
त्यागस्य च हृषीकेश पृथक्केशिनिषूदन ।।१।।

*arjuna uvāca*

*sannyāsasya mahābāho tattvamicchāmi veditum,*
*tyāgasya ca hṛṣīkeśa pṛthakkeśiniṣūdana. (1)*

Arjuna said :

I desire to know severally, O mighty-armed, the essence or truth of renunciation, O Hṛṣkeśa, as also of abandonment, O slayer of Keśi (Kṛṣṇa).

श्रीभगवानुवाच
काम्यानां कर्मणां न्यासं सन्न्यासं कवयो विदुः ।
सर्वकर्मफलत्यागं प्राहुस्त्यागं विचक्षणाः ।।२।।

*śrībhagavānuvāca*

*kāmyānāṁ karmaṇāṁ nyāsaṁ sannyāsaṁ kavayo viduḥ,*
*sarvakarmaphalatyāgaṁ prāhustyāgaṁ vicakṣaṇāḥ. (2)*

The Blessed Lord said:

The Sages understand sannyāsa to be the renunciation of work with desire; the wise declare the abandonment of the fruits of all actions as tyāga.

त्याज्यं दोषवदित्येके कर्म प्राहुर्मनीषिणः ।
यज्ञदानतपःकर्म न त्याज्यमिति चापरे ।।३।।

*tyājyaṁ doṣavadityeke karma prāhurmanīṣiṇaḥ,*
*yajñadānatapaḥkarma na tyājyamiti cāpare. (3)*

All actions should be abandoned as evil, declare some philosophers; while others (declare) that acts of sacrifice, gift and austerity should not be relinquished.

निश्चयं शृणु मे तत्र त्यागे भरतसत्तम ।
त्यागो हि पुरुषव्याघ्र त्रिविधः संप्रकीर्तितः ।।४।।

*niścayaṁ śṛṇu me tatra tyāge bharatasattama,*
*tyāgo hi puruṣavyāghra trividhaḥ saṁprakīrtitaḥ. (4)*

Hear from Me the conclusion or the final truth about this abandonment, O best of the Bhāratas; abandonment, verily, O best of men, has been declared to be of three kinds.

यज्ञदानतपःकर्म न त्याज्यं कार्यमेव तत् ।
यज्ञो दानं तपश्चैव पावनानि मनीषिणाम् ।।५।।

*yajñadānatapaḥkarma na tyājyaṁ kāryameva tat,*
*yajño dānaṁ tapaścaiva pāvanāni manīṣiṇām. (5)*

Acts of sacrifice, charity and austerity should not be abandoned, but should be performed; worship, charity, and also austerity, are the purifiers of even the 'wise'.

एतान्यपि तु कर्माणि सङ्गं त्यक्त्वा फलानि च ।
कर्तव्यानीति मे पार्थ निश्चितं मतमुत्तमम् ।।६।।

*etānyapi tu karmāṇi saṅgaṁ tyaktvā phalāni ca,*
*kartavyānīti me pārtha niścitaṁ matamuttamam. (6)*

But even these actions should be performed leaving aside attachment and the fruits, O Pārtha; this is My certain and best belief.

नियतस्य तु सन्न्यासः कर्मणो नोपपद्यते ।
मोहात्तस्य परित्यागस्तामसः परिकीर्तितः ।।७।।

*niyatasya tu sannyāsaḥ karmaṇo nopapadyate,*
*mohāttasya parityāgastāmasaḥ parikīrtitaḥ. (7)*

Verily, the renunciation of 'obligatory actions' is not proper; the abandonment of the same from delusion is declared to be tāmasika (dull).

दुःखमित्येव यत्कर्म कायक्लेशभयात्त्यजेत् ।
स कृत्वा राजसं त्यागं नैव त्यागफलं लभेत् ।।८।।

*duḥkhamityeva yatkarma kāyakleśabhayāttyajet,*
*sa kṛtvā rājasaṁ tyāgaṁ naiva tyāgaphalaṁ labhet. (8)*

He who, from fear of bodily trouble, abandons action because it is painful, thus performing a rājasika (passionate) abandonment, obtains not the fruit of abandonment.

कार्यमित्येव यत्कर्म नियतं क्रियतेऽर्जुन ।
सङ्गं त्यक्त्वा फलं चैव स त्यागः सात्त्विको मतः ॥९॥

*kāryamityeva yatkarma niyataṁ kriyate'rjuna,*
*saṅgaṁ tyaktvā phalaṁ caiva sa tyāgaḥ sāttviko mataḥ. (9)*

Whatever 'obligatory action' is done, O Arjuna, merely because it ought to be done, abandoning attachment and also fruit, that abandonment is regarded as sāttvika (pure).

न द्वेष्ट्यकुशलं कर्म कुशले नानुषज्जते ।
त्यागी सत्त्वसमाविष्टो मेधावी छिन्नसंशयः ॥१०॥

*na dveṣṭyakuśalaṁ karma kuśale nānuṣajjate,*
*tyāgī sattvasamāviṣṭo medhāvī chinnasaṁśayaḥ. (10)*

The abandoner, soaked in purity, being intelligent with all his doubts cut asunder, hates not disagreeable action, nor is he attached to an agreeable action.

न हि देहभृता शक्यं त्यक्तुं कर्माण्यशेषतः ।
यस्तु कर्मफलत्यागी स त्यागीत्यभिधीयते ।।११।।

*na hi dehabhṛtā śakyaṁ tyaktuṁ karmāṇyaśeṣataḥ,*
*yastu karmaphalatyāgī sa tyāgītyabhidhīyate. (11)*

Verily, it is not possible for an embodied being to abandon actions entirely, but he, who relinquishes the fruits of actions, is verily called a 'relinquisher' (tyāgī).

अनिष्टमिष्टं मिश्रं च त्रिविधं कर्मणः फलम् ।
भवत्यत्यागिनां प्रेत्य न तु सन्न्यासिनां क्वचित् ।।१२।।

*aniṣṭamiṣṭaṁ miśraṁ ca trividhaṁ karmaṇaḥ phalam,*
*bhavatyatyāgināṁ pretya na tu sannyāsināṁ kvacit. (12)*

The threefold fruit of action - evil, good and mixed - accrues after death, only to those who have no spirit of abandonment; never to total relinquishers.

पञ्चैतानि महाबाहो कारणानि निबोध मे ।
साङ्ख्ये कृतान्ते प्रोक्तानि सिद्धये सर्वकर्मणाम् ।।१३।।

*pañcaitāni mahābāho kāraṇāni nibodha me,*
*sāṅkhye kṛtānte proktāni siddhaye sarvakarmaṇām. (13)*

Learn from Me, O mighty-armed, these five causes for the accomplishment of all actions, as declared in the Sāṅkhya (Upaniṣad) system, which is the end of all actions.

अधिष्ठानं तथा कर्ता करणं च पृथग्विधम् ।
विविधाश्च पृथक्चेष्टा दैवं चैवात्र पञ्चमम् ।।१४।।

*adhiṣṭhānaṁ tathā kartā karaṇaṁ ca pṛthagvidham,*
*vividhāśca pṛthakceṣṭā daivaṁ caivātra pañcamam.* (14)

The seat (body), the doer (ego), the various organs of perception, the different functions of various organs of action and also the fifth, the presiding deity.

शरीरवाङ्मनोभिर्यत्कर्म प्रारभते नरः ।
न्याय्यं वा विपरीतं वा पञ्चैते तस्य हेतवः ।।१५।।

*śarīravāṅmanobhiryatkarma prārabhate naraḥ,*
*nyāyyaṁ vā viparītaṁ vā pañcaite tasya hetavaḥ.* (15)

Whatever action a man performs by his body, speech and mind, whether right or the reverse, these five are its causes.

तत्रैवं सति कर्तारमात्मानं केवलं तु यः ।
पश्यत्यकृतबुद्धित्वान्न स पश्यति दुर्मतिः ।।१६।।

*tatraivaṁ sati kartāramātmānaṁ kevalaṁ tu yaḥ,*
*paśyatyakṛtabuddhitvānna sa paśyati durmatiḥ. (16)*

Now, such being the case, verily, he who owing to his untrained understanding, looks upon his Self, which is alone (never conditioned by the 'engine'), as the doer, he, of perverted intelligence, sees not.

यस्य नाहङ्कृतो भावो बुद्धिर्यस्य न लिप्यते ।
हत्वाऽपि स इमाँल्लोकान्न हन्ति न निबध्यते ।।१७।।

*yasya nāhaṅkṛto bhāvo buddhiryasya na lipyate,*
*hatvā'pi sa imāṁllokānna hanti na nibadhyate. (17)*

He, who is free from the egoistic notion, whose intelligence is not tainted (by good or evil), though he slays these people, he slays not, nor is he bound (by the action).

ज्ञानं ज्ञेयं परिज्ञाता त्रिविधा कर्मचोदना ।
करणं कर्म कर्तेति त्रिविधः कर्मसङ्ग्रहः ।।१८।।

*jñānaṁ jñeyaṁ parijñātā trividhā karmacodanā,*
*karaṇaṁ karma karteti trividhaḥ karmasaṅgrahaḥ. (18)*

Knowledge, the known and the knower form the threefold impulse to action; the organs, the action, the agent form the threefold basis of action.

**ज्ञानं कर्म च कर्ता च त्रिधैव गुणभेदतः ।**
**प्रोच्यते गुणसङ्ख्याने यथावच्छृणु तान्यपि ।।१९।।**

*jñānaṁ karma ca kartā ca tridhaiva guṇabhedataḥ,*
*procyate guṇasaṅkhyāne yathāvacchṛṇu tānyapi. (19)*

Knowledge, action, and actor are declared in the science of temperaments (guṇas) to be of three kinds only, according to the distinctions of temperaments; hear them also duly.

**सर्वभूतेषु येनैकं भावमव्ययमीक्षते ।**
**अविभक्तं विभक्तेषु तज्ज्ञानं विद्धि सात्त्विकम् ।।२०।।**

*sarvabhūteṣu yenaikaṁ bhāvamavyayamīkṣate,*
*avibhaktaṁ vibhakteṣu tajjñānaṁ viddhi sāttvikam. (20)*

That, by which one sees the one indestructible Reality in all beings, undivided in the divided, know that knowledge as sāttvika (pure).

पृथक्त्वेन तु यज्ज्ञानं नानाभावान्पृथग्विधान् ।
वेत्ति सर्वेषु भूतेषु तज्ज्ञानं विद्धि राजसम् ।।२१।।

*pṛthaktvena tu yajjñānaṁ nānābhāvānpṛthagvidhān,*
*vetti sarveṣu bhūteṣu tajjñānaṁ viddhi rājasam.* (21)

But that knowledge, which sees in all beings various entities of distinct kinds, (and) as different from one another, know that knowledge as rājasika (passionate).

यत्तु कृत्स्नवदेकस्मिन्कार्ये सक्तमहैतुकम् ।
अतत्त्वार्थवदल्पं च तत्तामसमुदाहृतम् ।।२२।।

*yattu kṛtsnavadekasminkārye saktamahaitukam,*
*atattvārthavadalpaṁ ca tattāmasamudāhṛtam.* (22)

But that knowledge, which clings to one single effect, as if it were the whole, without reason, without foundation in truth, and narrow, that is declared to be tāmasika (dull).

नियतं सङ्गरहितमरागद्वेषतः कृतम् ।
अफलप्रेप्सुना कर्म यत्तत्सात्त्विकमुच्यते ।।२३।।

*niyataṁ saṅgarahitamarāgadveṣataḥ kṛtam,*
*aphalaprepsunā karma yattatsāttvikamucyate. (23)*

An action which is ordained, which is free from attachment, which is done without love or hatred, by one, who is not desirous of the fruit, that action is declared to be sāttvika (pure).

यत्तु कामेप्सुना कर्म साहङ्कारेण वा पुनः ।
क्रियते बहुलायासं तद्राजसमुदाहृतम् ।।२४।।

*yattu kāmepsunā karma sāhaṅkāreṇa vā punaḥ,*
*kriyate bahulāyāsaṁ tadrājasamudāhṛtam. (24)*

But that action, which is done by one longing for desires or gain, done with egoism, or with much effort, is declared to be rājasika (passionate).

अनुबन्धं क्षयं हिंसामनवेक्ष्य च पौरुषम् ।
मोहादारभ्यते कर्म यत्तत्तामसमुच्यते ।।२५।।

*anubandhaṁ kṣayaṁ hiṁsāmanavekṣya ca pauruṣam,*
*mohādārabhyate karma yattattāmasamucyate. (25)*

That action, which is undertaken from delusion, without regard for the consequence, loss, injury and ability is declared to be tāmasika (dull).

मुक्तसङ्गोऽनहंवादी धृत्युत्साहसमन्वितः ।
सिद्ध्यसिद्ध्योर्निर्विकारः कर्ता सात्त्विक उच्यते ।।२६।।

*muktasaṅgo'nahaṁvādī dhṛtyutsāhasamanvitaḥ,*
*siddhyasiddhyornirvikāraḥ kartā sāttvika ucyate. (26)*

An agent who is free from attachment, non-egoistic, endowed with firmness and enthusiasm and unaffected by success or failure, is called sāttvika (pure).

रागी कर्मफलप्रेप्सुर्लुब्धो हिंसात्मकोऽशुचिः ।
हर्षशोकान्वितः कर्ता राजसः परिकीर्तितः ।।२७।।

*rāgī karmaphalaprepsurlubdho hiṁsātmako'śuciḥ,*
*harṣaśokānvitaḥ kartā rājasaḥ parikīrtitaḥ. (27)*

Passionate, desiring to gain the fruits of actions, greedy, harmful, impure, full of delight and grief, such an agent is said to be rājasika (passionate).

अयुक्तः प्राकृतः स्तब्धः शठो नैष्कृतिकोऽलसः ।
विषादी दीर्घसूत्री च कर्ता तामस उच्यते ।।२८।।

*ayuktaḥ prākṛtaḥ stabdhaḥ śaṭho naiṣkṛtiko'lasaḥ,*
*viṣādī dīrghasūtrī ca kartā tāmasa ucyate. (28)*

Unsteady, vulgar, unbending, cheating, malicious, lazy, despondent and procrastinating, such an agent is said to be tāmasika (dull).

बुद्धेर्भेदं धृतेश्चैव गुणतस्त्रिविधं शृणु ।
प्रोच्यमानमशेषेण पृथक्त्वेन धनञ्जय ।।२९।।

*buddherbhedaṁ dhṛteścaiva guṇatastrividhaṁ śṛṇu,*
*procyamānamaśeṣeṇa pṛthaktvena dhanañjaya. (29)*

Hear (you) the threefold division of understanding and fortitude (made) according to the qualities , as I declare them fully and severally, O Dhanañjaya.

प्रवृत्तिं च निवृत्तिं च कार्याकार्ये भयाभये ।
बन्धं मोक्षं च या वेत्ति बुद्धिः सा पार्थ सात्त्विकी ।।३०।।

*pravṛttiṁ ca nivṛttiṁ ca kāryākārye bhayābhaye,*
*bandhaṁ mokṣaṁ ca yā vetti buddhiḥ sā pārtha sāttvikī. (30)*

That, which knows the paths of work and renunciation, what ought to be done and what ought not be done, fear and fearlessness, bondage and liberation, that understanding is sāttvika (pure), O Pārtha.

यया धर्ममधर्मं च कार्यं चाकार्यमेव च ।
अयथावत्प्रजानाति बुद्धिः सा पार्थ राजसी ।।३१।।

*yayā dharmamadharmaṁ ca kāryaṁ cākāryameva ca,*
*ayathāvatprajānāti buddhiḥ sā pārtha rājasī. (31)*

That, by which one wrongly understands dharma and adharma and also what ought to be done and what ought not to be done, that intellect (understanding), O Pārtha is rājasika (passionate).

अधर्मं धर्ममिति या मन्यते तमसावृता ।
सर्वार्थान्विपरीतांश्च बुद्धिः सा पार्थ तामसी ।।३२।।

*adharmaṁ dharmamiti ya manyate tamasāvṛtā,*
*sarvārthānviparītāṁśca buddhiḥ sā pārtha tāmasī. (32)*

That, which enveloped in darkness sees adharma as dharma, and all things perverted, that intellect (understanding), O Pārtha, is tāmasika (dull).

धृत्या यया धारयते मनःप्राणेन्द्रियक्रियाः ।
योगेनाव्यभिचारिण्या धृतिः सा पार्थ सात्त्विकी ।।३३।।

*dhṛtyā yayā dhārayate manaḥprāṇendriyakriyāḥ,*
*yogenāvyabhicāriṇyā dhṛtiḥ sā pārtha sāttvikī. (33)*

The unwavering fortitude by which, through yoga, the functions of the mind, the prāṇa and the senses are restrained, that fortitude, O Pārtha, is sāttvika (pure).

यया तु धर्मकामार्थान्धृत्या धारयतेऽर्जुन ।
प्रसङ्गेन फलाकाङ्क्षी धृतिः सा पार्थ राजसी ।।३४।।

*yayā tu dharmakāmārthāndhṛtyā dhārayate'rjuna,*
*prasaṅgena phalākāṅkṣī dhṛtiḥ sā pārtha rājasī. (34)*

But the fortitude, O Arjuna, by which one holds fast to duty, pleasure and wealth, from attachment and craving for the fruits of actions, that fortitude, O Pārtha, is rājasika (passionate).

यया स्वप्नं भयं शोकं विषादं मदमेव च ।
न विमुञ्चति दुर्मेधा धृतिः सा पार्थ तामसी ।।३५।।

*yayā svapnaṁ bhayaṁ śokaṁ viṣādaṁ madameva ca,*
*na vimuñcati durmedhā dhṛtiḥ sā pārtha tāmasī.* (35)

The constancy because of which, a stupid man does not abandon sleep, fear, grief, depression and also arrogance (conceit), that fortitude, O Pārtha, is tāmasika (dull).

सुखं त्विदानीं त्रिविधं शृणु मे भरतर्षभ ।
अभ्यासाद्रमते यत्र दुःखान्तं च निगच्छति ।।३६।।

*sukhaṁ tvidānīṁ trividhaṁ śṛṇu me bharatarṣabha,*
*abhyāsādramate yatra duḥkhāntaṁ ca nigacchati.* (36)

And now hear from Me, O best among the Bhāratas, of the threefold pleasure, in which one rejoices by practice and surely comes to the end of pain.

यत्तदग्रे विषमिव परिणामेऽमृतोपमम् ।
तत्सुखं सात्त्विकं प्रोक्तमात्मबुद्धिप्रसादजम् ।।३७।।

*yattadagre viṣamiva pariṇāme'mṛtopamam,*
*tatsukhaṁ sāttvikaṁ proktamātmabuddhiprasādajam. (37)*

That which is like poison at first, but in the end, like nectar, that pleasure is declared to be sāttvika (pure), born of the purity of one's own mind, due to Self-realisation.

विषयेन्द्रियसंयोगाद्यत्तदग्रेऽमृतोपमम् ।
परिणामे विषमिव तत्सुखं राजसं स्मृतम् ।।३८।।

*viṣayendriyasaṁyogādyattadagre'mṛtopamam,*
*pariṇāme viṣamiva tatsukhaṁ rājasaṁ smṛtam. (38)*

That pleasure which arises from the contact of the sense organs with the objects, (which is)at first like nectar, (but is) in the end like poison, that is declared to be rājasika (passionate).

यदग्रे चानुबन्धे च सुखं मोहनमात्मनः ।
निद्रालस्यप्रमादोत्थं तत्तामसमुदाहृतम् ।।३९।।

*yadagre cānubandhe ca sukhaṁ mohanamātmanaḥ,*
*nidrālasyapramādotthaṁ tattāmasamudahṛtam.* (39)

The pleasure, which at first and in the sequel deludes the Self, arising from sleep, indolence and heedlessness, is declared to be tāmasika (dull).

न तदस्ति पृथिव्यां वा दिवि देवेषु वा पुनः ।
सत्त्वं प्रकृतिजैर्मुक्तं यदेभिः स्यात्त्रिभिर्गुणैः ॥४०॥

*na tadasti pṛthivyāṁ vā divi deveṣu vā punaḥ,*
*sattvaṁ prakṛtijairmuktaṁ yadebhiḥ syāttribhirguṇaih.* (40)

There is no being on earth or in heavens among the devas (heavenly beings), who is totally liberated from the three qualities, born of prakṛti (matter).

ब्राह्मणक्षत्रियविशां शूद्राणां च परन्तप ।
कर्माणि प्रविभक्तानि स्वभावप्रभवैर्गुणैः ॥४१॥

*brāhmaṇakṣatriyaviśāṁ sūdrāṇāṁ ca parantapa,*
*karmāṇi pravibhaktāni svabhāvaprabhavairguṇaiḥ.* (41)

Of scholars (brāhmaṇas), of leaders (kṣatriyas) and of traders (vaiśyas), as also of workers (śūdras) O

Parantapa, the duties are distributed according to the qualities born of their own nature.

शमो दमस्तपः शौचं क्षान्तिरार्जवमेव च ।
ज्ञानं विज्ञानमास्तिक्यं ब्रह्मकर्म स्वभावजम् ।।४२।।

*śamo damastapaḥ śaucaṁ kṣāntirārjavameva ca,*
*jñānaṁ vijñānamāstikyaṁ brahmakarma svabhāvajam. (42)*

Serenity, self-restraint, austerity, purity, forgiveness and also uprightness, knowledge, realisation, belief in God; are the duties of the brāhmaṇas, born of (their own) nature.

शौर्यं तेजो धृतिर्दाक्ष्यं युद्धे चाप्यपलायनम् ।
दानमीश्वरभावश्च क्षात्रं कर्म स्वभावजम् ।।४३।।

*śauryaṁ tejo dhṛtirdākṣyaṁ yuddhe cāpyapalāyanam,*
*dānamīśvarabhāvaśca kṣātraṁ karma svabhāvajam. (43)*

Prowess, splendour, firmness, dexterity, and also not fleeing from battle, generosity, lordliness - these are the duties of the kṣatriyas, born of (their own) nature.

कृषिगौरक्ष्यवाणिज्यं वैश्यकर्म स्वभावजम् ।
परिचर्यात्मकं कर्म शूद्रस्यापि स्वभावजम् ।।४४।।

*kṛṣigaurakṣyavāṇijyaṁ vaiśyakarma svabhāvajam,*
*paricaryātmakaṁ karma śūdrasyāpi svabhāvajam.* (44)

Agriculture, cattle-rearing and trade are the duties of the vaiśyas, born of (their own) nature; and service is the duty of the ṣūdras, born of (their own) nature.

स्वे स्वे कर्मण्यभिरतः संसिद्धिं लभते नरः ।
स्वकर्मनिरतः सिद्धिं यथा विन्दति तच्छृणु ।।४५।।

*sve sve karmaṇyabhirataḥ saṁsiddhiṁ labhate naraḥ,*
*svakarmanirataḥ siddhiṁ yathā vindati tacchṛṇu.* (45)

Devoted, each to his own duty, man attains perfection. How, engaged in his own duty, he attains perfection - listen.

यतः प्रवृत्तिर्भूतानां येन सर्वमिदं ततम् ।
स्वकर्मणा तमभ्यर्च्य सिद्धिं विन्दति मानवः ।।४६।।

*yataḥ pravṛttirbhūtānāṁ yena sarvamidaṁ tatam,*
*svakarmaṇā tamabhyarcya siddhiṁ vindati mānavaḥ.* (46)

From whom is the evolution of all beings, by whom all this is pervaded, worshipping Him with one's own duty, man attains perfection.

श्रेयान्स्वधर्मो विगुणः परधर्मात्स्वनुष्ठितात् ।
स्वभावनियतं कर्म कुर्वन्नाप्नोति किल्बिषम् ।।४७।।

*śreyānsvadharmo viguṇaḥ paradharmātsvanuṣṭhitāt,*
*svabhāvaniyataṁ karma kurvannāpnoti kilbiṣam. (47)*

Better is one's own duty (though) destitute of merits, than the duty of another well performed. He, who does the duty ordained by his own nature incurs no sin.

सहजं कर्म कौन्तेय सदोषमपि न त्यजेत् ।
सर्वारम्भा हि दोषेण धूमेनाग्निरिवावृताः ।।४८।।

*sahajaṁ karma kaunteya sadoṣamapi na tyajet,*
*sarvārambhā hi doṣeṇa dhūmenāgnirivāvṛtāḥ. (48)*

One should not abandon, O Kaunteya, the duty to which one is born, though faulty; for, are not all undertakings enveloped by evil, as fire by smoke?

असक्तबुद्धिः सर्वत्र जितात्मा विगतस्पृहः ।
नैष्कर्म्यसिद्धिं परमां सन्न्यासेनाधिगच्छति ।।४९।।

*asaktabuddhiḥ sarvatra jitātmā vigataspṛhaḥ,*
*naiṣkarmyasiddhiṁ paramāṁ sannyāsenādhigacchati. (49)*

He, whose intellect is unattached everywhere, who has subdued his self, from whom desire has fled, he through renunciation, attains the supreme state of freedom from action.

सिद्धिं प्राप्तो यथा ब्रह्म तथाप्नोति निबोध मे ।
समासेनैव कौन्तेय निष्ठा ज्ञानस्य या परा ।।५०।।

*siddhiṁ prāpto yathā brahma tathāpnoti nibodha me,*
*samāsenaiva kaunteya niṣṭhā jñānasya yā parā. (50)*

How he, who has attained perfection, reaches Brahman (the eternal), that in brief, you learn from Me, O Kaunteya! That supreme state of Knowledge.

बुद्ध्या विशुद्धया युक्तो धृत्यात्मानं नियम्य च ।
शब्दादीन्विषयांस्त्यक्त्वा रागद्वेषौ व्युदस्य च ।।५१।।

*buddhyā viśuddhayā yukto dhṛtyātmānaṁ niyamya ca,*
*śabdādīnviṣayāṁstyaktvā rāgadveṣau vyudasya ca.* (51)

Endowed with a pure intellect, controlling the self by firmness, relinquishing sound and other objects and abandoning attraction and hatred....

विविक्तसेवी लघ्वाशी यतवाक्कायमानसः ।
ध्यानयोगपरो नित्यं वैराग्यं समुपाश्रितः ।।५२।।

*viviktasevī laghvāśī yatavākkāyamānasaḥ,*
*dhyānayogaparo nityaṁ vairāgyaṁ samupāśritaḥ.* (52)

Dwelling in solitude, eating but little, speech, body and mind subdued, always engaged in meditation and concentration, taking refuge in dispassion....

अहङ्कारं बलं दर्पं कामं क्रोधं परिग्रहम् ।
विमुच्य निर्ममः शान्तो ब्रह्मभूयाय कल्पते ।।५३।।

*ahaṅkāraṁ balaṁ darpaṁ kāmaṁ krodhaṁ parigraham,*
*vimucya nirmamaḥ śānto brahmabhūyāya kalpate.* (53)

Having abandoned egoism, power, arrogance, desire, anger and aggrandisement, and freed from the notion of mine, and therefore, peaceful - he is fit to become Brahman.

ब्रह्मभूतः प्रसन्नात्मा न शोचति न काङ्क्षति ।
समः सर्वेषु भूतेषु मद्भक्तिं लभते पराम् ।।५४।।

*brahmabhūtaḥ prasannātmā na śocati na kāṅkṣati,*
*samaḥ sarveṣu bhūteṣu madbhaktiṁ labhate parām.* (54)

Becoming Brahman, serene in the Self, he neither grieves nor desires; the same to all beings, he obtains supreme devotion towards Me.

भक्त्या मामभिजानाति यावान्यश्चास्मि तत्त्वतः ।
ततो मां तत्त्वतो ज्ञात्वा विशते तदनन्तरम् ।।५५।।

*bhaktyā māmabhijānāti yāvānyaścāsmi tattvataḥ,*
*tato māṁ tattvato jñātvā viśate tadanantaram.* (55)

By devotion he knows Me in essence, what and who I am; then, having known Me in My essence, he forthwith enters into Me - the Supreme.

सर्वकर्माण्यपि सदा कुर्वाणो मद्व्यपाश्रयः ।
मत्प्रसादादवाप्नोति शाश्वतं पदमव्ययम् ।।५६।।

*sarvakarmāṇyapi sadā kurvāṇo madvyapāśrayaḥ,*
*matprasādādavāpnoti śāśvataṁ padamavyayam. (56)*

Doing all actions, always taking refuge in Me, by My grace, he obtains the eternal, indestructible state or abode.

चेतसा सर्वकर्माणि मयि सन्न्यस्य मत्परः ।
बुद्धियोगमुपाश्रित्य मच्चित्तः सततं भव ।।५७।।

*cetasā sarvakarmāṇi mayi sannyasya matparaḥ,*
*buddhiyogamupāśritya maccittaḥ satataṁ bhava. (57)*

Mentally renouncing all actions in Me, having Me as the highest goal, resorting to the yoga of discrimination, ever fix your mind in Me.

मच्चित्तः सर्वदुर्गाणि मत्प्रसादात्तरिष्यसि ।
अथ चेत्त्वमहङ्कारान्न श्रोष्यसि विनङ्क्ष्यसि ।।५८।।

*maccittaḥ sarvadurgāṇi matprasādāttariṣyasi,*
*atha cettvamahaṅkārānna śroṣyasi vinaṅkṣyasi. (58)*

Fixing your mind upon Me, you shall, by My grace, overcome all obstacles; but if, from egoism, you will not hear Me, you shall perish.

यदहङ्कारमाश्रित्य न योत्स्य इति मन्यसे ।
मिथ्यैष व्यवसायस्ते प्रकृतिस्त्वां नियोक्ष्यति ।।५९।।

*yadahaṅkāramāśritya na yotsya iti manyase,*
*mithyaiṣa vyavasāyaste prakṛtistvāṁ niyokṣyati. (59)*

Filled with egoism, if you think, 'I will not fight', vain is this your resolve; (for) nature will compel you.

स्वभावजेन कौन्तेय निबद्धः स्वेन कर्मणा ।
कर्तुं नेच्छसि यन्मोहात्करिष्यस्यवशोऽपि तत् ।।६०।।

*svabhāvajena kaunteya nibaddhaḥ svena karmaṇā,*
*kartuṁ necchasi yanmohātkariṣyasyavaśo'pi tat. (60)*

O son of Kuntī, bound by your own karma (action), born of your own nature, that which, through delusion you wish not to do, even that you shall do, helplessly.

ईश्वरः सर्वभूतानां हृद्देशेऽर्जुन तिष्ठति ।
भ्रामयन्सर्वभूतानि यन्त्रारूढानि मायया ।।६१।।

*īśvaraḥ sarvabhūtānāṁ hṛddeśe'rjuna tiṣṭhati,*
*bhrāmayansarvabhūtāni yantrārūḍhāni māyayā. (61)*

The Lord dwells in the hearts of all beings, O Arjuna, causing all beings, by His illusive power to revolve, as if mounted on a machine.

तमेव शरणं गच्छ सर्वभावेन भारत ।
तत्प्रसादात्परां शान्तिं स्थानं प्राप्स्यसि शाश्वतम् ।।६२।।

*tameva śaraṇaṁ gaccha sarvabhāvena bhārata,*
*tatprasādātparāṁ śāntiṁ sthānaṁ prāpsyasi śāśvatam. (62)*

Fly unto Him for refuge with all your being, O Bhārata; by His grace, you shall obtain supreme peace (and) the eternal abode.

इति ते ज्ञानमाख्यातं गुह्याद्गुह्यतरं मया ।
विमृश्यैतदशेषेण यथेच्छसि तथा कुरु ।।६३।।

*iti te jñānamākhyātaṁ guhyādguhyataraṁ mayā,*
*vimṛśyaitadaśeṣeṇa yathecchasi tathā kuru. (63)*

Thus, the wisdom which is a greater secret than all secrets, has been declared to you by Me; having reflected upon it fully, you now act as you choose.

सर्वगुह्यतमं भूयः शृणु मे परमं वचः ।
इष्टोऽसि मे दृढमिति ततो वक्ष्यामि ते हितम् ।।६४।।

*sarvaguhyatamaṁ bhūyaḥ śṛṇu me paramaṁ vacaḥ,*
*iṣṭo'si me dṛḍhamiti tato vakṣyāmi te hitam. (64)*

Hear again, My supreme word, most secret of all; because you are My dear beloved, therefore, I will tell you what is good (for you).

मन्मना भव मद्भक्तो मद्याजी मां नमस्कुरु ।
मामेवैष्यसि सत्यं ते प्रतिजाने प्रियोऽसि मे ।।६५।।

*manmanā bhava madbhakto madyājī māṁ namaskuru,*
*māmevaiṣyasi satyaṁ te pratijāne priyo'si me. (65)*

Fix your mind upon Me; be devoted to Me; sacrifice for Me; bow down to Me; you shall surely then come to Me alone; truly do I promise to you, (for) you are dear to Me.

सर्वधर्मान्परित्यज्य मामेकं शरणं व्रज ।
अहं त्वा सर्वपापेभ्यो मोक्षयिष्यामि मा शुचः ।।६६।।

*sarvadharmānparityajya māmekaṁ śaraṇaṁ vraja,*
*ahaṁ tvā sarvapāpebhyo mokṣayiṣyāmi mā śucaḥ. (66)*

Abandoning all dharmas, (of the body, mind and intellect), take refuge in Me alone; I will liberate thee, from all sins; grieve not.

इदं ते नातपस्काय नाभक्ताय कदाचन ।
न चाशुश्रूषवे वाच्यं न च मां योऽभ्यसूयति ।।६७।।

*idaṁ te nātapaskāya nābhaktāya kadācana,*
*na cāśuśrūṣave vācyaṁ na ca māṁ yo'bhyasūyati. (67)*

This is never to be spoken by you to one who is devoid of austerities or devotion, nor to one who does not render service, nor to one who desires not to listen, nor to one who cavils at Me.

य इमं परमं गुह्यं मद्भक्तेष्वभिधास्यति ।
भक्तिं मयि परां कृत्वा मामेवैष्यत्यसंशयः ।।६८।।

*ya imaṁ paramaṁ guhyaṁ madbhakteṣvabhidhāsyati,*
*bhaktiṁ mayi parāṁ kṛtvā māmevaiṣyatyasaṁśayaḥ. (68)*

He who, with supreme devotion to Me, will teach this supreme secret to My devotees, shall doubtless come to Me.

न च तस्मान्मनुष्येषु कश्चिन्मे प्रियकृत्तमः ।
भविता न च मे तस्मादन्यः प्रियतरो भुवि ।।६९।।

*na ca tasmānmanuṣyeṣu kaścinme priyakṛttamaḥ,*
*bhavitā na ca me tasmādanyaḥ priyataro bhuvi. (69)*

Nor is there any among men who does dearer service to Me, nor shall there be another on earth dearer to Me than he.

अध्येष्यते च य इमं धर्म्यं संवादमावयोः ।
ज्ञानयज्ञेन तेनाहमिष्टः स्यामिति मे मतिः ।।७०।।

*adhyeṣyate ca ya imaṁ dharmyaṁ saṁvādamāvayoḥ,*
*jñānayajñena tenāhamiṣṭaḥ syāmiti me matiḥ. (70)*

And he, who will study this sacred dialouge of ours, by him, I shall have been worshipped by the sacrifice of wisdom, such is My conviction.

श्रद्धावाननसूयश्च शृणुयादपि यो नरः ।
सोऽपि मुक्तः शुभाँल्लोकान्प्राप्नुयात्पुण्यकर्मणाम् ।।७१।।

*śraddhāvānanasūyaśca śṛṇuyādapi yo naraḥ,*
*so'pi muktaḥ śubhāllokānprāpnuyātpuṇyakarmaṇām. (71)*

That man also, who hears this, full of faith and free from malice, he too, liberated, shall attain to the happy worlds of those righteous deeds.

कच्चिदेतच्छ्रुतं पार्थ त्वयैकाग्रेण चेतसा ।
कच्चिदज्ञानसम्मोहः प्रनष्टस्ते धनञ्जय ।।७२।।

*kaccidetacchrutaṁ pārtha tvayaikāgreṇa cetasā,*
*kaccidajñānasammohaḥ pranaṣṭaste dhanañjaya. (72)*

Has this been heard, O son of Pṛthā, with single pointed mind? Has the distraction, caused by your ignorance, been dispelled, O Dhanañjaya?

**अर्जुन उवाच**

**नष्टो मोहः स्मृतिर्लब्धा त्वत्प्रसादान्मयाच्युत ।**
**स्थितोऽस्मि गतसन्देहः करिष्ये वचनं तव ।।७३।।**

*arjuna uvāca*

*naṣṭo mohaḥ smṛtirlabdhā tvatprasādānmayācyuta,*
*sthito'smi gatasandehaḥ kariṣye vacanaṁ tava. (73)*

Arjuna said:

Destroyed is my delusion, as I have now gained my memory (knowledge) through your grace, O Achyuta. I am firm; my doubts are gone. I will do according to your word (bidding).

**सञ्जय उवाच**

**इत्यहं वासुदेवस्य पार्थस्य च महात्मनः ।**
**संवादमिममश्रौषमद्भुतं रोमहर्षणम् ।।७४।।**

*sañjaya uvāca*

*ityahaṁ vāsudevasya pārthasya ca mahātmanaḥ,*
*saṁvādamimamaśrauṣamadbhutaṁ romaharṣaṇam. (74)*

Sañjaya said:

Thus, have I heard this wonderful dialogue between Vāsudeva and the high-souled Pārtha, which cause the hair to stand on end.

व्यासप्रसादाच्छ्रुतवानेतद्गुह्यमहं परम् ।
योगं योगेश्वरात्कृष्णात्साक्षात्कथयतः स्वयम् ।।७५।।

*vyāsaprasādācchrutavānetadguhyamahaṁ param,*
*yogaṁ yogeśvarātkṛṣṇātsākṣātkathayataḥ svayam. (75)*

Through the grace of Vyāsa I have heard, this supreme and most secret yoga, directly from Kṛṣṇa, the Lord of yoga, Himself declaring it.

राजन्संस्मृत्य संस्मृत्य संवादमिममद्भुतम् ।
केशवार्जुनयोः पुण्यं हृष्यामि च मुहुर्मुहुः ।।७६।।

*rājansaṁsmṛtya saṁsmṛtya saṁvādamimamadbhutaṁ,*
*keśavārjunayoḥ puṇyaṁ hṛsyāmi ca muhurmuhuḥ. (76)*

O King remembering this wonderful and holy dialogue between Keśava and Arjuna, I rejoice again and again.

**तच्च संस्मृत्य संस्मृत्य रूपमत्यद्भुतं हरेः ।**
**विस्मयो मे महान्राजन्हृष्यामि च पुनः पुनः ।।७७।।**

*tacca saṁsmṛtya saṁsmṛtya rūpamatyadbhutaṁ hareḥ,*
*vismayo me mahānrājanhṛṣyāmi ca punaḥ punaḥ. (77)*

Remembering and again remembering, that most wonderful form of Hari, great is my wonder, O King; and I rejoice again and again.

**यत्र योगेश्वरः कृष्णो यत्र पार्थो धनुर्धरः ।**
**तत्र श्रीर्विजयो भूतिर्ध्रुवा नीतिर्मतिर्मम ।।७८।।**

*yatra yogeśvaraḥ kṛṣṇo yatra pārtho dhanurdharaḥ,*
*tatra śrīrvijayo bhūtirdhruvā nītirmatirmama. (78)*

Wherever is Kṛṣṇa, the Lord of yoga, wherever is Pārtha, the archer, there are prosperity, victory, happiness and firm (steady or sound) policy; this is my conviction.

ॐ तत्सदिति श्रीमद्भगवद्गीतासूपनिषत्सु
ब्रह्मविद्यायां योगशास्त्रे श्रीकृष्णार्जुनसंवादे
मोक्षसन्न्यासयोगो नाम अष्टादशोऽध्यायः

*om tatsaditi śrīmadbhagavadgītāsūpaniṣatsu*
*brahmavidyāyāṁ yogaśāstre śrīkṛṣṇārjunasaṁvāde*
*mokṣasannyāsayogo nāma aṣṭādaśo'dhyāyaḥ.*

Thus, in the Upaniṣads of the glorious Bhagavad-gītā, in the science of the eternal, in the scripture of yoga, in the dialogue between Śrī Kṛṣṇa and Arjuna, the eighteenth discourse ends entitled:

THE YOGA OF LIBERATION THROUGH RENUNCIATION

OM TAT SAT

* * *

*I found the world-famous Guru due to merits acquired in my countless lives. I bow to Him, by whose grace my mind has attained peace.*

*The gratitude in my heart can never be expressed fully inspite of my best efforts. O teacher! Be gracious and bless me with devotion of nature of Supreme love to Your feet.*

# श्रीमद्-भगवद्-गीता आरती

जय भगवद्गीते, मैया जय भगवद्गीते।
हरि-हिय-कमल-विहारिणि, सुन्दर सुपुनीते॥
मैया जय भगवद्गीते॥

कर्म-सुमर्म-प्रकाशिनि, कामासक्तिहरा।
तत्त्वज्ञान-विकासिनि, विद्या ब्रह्म परा॥ मैया... ॥

निश्चल-भक्ति-विधायिनि, निर्मल मलहारि
शरण-रहस्य-प्रदायिनि, सब विधि सुखकारि॥ मैया... ॥

राग-द्वेष-विदारिणि, कारिणि मोद सदा।
भव-भय-हारिणि, तारिणि, परमानन्दप्रदा॥ मैया... ॥

आसुर-भाव-विनाशिनि, नाशिनि तम-रजनी।
दैवी सद्गुणदायिनि, हरि-रसिका सजनी॥ मैया... ॥

समता, त्याग सिखावनि, हरि-मुखकी बानी।
सकल शास्त्रकी स्वामिनि, श्रुतियोंकी रानी॥ मैया... ॥

दया-सुधा बरसावनी मातु! कृपा कीजै।
हरिपद-प्रेम दान कर, अपनो कर लीजै॥ मैया... ॥

# Śrīmad Bhagavadgītā Āratī

Jaya Bhagavadgīte, Maiyā Jaya Bhagavadgīte,
Hari-Hiya-Kamala-Vihāriṇi, Sundara Supunīte.
- Maiyā Jaya Bhagavadgīte.

Karma-Sumarma-Prakāśini, Kāmāsaktiharā,
Tattvajñāna-Vikāsini, Vidyā Brahma Parā.
- Maiyā Jaya Bhagavadgīte.

Niścala-Bhakti-Vidhāyini, Nirmala Malhāri,
Śaraṇa-Rahasya-Pradāyini, Saba Vidhi Sukhkārī.
- Maiyā Jaya Bhagavadgīte.

Rāga-Dveṣa-Vidāriṇi, Kāriṇi Moda Sadā,
Bhava-Bhaya-Hāriṇi, Tāraṇi, Parmānandapradā.
- Maiyā Jaya Bhagavadgīte.

Āsura-Bhāva-Vināśini, Nāśini Tama-Rajnī,
Daivī Sadguṇadāyini, Hari-Rasikā Sajnī.
- Maiyā Jaya Bhagavadgīte.

Samatā, Tyāga Sikhāvani, Hari-Mukhkī Bānī,
Sakala Śāṣtrakī Svāmini, Śrutiyoṁkī Rānī.
- Maiyā Jaya Bhagavadgīte.

Dayā-Sudhā Barsāvani, Mātu! Kṛpa Kījai,
Haripada-Prema Dāna Kara, Apano Kara Lījai.
- Maiyā Jaya Bhagavadgīte.

# श्री चिन्मय आरती

आरति श्रीचिन्मय सद्गुरु की।
दिव्य रूप मूरति करुणा की॥
आरति सद्गुरु की॥
चरणों में उनके शान्ति समाए।
शरणागत की भ्रान्ति मिटाए।
पाप ताप सन्ताप हरनकी।
आरति श्रीचिन्मय सद्गुरु की॥
आरति सद्गुरु की॥
वेद् उपनिषद् गीता को गाया।
धर्म सनातन फिर से जगाया।
शुद्ध नीति प्रीति शङ्कर की।
आरति श्रीचिन्मय सद्गुरु की॥
आरति सद्गुरु की॥
सिद्धबाड़िकी तपोभूमि में।
नित्य विराजे गुरु हमारे।
भक्त हृदय आनन्द स्रोत की।
आरति श्रीचिन्मय सद्गुरु की॥
आरति सद्गुरु की॥
बोलिए सद्गुरुनाथ महाराज की जय॥

## Śrī Chinmaya Āratī

ārati śrīcinmaya sadgurukī,
divya rūpa mūrati karuṇākī.
ārati sadgurukī.

caraṇoṁ meṁ unake śānti samāye,
śaraṇāgatakī bhrānti miṭāye,
pāpa tāpa santāpa haranakī,
ārati śricinmaya sadgurukī.
ārati sadgurukī.

veda upaniṣad gītā ko gāyā,
dharma sanātana phira se jagāya,
śuddha nīti prīti śaṅkarakī,
ārati śrīcinmaya sadgurukī.
ārati sadgurukī.

siddhabāḍikī tapobhūmi meṁ,
nitya virāje guru hamāre,
bhakta hṛdaya ānanda srota kī,
ārati śrīcinmaya sadgurukī.
ārati sadgurukī.

boliye sadgurunātha mahārāja kī jaya.